4/28/01

*To my colleague-to-be Clarence,
with [...] respect —
the beginning [...],
friendship —Erv*

the refuge of affections

COLUMBIA STUDIES IN CONTEMPORARY AMERICAN HISTORY

COLUMBIA STUDIES IN CONTEMPORARY AMERICAN HISTORY
WILLIAM E. LEUCHTENBURG AND ALAN BRINKLEY, GENERAL EDITORS

Lawrence S. Wittner, *Rebels Against War: The American Peace Movement, 1941–1960*
1969

Davis R. B. Ross, *Preparing for Ulysses: Politics and Veterans During World War II*
1969

John Lewis Gaddis, *The United States and the Origins of the Cold War, 1941–1947*   1972

George C. Herring, Jr., *Aid to Russia, 1941–1946: Strategy, Diplomacy, the Origins of the
Cold War*   1973

Alonzo L. Hamby, *Beyond the New Deal: Harry S. Truman and American Liberalism*
1973

Richard M. Fried, *Men Against McCarthy*   1976

Steven F. Lawson, *Black Ballots: Voting Rights in the South, 1944–1969*   1976

Carl M. Brauer, *John F. Kennedy and the Second Reconstruction*   1977

Maeva Marcus, *Truman and the Steel Seizure Case: The Limits of Presidential Power*
1977

Morton Sosna, *In Search of the Silent South: Southern Liberals and the Race Issue*   1977

Robert M. Collins, *The Business Response to Keynes, 1929–1964*   1981

Robert M. Hathaway, *Ambiguous Partnership: Britain and America, 1944–1947*   1981

Leonard Dinnerstein, *America and the Survivors of the Holocaust*   1982

Lawrence S. Wittner, *American Intervention in Greece, 1943–1949*   1982

Nancy Bernkopf Tucker, *Patterns in the Dust: Chinese-American Relations and the
Recognition Controversy, 1949–1950*   1983

Catherine A. Barnes, *Journey from Jim Crow: The Desegregation of Southern
Transit*   1983

Steven F. Lawson, *In Pursuit of Power: Southern Blacks and Electoral Politics, 1965–1982*
1985

David R. Colburn, *Racial Change and Community Crisis: St. Augustine, Florida,
1877–1980*   1985

Henry William Brands, *Cold Warriors: Eisenhower's Generation and the Making of
American Foreign Policy*   1988

Marc S. Gallicchio, *The Cold War Begins in Asia: American East Asian Policy and the
Fall of the Japanese Empire*   1988

Melanie Billings-Yun, *Decision Against War: Eisenhower and Dien Bien Phu*   1988

Walter L. Hixson, *George F. Kennan: Cold War Iconoclast*   1989

Robert D. Schulzinger, *Henry Kissinger: Doctor of Diplomacy*   1989

Henry William Brands, *The Specter of Neutralism: The United States and the Emergence
of the Third World, 1947–1960*   1989

Mitchell K. Hall, *Because of Their Faith: CALCAV and Religious Opposition to the Vietnam War*   1990

David L. Anderson, *Trapped By Success: The Eisehower Administration and Vietnam,
1953–1961*   1991

Steven M. Gillon, *The Democrats' Dilemma: Walter F. Mondale and the Liberal Legacy*
1992

Wyatt C. Wells, *Economist in an Uncertain World: Arthur F. Burns and the Federal
Reserve, 1970–1978*   1994

Stuart Svonkin, *Jews Against Prejudice: American Jews and the Fight for Civil Liberties*
1997

Doug Rossinow, *The Politics of Authenticity: Liberalism, Christianity, and the New Left
in America*   1998

the refuge of affections

FAMILY AND AMERICAN REFORM POLITICS, 1900–1920

Eric Rauchway

COLUMBIA UNIVERSITY PRESS NEW YORK

Copyright © 2001
Columbia University Press
All rights reserved

Library of Congress Cataloging-in-Publication Data
Rauchway, Eric.
    The refuge of affections : family and American reform politics, 1900–1920 /
Eric Rauchway.
        p. cm. — (Contemporary American history series)
    Includes bibliographical references and index.
    ISBN 0–231–12146–6 (cloth : alk. paper) — ISBN 0–231–12147–4 (pbk. :
alk. paper)
        1. Social reformers—United States—Biography. 2. Family—United
States—History. 3. Progressivism (United States politics) I. Title. II. Series.

HN57 .R28 2001
303.48′4′092273—dc21   00–045170

⊗
Casebound editions of Columbia University Press books are printed
on permanent and durable acid-free paper.
Designed by Chang Jae Lee
Printed in the United States of America
c 10 9 8 7 6 5 4 3 2 1
p 10 9 8 7 6 5 4 3 2 1

for M.E.A. *and* A.S.R.

CONTENTS

ACKNOWLEDGMENTS

To acknowledge every considerable debt I have incurred in writing this book would fill another volume: so for incorporating several benefactors under collective names and, despite care and sincerely felt gratitude, possibly omitting others, I apologize.

For invaluable critical advice and encouragement during the writing of this book, I thank Glenn Altschuler, Alan Brinkley, Scott Casper, George Fredrickson, David Kennedy, Elizabeth Raymond, and Paul Robinson.

For assistance in formulating my ideas about Dorothy Whitney Straight, I thank the editors of the *Journal of Women's History*, especially Toni Mortimer. I am also grateful for the journal's permission to reprint portions of my article "A Gentlemen's Club in a Woman's Sphere," *Journal of Women's History* 11, no. 2 (1999): 60–85, some altered parts of which reappear here in chapter 1.

I have also benefited from collections in the Hubert Howe Bancroft Library of the University California at Berkeley, the Bodleian Libraries of Oxford University, the Nicholas Murray Butler Library of Columbia University, the Hoover Institute in Stanford, California, the Carl A. Kroch Library of Cornell University, the Rose Reading Room and the Science, Industry, and Business Library of the New York Public Library, and the Roy O. West Library of DePauw University. In those cases where permission to reproduce was necessary, I am grateful to the archives for that permission.

Friends and friendly strangers gave direction and assistance both expert and material, too, and for these I thank Catherine Atwell, Louis Auchincloss, Gould Colman, Kevin Fowler, Lawrence Goldman, Walter LaFeber, John McWhorter, Elizabeth Ochester, Michael Srba, Michael Straight, and William Summerhill, and for always having a place for me to go, the family Rauchway.

I should also like to thank the anonymous readers and editorial staff of Columbia University Press, ably headed by Kate Wittenberg, for their help and advice.

Most of all I thank M. E. A. and A. S. R., to whom the book is dedicated.

ABBREVIATIONS AND MANUSCRIPT CITATIONS

In the case of personal names, for consistency's sake a single abbreviation is used for each person, even though this means identifying women with a full, married monogram on items predating the marriage.

BB	Beatrice Bend
BIW	Benjamin Ide Wheeler
CAB	Charles Austin Beard
HC	Herbert Croly
MRB	Mary Ritter Beard
LSM	Lucy Sprague Mitchell
WCM	Wesley Clair Mitchell
DWSE	Dorothy Whitney Straight (later Elmhirst)
WDS	Willard Dickerman Straight
Beard Papers	Charles and Mary Beard Papers in the Roy O. West Library of DePauw University, Greencastle, Indiana

DWSE Papers   Dorothy Whitney Straight Elmhirst Papers
              (#3725 and #3782) in the Division of Rare and
              Manuscript Collections, Carl A. Kroch Library,
              Cornell University, Ithaca, New York

Gay Papers   Edwin F. Gay Papers in the Hoover Institution
              on War, Revolution, and Peace,
              Stanford, California

HMS Papers   Henry Morse Stephens Papers, Hubert Howe
              Bancroft Library, University of California,
              Berkeley, California

LSM Papers   Lucy Sprague Mitchell Papers in the Nicholas
              Murray Butler Library of Columbia University,
              New York

LSM Oral   Lucy Sprague Mitchell Oral History
History   in the Oral History Collection of Columbia
              University, New York, and the Hubert Howe
              Bancroft Library, University of California,
              Berkeley, California

Presidents'   Presidents' Papers at the Hubert Howe
Papers   Bancroft Library, University of California,
              Berkeley, California

WCM Papers   Wesley Clair Mitchell Papers in the Nicholas
              Murray Butler Library of Columbia University,
              New York

WDS Papers   Willard Dickerman Straight Papers (#1260) in
              the Division of Rare and Manuscript
              Collections, Carl A. Kroch Library,
              Cornell University, Ithaca, New York

the refuge of affections

INTRODUCTION

She had thus arrived, through miscalculations and misplaced hopes, at the age when women have no part to play in life but that of mother, a part that requires sacrificing one's self to one's children, and placing all one's unselfish interests in another household,—the last refuge of human affections.
                                           —Honoré de Balzac, *The Marriage Contract.*[1]

Imagine a family portrait: what you now see with your mind's eye may depict your family, or a generic family, or the ideal family. However you conceive what you see, the family on your mental canvas will consist of individual people bearing various relationships to each other. But no matter how generously you crop your picture, it cannot contain an entire network of such relationships. Wherever you put the frame, there is always someone just outside it (or, perhaps, sitting at the easel) who is yet related to someone inside.

The limits to what we mean by family are always somewhat arbitrary and also easily redrawn to include new people: we marry, we procreate, we adopt, we discover new relatives, we take in lost souls and often assimilate close friendships to our meaning of family. (We also, though more rarely and more painfully, cut people out of this definition as well.) When we redefine our families, we exercise a special version of our basic right of association, which is why we often feel uneasy when someone holding a position of public authority tells us what families are supposed to look like. Families are never so clearly defined as political rhetoricians would like them to be. They occupy an indefinite and messy middle ground between our private affairs and our public business, and anything crossing from one of those categories to the other must cover some unsteady footing. In recent years, perhaps because of the public emphasis on the nuclear (or "normal") family, Americans have tended to think of this traffic as running one way: public events (welfare legislation, wars, business cycles, social policy, health-insurance requirements) push at our families, and we react. But American families have not always been so buffeted, nor has the ideal of the American family always been so narrowly drawn. For historians—and for all of us interested in the nature of the society we inhabit—families are (as one scholar says) "the missing link for understanding the relationship between individuals and social change."[2] Social forces and political currents tug at this link, but individuals have often pulled back quite as hard, and the purpose of the connection—a yoke, a leash, reins, a lifeline—changes as one side or the other gains an upper hand.

In our time, the use of the word *family* in political language has become a characteristic trait of political and cultural conservatism throughout the United States and Europe. We hear the word and immediately feel the censorious gaze of authority sweep over the messiness of our own affairs. But the family has a history as a transformative institution specifically designed to bridge the gap between private and public morality, and it has often—not only within the last twenty years or so—been a metaphor for the larger society. During the Progressive period at the start of the twentieth century, a generation of reformers began self-consciously to adapt traditional institutions to a modern and rapidly changing world, and in the process they took an especially keen interest in the meaning and purpose of families. The Progressive approach to these issues has not always been clear in historical memory, in large part because students of the period have not been sensitive to the artful ways in which Progressives used their idea of family to describe the appropriate relation between private lives and public action and between social elites and dependent classes, and also to give political meaning to the power of education— the principal Progressive method of child rearing—as a means of reform.

This book contains a history of three families, each of them a self-conscious creation of a married couple determined to make their lives together the basis for a career of political and social reform. It includes analyses of how these reformers used their ideas about family and social obligation to create the *New Republic* periodical, Ruskin College Oxford, the Bank Street Schools, and the New School for Social Research, among other efforts that all embodied (and to some greater or lesser extent continue to embody) this familial ethos. It also contains a variety of children: natural, adopted, and metaphorical. With all these elements it essays an explanation of what was progressive about Progressivism: the use of the family (in fact and in metaphor) as an engine to diffuse wisdom outward and pass it on to the next generation. In some cases, family ideals suited progressive purposes, and in others they did not. As an animating vision and a model for social relationships, the progressive family had limited utility. And like all animating visions, it depended less on logical persuasion than on felt inspiration. Logic can be reiterated, and its persuasive power demonstrated, but inspiration can only be reconstructed and its persuasive power felt with an imaginative sympathy. For this reason, this book depends considerably on narrative to make its case. But this introduction (by contrast) sets forth the intellectual context for the history that follows.

When historians of the United States talk about Progressivism, we refer to a politics of social responsibility that emerged in the United States at the turn of the twentieth century, analogous to but distinct from similar tendencies in other industrialized countries. Throughout Europe, North America, and the Antipodes—wherever railroads and telegraphs, steel rails and copper wire had begun to wring modernity from tradition—citizens struggled accordingly to reformulate their ideas about how society worked and what it was for. This struggle invariably began with a renunciation of old ways and the inauguration of a search for new morally and politically acceptable habits that made room for modern life. In many societies, the renunciation of the old meant moving away from conservative, organic ideas about social obligations and toward the recognition of individual liberties. Sometimes the renunciation of the old also meant relinquishing the revolutionary socialism of the earlier nineteenth century and embracing a democratic socialism that recognized the legitimacy of political processes. But in the United States, where neither true conservatism nor true radicalism had really flourished, the renunciation of old ways took on the form of an attack on traditional liberalism and a groping toward some conception of society that would permit a definition of social responsibility—of what citizens in a modern America might conceivably owe to each other as a matter of decency and duty—that might fit within the frame of liberal prejudices on which the thin canvas of American institutions was stretched. In a society where the dollar was almighty and the only really legal relationship was a contractual one, Americans struggled to explain what kinds of obligations might comprise a community life worth living.[3]

For many years, Progressive-era Americans' "search for a public interest that would transcend particularity," or their "quest for union and meaning amid a decaying culture," has seemed to historians simply, in the words of one interpreter, a "search for order"—an order preferable only for its orderliness, without respect for liberty or regard for individual fulfillment.[4] During this quest, states and state agencies (like courts and orphanages) acquired the power to look into even the most private of affairs so long as they evinced an interest in the welfare of children. The increasing power of the state to interfere with families has often seemed to buttress the orderly interpretation, seeming to expose Progressive reformers as coolly willing "to organize both sexual life and social life according to the principles of modern science."[5] This interpretation seems to me to mix results with intentions, and to confuse the brackish trickle of the Progressives' legacy with its major tributaries. Progressives sought an organizing principle for society that would accommodate liberties, encourage individual self-fulfillment, and, most important, erode invidious social distinctions. They turned—and returned—to the family because it was a unique form of social order that fulfilled itself in its dissolution—in the release of grown children, now self-governing adults, into the society. For them the family was not a shelter from a harsh society, but a starting point in transforming such a society.

There were several structural features to the American case that encouraged Progressives to think about family rather than other species of social bonds. In the past, American political thinkers had expended their intellectual elbow grease on erasing arbitrary claims to citizens' duty. No king or sovereign parliament, let alone local baron, could constrain the liberty of a citizen: only he himself (or, as women gained rights through the nineteenth century, she herself) could do that, by making a contract with another. Within the realm of contracts made, there were clear obligations people had incurred. But without contract—without money and property at stake—there were precious few ways to command an American's sense of duty. Christianity had tended to provide a certain dutiful leaven to Americans' daily bread. But by the turn of the twentieth century, even the traditional Protestant denominations, historically the conscience of American liberalism, had succumbed to such theological attenuation that they hardly dared compel believers to consider other members of the community of Christ as their brothers and sisters, without a wholesale rewriting of the gospel to make it social. The contagion of liberty had sapped the strength of all traditional institutions, even God's. New institutions would have to anticipate this assault, and to make room for liberty in their conception of duty.

Apart from the prevalence of liberal prejudices, the American case featured two further distinctive tendencies that determined its different political progress. First, the industrial problem that American Progressives confronted was not nearly so clearly a problem of labor as it was one of immigration. Between 1890 and 1914, the United States drew about fifteen million immigrants principally from countries in South and East Europe. Peasants and craftsmen left when shaken from their traditional places by industrialization, seeking higher wages and good (or good enough) work, which they expected to find in America. They left when pogroms or political upheaval stigmatized their people, expecting to endure less brutal stigmatization in America. The appearance of these immigrants, so different from the German, English, and other West European populations already well-represented in America, shook existing conceptions of who belonged, and how they belonged, to an American community. Did transients belong? Did believers in other gods? Did speakers of foreign tongues? And if so, how could they learn to belong responsibly—to act as citizens, self-governing and informed of their rights? American Progressives tended to address these questions first, whereas their European and Antipodean counterparts concerned themselves more with the emergence of a native-born industrial working class—a different, no more tractable, but largely internal phenomenon that raised different questions about the nature of society.[6]

Progressivism in America also involved women much more thoroughly than the concurrent social politics of other countries did. The most important instance of women's role in Progressivism was the settlement-house movement, which saw middle-class, university-educated women living together in large houses in urban, immigrant neighborhoods for the purpose of educating and enlightening the newly arrived Americans. Although the settlement houses borrowed heavily and explicitly from English precedent, the English version of these houses relied much more extensively on reform-minded men with connections to Oxford University and other elite institutions than their American counterparts could, or would, do; in the United States, the houses comprised primarily unmarried and independent-minded women, such as Jane Addams, Lillian

Wald, and Florence Kelley.[7] The presence and political influence of the settlement-house women inspired a younger generation of American women to think beyond their duty to their families to their duty to society—and even their duty to themselves.

Both these latter two characteristics of Progressivism—the importance of immigrants and of women—made the issue of family into a matter of political discussion, and sometimes of controversy. Even though immigrants did not always arrive as the poorest of the poor, homeless and all but wholly ignorant of the world, reformers tended to see them that way: they believed the newcomers needed comfort and education, and an explanation of how the United States worked, so they might become independent, self-governing citizens. And nobody could better supply these needs than the well-educated, well-connected, and unmarried daughters of a professional class whose universities were open to them but whose professions were not. These women invented careers of their own, serving evident social needs. But mothering whole communities precluded (so one argument went) mothering one's own children. A settlement-house worker could have one or the other, but not both—certainly not easily. The women of the settlement houses tended to describe their careers as substitutes for family relations, and for many years historians have echoed this contemporary judgment, often referring explicitly to the writings of Jane Addams. Addams was one of the most eloquent of Progressive reformers and the best-known of the settlement-house workers, famous for her success in establishing and promoting Hull House in Chicago, where middle-class women lived and worked in the heart of one of the city's poorest immigrant districts. She justified the living and working arrangement of Hull House by identifying a conflict between social roles that tore at the consciences of educated middle-class women. These women's families believed they had a claim on them to serve as caretakers for older relatives and for children and also as marriageable links up the social ladder. But (Addams argued) educated women themselves recognized that the society in which they lived—and that had given them advantages so much greater than those it had given their fellow-citizens—required different behavior of them than it had of their mothers. Society, newly teeming with undereducated immigrants preyed upon by party bosses and ruthless employers, demanded that educated women give their time to the remedy of these public ills, rather than to the private matters of the household. Addams's counterposition of the family and the social claim suggested that even though it might be personally painful for them to do it, women had an obligation to forgo their traditional familial roles to serve a morally superior social role. She framed the choice in terms of sacrifice—"in the effort to sustain the moral energy necessary to work out a more satisfactory social relation, the individual often sacrifices the energy which should legitimately go into the fulfilment [sic] of personal and family claims, to what he considers the higher claim"—and she tended to use gender-neutral language, but the predicament she described and the solution she outlined specifically addressed the concerns of educated women. There appeared to be a basic conflict between women's familial role and their reform work, and indeed doing the latter sort of work often required that women forgo families and children of their own, even should they greatly want them.[8]

Scholars of the period have therefore habitually identified the conflict between family and social claims as a felt, present discomfort that spurred educated women to take up public roles as reformers—and also to decide not to marry, or to divorce, so as to free themselves from the family claim. Contemporary observers identified an increasing number of divorces between 1890 and 1920 as evidence of women's increased freedom—for good or ill, depending on the politics of the observer. Historians have tended to identify the increase in divorces as marking a shift in the way Americans tended to view marriage. Through the course of the nineteenth century, as Americans tended more and more to move to cities, American families had been changing from self-contained economic and social institutions to arrangements increasingly dependent on market economies and large institutions for their daily bread and for the activities that took up the bulk of their waking time. The marriage, which had been chiefly an economic and social institution, came now to symbolize, and provide, a primarily emotional satisfaction—and if it could not do that, then Americans felt licensed to dissolve the relationship. Indeed, historians have tended to see the increased divorce rate as evidence that divorce functioned as a necessary safety valve for this more emotionally intense variety of marriage.[9]

Women reformers' decisions not to marry, or to divorce, meant they spent less time in the company of men. Historians have suggested this separation reinforced an apparent division between the moral values of men and of women in the period. As one writes, "In reality there may have been *two* Progressive eras, one based on the cultural politics of men, the other based on the cultural politics of women."[10] Men were supposed to be interested in economics and politics, in rationalizing the workings of the economy through financial reforms, regulating industry, and providing benefits for male laborers. These were traditional, public concerns and thus traditionally the province of men. Women by contrast were supposed to be interested in abolishing child labor and making working conditions for women more humane—reforms that, though they impinged on public matters, grew directly out of women's traditional, private concerns with home and family.

The study of women's separate reforms has from its beginning been linked to a set of assumptions, not always explicit, about women's distinctive role in politics. These assumptions derive from the axiom that introducing women's voices into political debate did not merely increase the quantity of that debate but changed its basic quality. Women's politics were different because they had different histories from men and played different social roles. Women had greater material interest in the welfare of children than men did. Therefore, historians discovered, the politics that women brought into public debate from their distinctively female institutions were distinctively female politics: maternalist politics, as we have come to describe them. Thus women fulfilling the social claim were not only transferring their moral energy from the private to the public sphere (as Addams wrote) but transferring their mothering role along with that energy. By drawing on cultural assumptions about women's specific authority as mothers, women reformers were able to see maternalist policies created, followed by government agencies to implement those policies, and finally were able to run those agencies themselves in keeping with their own convictions. The best example here is the federal Children's Bureau, which grew directly out of conversations in Hull House and the Henry Street settlement house, and which was ultimately run by settlement worker Julia Lathrop. The bureau fed a hunger for helpful information on bringing children up in American cities, and served as a library and counselor to its client mothers.[11]

That women reformers had a specific material interest in identifiable women's issues (especially those relating to the rearing of children) does not logically entail their pursuing these interests in a distinctively feminine manner. But it might be reasonable to suppose that focusing on these specific issues often went hand-in-hand with the assumption that they were the most important, and even the defining, issues of public policy. On this ground, the historiographical school of the maternalist state has grown, rooting itself in the thesis that women reformers believed themselves especially suited, by virtue of their virtue (so to speak), to pursue a politics of public welfare based on the nurturing of dependent classes of citizens. The maternalist state never became reality, but (the argument goes) its outlines eventually provided the basis for the modern welfare state. This thesis has relied on the observation that women reformers in the Progressive period had launched themselves on a "project of authorizing and constructing their identities as women committed to making society in their likeness";[12] that is to say, women sought to re-create society as feminine and maternal, because it reinforced their convictions about the moral virtue of femininity and motherhood.

This elevation of women's politics from historically contingent practice to ideologically informed culture has allowed historians to speak, relying on a common understanding of the term, of "the maternalist politics that fueled Progressivism nationally," and has also led to the emergence of *maternalist* as a noun to denote a Progressive reformer.[13] And these maternalist reformers appear to have fought masculine, paternalist reformers. Women did not enter the political lists unopposed, and the maternalist state did not suit all politicians or even all reformers. The women's movement did not therefore fall from prominence after suffrage: it was pushed off by masculinists, advocates of a paternalist state and a politics antithetical to maternalism. Though the literature on this subject is not yet so diverse as the literature on women's reform politics, it covers a newly militant Protestantism (in which male reformers "condemned the women's movement in no uncertain terms" and reacted by campaigning to retake the moral authority of the churches from women) and a new, politically informed interest in fatherhood (in that men launched a "male recapture of the domestic space").[14]

Thus it has become possible to see male reformers as the opponents of a female agenda: the two Progressive eras that historians identify were not only contemporaneous and distinct, but at odds. Either male reformers drove female reformers out of the public sphere or, acting as the agents of a hegemonic political culture, they absorbed maternalist initiatives into their own agendas and deprived them of their distinctive and subversive character: "Male politicians used maternalist rhetoric . . . merely as a cloak for paternalism."[15]

The problem with so thoroughly gendered a history of Progressivism is that it places explanatory burdens on the thoughts of reformers that they cannot reasonably be expected to bear. It requires us to believe that for any given Progressive, his or her most important filter for translating private morality into public action was a masculine or feminine understanding of duty. But at bottom, it is difficult to distinguish, case by case, women's politics from men's, and it is even more problematic to suggest that in practice there is a gendered difference in political action. Most historians will therefore still stop "short of making a general argument that women behave differently than men under bureaucratic conditions or that a female-dominated state would look different."[16] Even when trying explicitly to explain such differences, scholars find it difficult: one writes that maternalist agencies were "female-dominated public agencies implementing regulations and benefits for the good of women and their children," and that paternalist ones were those "in which male bureaucrats would administer regulations and social insurance 'for the good' of breadwinning industrial workers."[17] The use of judgmental quotation marks here flags the principal difficulty with a thesis of rigorous opposition: it presumes different, gendered notions of "the good" that remain indefinite and are hard to find when we descend to cases. If the Progressive idea of the social good differed from men to women, we *should* find women and men defining themselves within their gender, and reasoning out from that notion of gendered virtue to a corresponding notion of public good.

Language that suggests this mode of thought does indeed sometimes crop up in the period. But in theory at least there is a great gulf between noting the prevalence of maternalist language and asserting the existence of a maternalist ideology. The former observation refers to persuasive rhetoric: reformers would appeal to maternal analogies much as they might appeal to agrarian, republican, or classical analogies, none of which necessarily signifies motive or belief. A politician could refer to motherhood because of its persuasive power without necessarily believing maternal values should determine social policy.[18] The latter assertion refers to a set of principles that governs the way Progressives saw the world: women reformers believed themselves the keepers of maternal values and therefore applied these values to the project of reform.

Despite this distinction, which makes a difference if we are concerned to discover what Progressives really wanted to achieve, historians sometimes move easily from the former idea to the latter. It is often a key element of such analyses that women reformers "thought of themselves" in distinctly virtuous, gendered terms—that they had "a remarkable kind of maternalist political consciousness."[19] This argument depends exclusively on what the reformers believed about themselves. Again, descending to cases it is awfully difficult to make this suggestion stick. To take a specific example that historians sometimes use, it might be possible to argue that Mary Ritter Beard involved herself with projects that constructed women's identity as virtuous, both privately and publicly, and so worked in such efforts as were "closely linked to the traditional female sphere."[20] But Beard's career does not fit this interpretation. As Beard herself wrote, though there were bourgeois women who defined themselves with reference to the traditional sphere (setting themselves apart from laborers on one hand and the luxurious rich on the other), "this list does not complete the types of modern women"—and as for herself, she was not on it. She believed Progressive reform represented "a long journey from women's old spheres," that the reforms of "club women" had "broken down the walls of the traditional sphere," and that ultimately she could no longer countenance "the non-historic historiography of feministic dialectics devised in 1848."[21] Throughout her career she made it clear she did not imagine herself applying the moral lessons of women's sphere to the larger world, but rather rejected the notion of that sphere as a limit to her political activity.

And Mary Beard was neither alone nor eccentric. As one historian writes, there were important and influential women reformers of the Progressive period who "did not talk about a female temperament. . . . In addition, although the institutions they characteristically developed were women-centered . . . they shared interests, methodologies, and cooperative projects with male social scientists."[22] For such women the dissolution of a fixed feminine identity was the essence of progress, a project linked to the development of research-oriented social sciences and the revelation that femininity had a history that might or might not be useful, depending on the occasion.[23]

Furthermore, similar analytical problems appear on the masculine side of the Progressive divide. Even though it is difficult to distinguish the politics of men from the politics of women, there is no question that there was a language of masculinity that had a definite rhetorical appeal in the period. But to suggest that it governed male reformers' perception of their identity and their proposed political activities is to take a further, and unwarranted, leap in logic. For one thing, a considerable proportion of the literature on masculinity and Progressivism (as indeed of the literature on Progressivism itself) depends heavily on the biography of Theodore Roosevelt. Despite his undeniable political influence, Roosevelt was exception to a variety of rules about identity in his own time. He spent a tremendous amount of time and energy on his manly image because early in his career he fell prey to a popular linkage between aristocratic airs and effeminacy, a link that earned him the sobriquets "Rosy Roosy," "Jane Dandy," "Oscar Wilde," and "the exquisite Mr. Roosevelt."[24] Roosevelt used a theatrical masculinity as a preemptive strike to forestall such accusations aimed at his upbringing. He believed he had to do this because he was a public figure. It does not necessarily follow that these masculine ideas governed his ambitions or desires, let alone those of contemporary men who did not have to suffer the slings and arrows of political publicity the way a president did. And in the case of more ordinary men of the period, historians have documented the disjunction between masculine rhetoric and middle-class reality. The rhetoric of the strenuous life was little more than "vigorous fantasy life masking but not contradicting masculine domesticity." Men could go to exotic places in their dream lives if they had to, but they did not expect to live there (a conclusion warranted even by the example of Roosevelt, who was, as it turns out, extremely domestic).[25]

Given this series of objections to a strictly gendered interpretation, the existence and eminence of married Progressive couples requires a closer look. In each of these couples, a man and a woman reformer worked each alongside the other, together and in parallel. Just what did these men and women think they were doing together if they were involved in gendered, separate worlds of reform? A dismissive critic might say that Charles and Mary Beard simply were special—or that Lucy Sprague and Wesley Clair Mitchell were, or Dorothy Whitney and Willard Straight. But once we start looking, reform couples crop up everywhere. Consider not only these three (the three in this study) but also (for example) Bruce and Rose Bliven, Heywood Broun and Ruth Hale, Robert and Martha Bruère, Clarence and Ruby Darrow, Bruce and Betty Gould, Ernest and Agnes Hocking, Frederic and Marie Jenny Howe, Harry and Belle Moskowitz, Herbert and Elsie Clews Parsons, Amos Pinchot and Ruth Pickering, Raymond and Margaret Dreier Robins, Robert and Mary Church Terrell, Stephen and Louise Waterman Wise, and Robert M. and Belle Case La Follette, among others.[26]

It would of course be possible to explain the mere fact of such couples within a separatist, gendered analysis by arguing that these marriages had distinct public and private components, and that the lines of gender divided these marriages even if political convenience kept them together (when they did stay together). In such a framework, the archetypal married Progressives would look something like Eleanor and Franklin Roosevelt. "Most Rooseveltians are either Franklinites or Eleanorites," as one writer observes, just as we have come to see most Progressives as either masculinist or feminist. The two Roosevelts moved in different worlds, though they were joined under the loose-fitting mantle of Progressive, and later New-Deal-inflected, liberalism. They had different allies, friends, and (it appears) extramarital lovers. They worked together like executives of the same company, and Eleanor was its traveling representative: "She is forever on the move, on the firm's behalf of course, but there are hints she would rather be anywhere than at his side."[27] He betrayed her, and she never forgave him. Before the critical episode, Eleanor had been scarcely political, "only marginally involved in the fray," and without her own voice. Afterward, and in some way because of what it suggested to her, she became active on her own behalf.[28]

So far we have a neatly divided, gendered, yet married pair of Progressives. But in no way could we honestly characterize the Roosevelts as believing their relationship should serve as a model for social relationships generally. If they had not thought of themselves as worlds apart from ordinary people before their private crisis of 1919–20, they certainly did afterward. Like many powerful people, they believed their personal relations were their own business, as they carried on their operations in a "divided . . . house."[29] Americans have monumentalized their sense of this division in the Roosevelt memorial in Washington. It is the only presidential memorial to feature a First Lady at all, but in it the massive bronze FDR sits by a gigantic replica of his little dog Fala, while Eleanor appears around the corner and considerably smaller, in a recessed cupboard of her own. They remain apart from each other, and from us.

If the Roosevelts were our template—if there were a barrier in these marriages between personal identity and public mission—then a thesis of distinct, gendered paradigms could incorporate the bare fact of Progressive marriages. But such a thesis cannot account for the conscientious attempt to apply the relations implicit in marriage and family to larger social relations, which is an attempt we find Progressives of all kinds making. For example, Jane Addams is, as we have seen, best known for her explanation of the opposition between the family claim and the social claim not least because she dedicated her own life to the fulfillment of the social claim. But the argument she made to justify her politics does not go a further step and suggest a contradictory division between family and society or between private and public morality—indeed, quite the opposite.

Addams identified her generation as belonging to a peculiar historical moment when secular social trends challenged the institution of the
family. Because middle-class women had now attained university degrees
they now possessed a measure of power and privilege. Further, because
their society's promise of substantive equality was threatened by the pres-
sures of immigration and industrialization as well as by the obviously
inadequate responses to these developments, duty called: such educated
women could not afford to consider themselves solely as creatures of their
own homes. Addams believed that "our democracy is making inroads on
the family . . . and a claim is being advanced which in a certain sense is
larger than the family claim." But this observation led her to urge a transformation, rather than an abandonment, of the family claim. "The family, like every other element of human life, is susceptible of progress, and
from epoch to epoch its tendencies and aspirations are enlarged."[30]

Addams's own experience highlighted the shortcomings of America's
allegedly democratic society, and nothing revealed these shortcomings
better than the contact between reformers and their intended reformees.
When educated U.S.-born women in their confining corsets and petti-
coats stood face-to-face with the overalled and soft-capped workers who
had only just arrived on American shores, they knew they teetered on the
brink of a social and cultural divide. But the vertigo they felt did not permit them to step back, Addams reasoned. It meant they must press forward to bridge the gap. That uncomfortable meeting between two cultures was the "point of contact in our modern experience which reveals
so clearly the lack of equality which democracy implies." The solution,
Addams believed, was to alter the character of social relations to eliminate the gulf between the two classes of people. Reformers must come to
"care for the unworthy among the poor as we would care for the unworthy among our own kin. . . . To say that it should never be so, is a comment upon our democratic relations to them which few of us would be
willing to make." Thus, as she wrote, "the family in its entirety must be
carried out into the larger life."[31]

Addams would carry these convictions about the proper nature of
social relations into party politics, delivering a speech nominating
Theodore Roosevelt for the presidency at the Progressive Party convention in 1912. Addams, who mistrusted Roosevelt for his belligerency,
sought influence by compromising her pacifist principles.[32] They did,
however, share more than political opportunism. When Roosevelt could

be pried away from the lure of war, he shared Addams's vision of social relations.

If in time of war Roosevelt yielded too easily to a worse self, this tendency only highlights by contrast the open, liberal approach to social and family relations that mark him as a Progressive. For example, in a 1917 investigation of the relationship between middle-class society and the working-class or immigrant family, he reported himself fascinated by the adaptive philosophy of the Juvenile Workers' Bureau, which (he wrote) "never commits the dreadful fault of reducing all cases to the same test. It tries to keep the family together, so long as there is any possibility of good coming from the effort; but where necessary it unhesitatingly protects and separates the boy or girl from the drunken mother or brutal father." In dealing with illegitimate children, the juvenile courts had also played to Roosevelt's open-mindedness. "I was myself sufficiently under the rule of tradition to assume that the desirable thing was to secure the marriage of the parents; but the lady who was chief of the woman's division of the criminal department explained to me that in actual practice this had not been found desirable."[33] Roosevelt approved of an open approach to families that responded to social needs. For him, family also expanded outward into society: "the meaning of free government" included his notion that what he called "the parent class" had to foster independence not only in their own children but in "the people as a whole."[34]

Given Roosevelt's approval of this elastic approach to families and his criticism of "wooden and cramping formalism" in familial morality, the increasingly dogmatic pronouncements he made in his warrior mode are the more shocking. As war encouraged him to do so, he emphasized the imposition of state duty on family structure. "Patriotism . . . consists in putting duty before the question of individual rights. This must be done in our family relations," he wrote, and he advocated cramping and formal masculine-soldier and feminine-mother roles for men and women. These roles ossified into gender-specific fighting and nurturing roles whenever Roosevelt elevated himself to rhetorical dudgeon, which he did more and more as World War I wore on. When aroused to this demagogic degree, Roosevelt's familial metaphors grew ever more rigid and righteous, as when he compared internationalists to philanderers who love other women as much as they love their own wives.[35] Roosevelt's reaction to war provides us with a clear-cut example of the great threat that war posed to Progressivism: it changed the way citizens constructed their social obligations and destroyed their hopes of re-creating families as sources of social reform.

Had Addams simply advocated nurturing roles for women—had Roosevelt advocated only the mother/soldier vision of the family that he thought necessary in time of war—then it would be necessary to describe the Progressive vision of family as essentially conservative.[36] But both of them promoted an expansive vision of the family, extending beyond domestic walls into the larger society and forging kinship ties across class lines, and both of them referred to this idea of family when they discussed the potential of reform projects. Further, the socialized morals of the liberal family, advocated by both Addams and Roosevelt (in time of peace), helped during the Progressive period to foster the use of marriage and family as ideal models for a liberal society, and even the self-conscious remodeling of actual marriages and families in keeping with these political ideals. Familial language and ideals were only one of the tropes available to Progressives—there were Jefferson-inspired agrarian metaphors, and new, tentative imperialist metaphors—but marriage and family were ideals sufficiently close to urban-American norms to allow optimistic experimentation in everyday life. By looking at the three families in this study—the Beards, the Mitchells, and the Straights—it will be possible to outline the utility and the limits of the family as an organizing principle for Progressive politics.

As defined in liberal philosophy and practice, the family is a paradoxical institution. Parents legitimately enjoy authority over children only so long as they cultivate in their children an ability to live independently. Thus the family is a form of hierarchical social order that can justify its existence only when it undoes itself. If we understand how this conception of the family underlay Progressives' sense of their social obligations, we will be able to see that Progressives did not desire either order or individualism per se. Rather, they sought to impose on society a moral system whose end was a progressively wider diffusion of rights and goods among the populace. As a model engine for this diffusion, the liberal family promoted this spread of liberties by a repeatable devolution of power from those who had it to those who could. The partnered marriages such as those in this study provided the beginnings of such families and the core of reformist institutions that fulfilled similar roles with respect to their dependents.[37]

A liberal understanding of family was the heart of a moral system that sensibly organizes the Progressives' politics. It contained assumptions about human nature: that human beings require education, so that once they comprehend the truth they will act morally upon it. It contained assumptions about the appropriate relations between social equals: that spouses and members of the same generation act not only on contracts they make with each other, but out of a commitment to each other's self-fulfillment. It contained assumptions about appropriate relations between the powerful and the powerless: that parents govern children only because they teach children to govern themselves. The ideal liberal family (unlike, for example, the tribal family) had permeable boundaries. Its relations extended out into society to provide assistance and education to the needy and at the logical extreme to the adoption of the orphaned. Further, society extended into it, giving rights to children and responsibilities to parents. The liberal family was a model for society as Progressives imagined it should be. Most important, because families entail narratives of maturation and succession, they provided an explanation for how progress from the old to the new was supposed to occur. Children grew up, attained their independence, and built on the inheritance they received from their parents. Authority devolved from one generation to the next, but knowledge continued. In short, the liberal family tells us what was progressive about Progressivism. As we look closely at Progressive couples with attention to their ideas about themselves and their lives as reformers, we see these families forming, growing, and attempting to extend their influence out into society and onward into the future.

The favorite Progressive reform was a new school, a research bureau, a new publication, or an information clearinghouse. These measures are better characterized as educational than as interventionist. Even at their most activist, what Progressives most wanted was to teach, to make society "a school where democratic experiments could be worked out as they should be."[38] Why? In part, of course, because it was financially and politically cheaper to teach than to do. Institutions of education were more politically acceptable and less accountable than programs that could compose what we might think of as a prototypical welfare state. But in their political cheapness, these measures for education reflected widespread and influential values. These institutions of reform acted toward their dependents as liberal parents did toward their children, teaching them to achieve their independence. Even when such reforms became arms of the state—like the federal Children's Bureau—they spent their time principally gathering and disbursing information. In the bureau's most active mode, it represented the state in the role of a library or an advice columnist, and its dependents—the mothers who relied on it—leaned on it of their own accord and did so only as long as they needed to.[39]

Traditionally, historians have seen the Progressive period as one in which the state increasingly encroached on American families. New state agencies and courts and new welfare legislation appeared designed to regulate the family in the interest of social order. Over the course of the nineteenth century, marriage had changed legally so that women no longer merged into a single legal being with their husbands: they were by 1900 generally recognized as independent, contracting beings with a legal existence of their own. Children, too, had a new legal status, serving no longer merely as extensions of the parental will but emerging as legally distinct persons with their own rights. This newly liberalized legal vision of the family was qualified by an often implicit but (some historians argue) widely understood set of norms: freedom within marriage was a privilege extended to those who generally adhered to social norms and kept up a standard, monogamous relationship that did not challenge taboos of race, class, or politics. "Family savers," as one historian calls them, re-created marriage as a cultural training ground for conservative social values. The involvement of the state in family affairs thus became a way for the powerful to impose orderly behavior on the powerless.[40]

There are at least two problems with identifying Progressive reformers who sought to extend families out into society, and vice versa, with this repressive cultural regime of familial law and order. First, it assumes that the policy regime that emerged necessarily reflected Progressives' desires regarding the family. This assumption attributes motives on the basis of consequences and entirely cuts out the rebellious nature of Progressive thought. Progressives drew their ideas about families from their experience, as indeed they did all their ideas about reform, and they found their experience at odds with social norms. They clamored loudly to see those norms changed, and they changed them within their own lives. If this process of ferment led to the state taking a more interfering, activist role in family life, it is not because Progressives wanted it, but because unforeseen consequences resulted, as they often do, from political agitation. And indeed, these unforeseen consequences almost always arise not because of the ideas behind proposed reforms, but because those ideas are invariably transformed by powerful interests in the course of making policy. This suggests the second problem: we often tend to blame the unhappy results of policy regimes on the ideas that inspired them, rather than on the incidents and the systems that see those ideas translated into policies. There is in modern life a considerable divide between even the best educated, most articulate private members of society and the makers of policy—a divide occasionally bridged, but rarely closed. The Progressive period was no exception. Reformers who sought to make their families into engines for transforming society saw instead the state—in its rude health after a world war—exert increasing control over social relations.[41]

If Progressives were principally interested in the development of a welfare state, they would have been morally derelict in leaning on families and familial relations when they should instead have been arguing for a stronger state. But they may well have wanted something different from a stronger state. They liked to use phrases like, "not toward socialism, but toward socialization," as Willard Straight wrote. To us this locution may sound temporizing, but there was more coherence than compromise in this belief. "Paternalism in any form—no matter how beneficial its results—will not ultimately be acceptable," Straight wrote. "What has hitherto been termed philanthropy—like commerce and industry and politics—will tend gradually to conform to a more democratic ideal." As the Progressives tended to do, Straight envisioned a parenting role—an imbalance of power—ending through fulfillment in a more nearly egalitarian society.[42]

When Progressives applied the basic familial narrative of maturation (from dependence to independence) to their reform projects, they were also applying the lessons of their own experience. In telling their own stories they tended to emphasize their equivocal relations to social norms, including those defined by gender, and also to traditional familial duties. They believed that in the course of their own education they had learned to move beyond these limits. When they brought up the matter of gender, they discussed their lives in terms of either exemption from or manipulation of social expectations. They described their coming-of-age experiences—their attaining of independence—in terms of a conversion from traditional roles. "If the incident hadn't occurred," Mary Ritter Beard said about her own political awakening, "I might have gone on giggling my way through life."[43] They dedicated themselves to reproducing this moment of realization for others, hoping they might similarly mature.

Their experience of awakening made them uncomfortable with their prescribed roles—giggling ingenue, marriageable debutante, swaggering imperialist, and so on—and it forced them to reassess their relationship to the family as an institution. For some women, mostly for women a little older than those considered here, this process of reassessment led them to forsake marriage: they could not pursue a career as reformers and marry as well. But for women and educated men a little younger than that pioneering generation, it seemed possible, and even desirable, to reconcile these two demands. Women and men of the Progressives' generation were able—when income and education permitted—to see themselves as "choosing to marry," rather than being forced into it. Historians have sometimes regarded the increase in marriages among this generation—following on the decrease in marriages among the first generation of university-educated women—as an example of a population regressing to the mean. But the variables of income and education, which both had to be high for these self-consciously partnered marriages to work, suggest that this population did not consist of the sort of people who regress to means, but rather of the sort who conscientiously challenge them.[44]

One of Wesley Clair Mitchell's favorites among his own essays dealt with this contradiction between logic and experience in understanding the meaning of marriage. It seemed logical to him, as it had seemed to other activists, that the family as an institution could not survive close rational analysis. It was economically inefficient. Yet it stubbornly persisted.

Any thinking person could see (Mitchell believed) that the antiquated family structure really should yield to a consumers' "commissariat with its trained corps of purchasing agents and chemists, each giving his whole working day to the buying or testing of meats, vegetables, or groceries. Then there would be the departments of buildings and grounds, of furnishing, of fuel and lighting, of the laundry, of clothing, of the nursery and the like." Instead the business of consumption remained limited to the single household presided over by a mother, who with the best will in the world could not match the expertise of producers or the wiles of marketers. But as adaptive as Americans proved in other circumstances, here they did not change. Mitchell wanted to know why.

He offered a disarmingly simple answer. We have not abandoned the family "because we have not wanted to," he said. "Our race-old instincts of love between the sexes and parental affection, long since standardized in the institution of monogamy, are a part of experience at once so precious and so respectable that we have looked askance at every relaxation of the family bond, whatever material advantages it has promised." The family, Mitchell believed, had become an integral part of the complex of feelings and presumptions through which Americans examined the world. Mitchell admitted his consciousness of these prejudices, but refrained from offering a prescriptive answer to the deeper question: not, ought we to do away with families—for the answer to that was obviously, rationally, yes—but, ought we to want to? He could not be sure. The relationships implied in families seemed to him more important than the rational goals of a sound, efficient economy. "The ultimate problem of what is worth while to strive for is not to be solved by sounder organization, by better training, or by the advance of science."[45]

It was not therefore through logical persuasion or the accumulation of data, not through a gospel of efficiency or an appeal to civic virtue, that reformers could get what they wanted from American life. In the advance of innovation on the political arena, mere reasoning (as the philosopher Isaiah Berlin observed) is "an ancillary weapon, not the principal means of conquest: that is the new model itself, which casts its own emotional or intellectual or spiritual spell upon those who are converted."[46] The liberal family was this model. It supplied a set of generally unquestioned presumptions about proper social relations. Rational economics and politics notwithstanding, the structure of the family, separate from though not immune to the corrosive effects of liberal political economy, told Progressives "what is worth while to strive for." When applied to social problems, it made possible what Mitchell called a "slow modification of the broad social conditions." The extension of family obligations into society allowed a community to move toward "socialized spending of money with a neighborhood instead of a family as the unit." The family expanded, however slowly, outward. The boundaries between it and the larger society blurred, though they remained. Thus progress occurred, preserving what middle-class Americans, in Mitchell's homely phrase, "wanted to."[47]

For a time Progressives found themselves able to create not only marriages and families that fulfilled their ambitions but also reform enterprises that grew out of their households and expanded their sphere of influence. Their ability to do so depended on their belief that what was true of them was true of everyone; that anyone who knew what they knew would call for the same political action that they did; that society consisted of "like-minded and mutually supportive citizens."[48] If it were so, then Progressives' experience of revelation, of conversion, and of liberation from confining social convention could be repeated endlessly throughout an apparently diverse society. So they created programs of education and supervised living based on their faith in a common human need for liberation from dependence on such social conventions.

This faith in human commonality persisted until something dramatic interfered with it: World War I. The effort to mobilize the U.S. populace undermined the Progressives' faith in the educability and enlightenment of the ordinary citizen. Reformers who had previously believed they were making progress by increasing the spread of knowledge now confronted instead an "intensely emotional, unreasoning, partisan, and cruel attitude," as Dorothy Whitney Straight wrote.[49] But the war did more than cause them to question their faith in the common man. More important, it forced them to confront the intransigence of gender norms as cultural myths that limited the behavior of people of their own class. In time of war, the state can draw on such myths to mobilize the population, in effect socializing human resources by an appeal to gender: men become warriors; women become self-sacrificing keepers of the home front. Wartime propaganda and special wartime education programs—such as those to ready boys for war work—threatened Progressives' special province and put the state in a position to "clip children" to fit its mold, as Lucy Sprague Mitchell charged.[50] Facing such obstacles, Progressive efforts to transcend or circumvent social dictates had to halt or face charges of disloyalty. At that point, having grown tired of the he-men and the virtuous women, Progressives withdrew to seek different, less public and less loud, avenues of reform: "Please, let me depart quietly," Mary Ritter Beard wrote.[51] The mobilization of state and society for war forced a reconsideration of the means and probable end of education as a social reform, especially the utility of the family metaphor as a way of transforming social processes.

If this story ends on a minatory note, it begins in a crescendo of hope and ambition. The liberal vision of the family inspired Progressive politics at a time when middle-class Americans had every reason to believe that the blessings they had enjoyed all their lives would apply not only to their children, but to the children of their less-fortunate neighbors as well. In the absence of harsh evidence to the contrary, and in the presence of their own remarkable experience, it was possible for them to believe that the story of their own independence could become everyone's story. Despite the shame of certain neighborhoods, Americans at the turn of the century had good reason to believe their cities were becoming cleaner, more democratic, and better run—that "democracy could work in an urban America."[52] Immigrants of this generation, like those of 1848, would become solid, dependable U.S. citizens. Combinations of capital would yield to public pressure. The end of Spain's colonization of the Western Hemisphere in 1898 might even mean the beginning of a new international era of democratization, when American ideals and institutions would spread on their own merits. In this atmosphere, Progressives set about making their own destinies—a project in which they were left to themselves until the war.

Though each of the cases considered here has its individual hallmarks, they share the same important elements. First, the men and women involved had to reckon with prevailing social prescriptions for their behavior. As men or as women, they were supposed to fulfill certain roles both in society and in their families. They had to decide for themselves how they would ignore or modify these descriptions so they could pursue careers as reformers. Hence the prominence, in each of their own stories about themselves, of the rhetoric of conversion or transformation, revealing their underlying assumption that they had avoided becoming ordinary burghers by becoming reformers.

Second, they had to decide how they would allow their newly chosen roles to shape their lives. If they would not set aside marriage in favor of a reformist career, then how would they incorporate the two? Their hortatory writings on how and why one should pursue a career as a reformer reveal their keen and sometimes painful interest in preserving the social bonds they believed exemplified by family, and extending these bonds into the otherwise heartless public sphere.[53]

Third, having created for themselves marriages that answered their own political and social needs, they set about pushing the boundaries of these marriages outward by making them the model for and the center of institutions that propagated reform-by-education. Each of them saw their own families as the bases for a progressively improving society.

Fourth, and most revelatory about what they expected and why they did not get what they wanted, they withdrew from active politics, reconsidered their agendas, and even retreated from their optimistic positions when the war came. The deleterious effect of World War I has for a long time been a commonplace of Progressive historiography. But the effects of the war were intimately tied up not only with shifts in discourses on gender and reform, but also with changes in the meaning of social structures, including the family, on which Progressive reformers had come to depend.[54]

For Charles and Mary Beard, marriage meant intellectual and political collaboration and parallel career development. They became formidable political activists, cultural critics, and popular historians, in each of these enterprises working with or alongside each other. Though famously secretive about the details of their private lives, they often exploited their personal histories and experiences for exemplary tales, and they were always quite clear on the essential relations of private relations to public ones. As Mary Ritter Beard wrote when they were young, marriage had historically been "at first domestic tyranny on the part of the man, and then an approach to voluntary co-operation, until we come to present-day conditions . . . when both parents are able to unite in one common ideal for the race." Though they later stopped referring quite so often to "the race," their commitment to the cooperative project persisted.[55]

Lucy Sprague and Wesley Clair Mitchell earned their reputations separately before joining each other in a negotiated partnership that they designed to include a combined commitment to social reform encompassing the education of their natural and adopted children as well as other children schooled in their house and adults enlightened by their writings. As Wesley Clair Mitchell believed, though marriage might be rationally "backward," it plainly would not yield to logic, and so instead must expand outward into society, carrying with it the elements of human relations that were most attractive.[56]

Dorothy Whitney and Willard Straight also launched themselves on their joint enterprise after establishing themselves independently, and they did so with the intention of gaining access to new worlds through each other. They created institutions together—the *New Republic* and the New School for Social Research, among others—to extend outward into the greater world the little society they had created for themselves and their children, a world of liberalized familial commitments they called "the greatest thing." As Herbert Croly (their friend and Willard's biographer) wrote, their "marriage . . . modified his relations to the world," and as her diaries and letters attest, it did the same for her.[57]

When Progressives compared themselves with conservatives on the one hand and radicals on the other, they had to explain where they fit and what they wanted, and in doing so they resorted to the various tenets of liberalism. Liberalism is itself a philosophical construct often susceptible to charges of weakness, for liberalism seems only to prescribe the absence of restrictive social ties, to expel from public consideration all pleas for organic connection; conservatives commonly charge that liberalism is only plausible as a means of opposition.[58] Corrosive though liberalism may be in the public sphere—a threat to churches and other arbitrary moral authorities—it relies on the resistance of the family to its otherwise universally solvent philosophy. If a liberal society could remain a closed system comprising a static population, it might preclude all possible inequity. But populations change and incorporate new citizens, who in the first years of their entry into society necessarily require education—in other words, children are born, and (Rousseau notwithstanding) they need bringing up. Liberalism relies on the family to meet this need, and at the turn of the century, with society taking in new citizens by the expansion of suffrage and the absorption of new immigrants, U.S. liberalism relied on the metaphor of the family to explain this process of inducting new citizens. This idea shows the centrality of family to a particular historical period in the development of American liberalism.

Wesley Clair Mitchell dismissed efficiency, scientific progress, and social order as sufficient motivating visions for reformers. None was especially inspirational, for none could itself sum up a more desirable system of social obligations. Yet they have loomed over scholarship during nearly a century's backward glances. Even the widespread destabilization of various philosophical certainties—another, essential factor in making way for Progressivism's emergence—could only establish the conditions necessary for a new social model to emerge. It could help Progressives explain that there was in fact a breach, but it could not propel them into it to close up the gap. For that they needed a vision of what social relations were supposed to look like. Formal political theory in the United States, liberal as it was, precluded almost every assertion of organic social relations that theorists could imagine. And what was more important, the character of everyday life had often enough vindicated the assumptions of liberal theory that Americans tended, even when not paying much attention, to assume they lived in a liberal society. This often unreflective assumption, which historians sometimes call "vernacular liberalism," included the notion that the bonds of affection originated in the home, but did not dogmatically assert that they must confine themselves to that refuge. They might, however slowly, extend their influence progressively outward.[59]

Current scholarship leads us to believe that gender—either masculinity or femininity—was the principal means by which Progressives translated private morality into public action. If this were true, then married Progressives would be indulging themselves in quirky personal partnerships that had nothing to do with their politics. But looking at such marriages, we see that it is not so: instead, Progressives married with the explicit intention of making their new families into engines of reform. Indeed, examination of these families makes it possible to go further and say that the idea of family was itself the means for translating private morality into public action.

So what difference does it make if Progressivism relied on a liberal politics of family? At the level of our everyday interest in the history of our society, it tells us something new—or it reminds us of something we tend to forget—about families and politics. *Family* has multiple possible political meanings that pervade our perceptions of our society, whether we think of ourselves as liberal, conservative, or neither. And historically, liberals have been quite as willing as conservatives to suggest that their vision of family should inform the political agenda. As for our understanding of Progressivism in particular, it reminds us of the loose, open, and often nonstatist character of proposed Progressive reform. Because Progressives thought of society as ideally working like a liberal family, they did not always or even often think immediately in terms of using the state to fix society's problems, even when they looked at areas—such as foreign policy—in which we are used to thinking of the state as preeminent.

At the level of professional historical scholarship, the familial idea has further specific implications. First, it suggests that Progressivism has deep roots in the structure of the bourgeois family—roots whose extent will surprise nobody who has studied the family in the nineteenth century.[60] Throughout the 1800s, the structure of the bourgeois family and its focus on preserving both property and status fueled a variety of reform movements, including abolitionism and early feminism. This connection helps explain the persistence of the family as an institution and a source of political discomfort: if the family were as inherently conservative an institution as we sometimes appear to think, we would have no qualms in surrendering it. If family relations were as politically beside the point as logic suggests they should be, they would remain outside the realm of public debate. Neither of these conditionals holds, because families are indeed little commonwealths and tell us much about how our society conceives the legitimate sources and uses of authority.

Second, this thesis suggests that we should not immediately mark as suspect all historical claims on the idea of civilization. The idea of the liberal family encapsulated for Progressives the appropriate relations between powerful and powerless people in society, a relation akin to the process of civilization as described by their contemporaries. For Progressives, *civilization* referred to the notion of social progress tending toward the equitable treatment of all citizens, and they frequently invoked it to refer not only to the construction of a desirable society in the United

States but also to the extension of ideal social relations overseas. Despite the current fondness of some politically active and conservative historians for the word *civilization*, it is worth recalling the term's roots in liberal thought. It invoked for Progressives the idea of a literally civilized—that is to say, urban—society pushing itself to greater achievements not merely in the building of bridges and tunnels but of institutions to further the cause of self-government. Charles Beard would use the word to praise top-down efforts to foster "grass-roots democracy"—reforms like those the Progressives had undertaken to diffuse power and knowledge from the centers of education to the populace.[61]

Third, it suggests that we should reenvision separate female institutions as part of a continuum of new ways of living, a complement and not a counterpart to the restructured Progressive family. The evidence relating to the construction of such families persuades me that the preceding existence of strong, separate, female institutions and a women's design for living made these marriages possible, if not inevitable. The examples and ideas of the settlement-house women encouraged a widespread reevaluation of women's political and social role—yet women did not as a consequence entirely abandon the institution of marriage. Instead, educated women discovered they could determine their relationship to men and to the conventionally masculine worlds of politics and economics by using the settlement houses and the suffrage movements as points of reference, a way of determining what else was possible.[62] They could then undertake marriage while preserving their independence, entering the world of politics rather than sheltering themselves from it. They thus redefined the family as a society rather than as a haven from it. This point also helps to explain the persistent commitment that thinking liberals have shown to the family and their willingness to associate it with liberty rather than with repression.[63]

Fourth, it suggests why the war should have had a disheartening effect on Progressive idealism: it reinforced conceptions of family and of gender inconsistent with Progressive ambitions. When the war began and the superpatriots and the "he-men" began defining what real men and real women were supposed to do, Progressives felt themselves forced to change their tactics, lest they find themselves insufficiently patriotic during wartime. War cruelly limited dreamers and dissenters alike, and it made it more difficult to differ from social norms than it had been in peacetime.[64]

The centrality of the family as an interpretive metaphor also gives us insight into the reasons for both the successes and the limits of Progressive reforms. Wherever we look into Progressive activities, we find more or less explicit notions about the appropriate relations between the privileged and the underprivileged, the elite and the larger public. American reformers, clinging gamely to the promise of American life (that an equal creation of all men and women should fulfill itself in an equally rewarding life for those men and women) could not reconcile themselves to the possibility of persistent inequities. Therefore they stood by the narratives of maturation and the achievement of independence that were the hallmark of liberal familial thinking. The only way to justify their persistent social superiority was to act deliberately to undermine it by educating their charges to become independent of their supervision. As they drew on their own experience, and acted as if it could be endlessly repeated, they believed they were extending the promise of equality ever outward. But this relation between elites and the public they served depended on time for its vindication, and instead the passage of time brought impatience, anger, and of course war, whose regimentation of society stopped the precession of knowledge and independence from one generation to the next.[65]

Last, and least hopefully, this interpretive tack implies the irretrievability of Progressivism per se, contrary to a considerable recent literature betting on its imminent resurrection.[66] The Progressives grew up in an explicitly imperialist world, where they believed their ambitions stood an excellent chance of global fulfillment. However paradoxical it may sound, when we descend to cases we see that these ambitions rested less on the increase of state power than on the spread of American institutions and customs—on the family and its relations to society, on small institutions more than on the central state. Progressives optimistically believed that beyond minimal cleanliness and shelter, all anyone really needed was to know better, to abandon ancient superstitions about social obligations (to the church, to Old World authority, to patriarchal families). They could hopefully launch their educational enterprises only because they believed that education was all any group really required to free themselves, that the proper education would create critically thinking, intelligently-self-governing citizens. Like the good liberals they were, they brought up their children in keeping with this precept, and they believed that if any social class needed bringing up or uplifting, the same principles should apply. They lived in an America where this sort of bourgeois condescension was acceptable, because without condescension there could be no perception of weakness on the part of other classes and thus no call for reform. They lived in an America where self-government meant self-discipline and individual independence, for the bonds between parents and children could only justify their existence if they ensured their ultimate dissolution. They lived in an America that did not yet tend toward statist solutions to social problems. Their America, in short, was not ours. Still, comparisons with an America not our own are useful because they help us to remember that current social reality does not result from immutable principle and may prove susceptible of change.

One

DOROTHY WHITNEY AND WILLARD STRAIGHT

You marry to get married . . . not because you want to change the world.
—Marianne Gingrich[1]

Even before it began publishing in 1914, the *New Republic* had become the focus of Progressive attention. The infant journal out of New York City seemed to speak for a generation of reformers ambitious to transform American society. Whatever its intellectual merits, it owed its prominence to the joint intentions and extensive connections of its married publishers, Dorothy Whitney and Willard Straight, who created it to fulfill the shared elements of their reform agendas and thus to give their marriage a public presence. These shared elements comprised a set of convictions about their duty to the benighted, who were in this case a public that required education on political matters so that it could manage its own affairs and become truly self-governing. While the Straights were planning the venture, they gave it the politically purposeful subtitle *A Journal of Liberal Democracy* (which later became the blander *Journal of Opinion*). The original subtitle revealed their intentions: within the framework of liberalism, the only legitimate role for the powerful was the adoption of the powerless as their temporary charges, to encourage their independence. Elites had to foster democratic self-government, though it meant ultimately undermining their own privileged standing. In this respect they behaved like proper liberal parents, the legitimacy of whose authority rested on their willingness to see to its eventual dissolution. The Straights shaped the *New Republic* as an institution and as the source of an ongoing critical social commentary to serve these purposes. Their confidence in this mission attracted and inspired innumerable Progressives precisely because the ideas they expressed echoed and amplified the experiences of their generation.

Like many of their contemporaries, both Dorothy Whitney and Willard Straight had, when younger, tried to change the world they knew, and they both succeeded within limits. Both established reform projects that addressed the relations between powerful and powerless classes of people and aimed at the ultimate independence of dependent classes. Neither found the limits on their activities satisfying and so both sought new ways of achieving the changes they desired. They found that marriage to each other afforded them, if only for a time, the chance to forge a partnership dedicated to the transformation of social relations.[2]

THE BENEVOLENT METROPOLIS

Dorothy Whitney was born in 1887 to a pair of singularly agile social climbers. William Collins Whitney married one fortune (in the person of Flora Payne) and then promptly made another of his own. He did both easily, and then unlike so many of his peers he turned his attention away from money to things he enjoyed: remaking the Metropolitan Opera House into a showplace for Manhattan society, remaking muddy Saratoga into a mecca for the horsey set, and making and remaking Grover Cleveland into the President of the United States. Throughout it all, Flora served as his partner by playing hostess to society, for that was how social climbers cemented their gains: through invitations made and accepted. Their marriage worked publicly, though privately it was (in his words) a "failure" that they kept up "for the sake of the children and society."[3]

Their concern for their children and their concern for society coincided, because for the upwardly mobile the plateau never comes unless the next generation can feel at home on the family's new height. Thus their attention to proper schools for boys; proper finishings, debuts, and betrothals for girls. In light of this pattern, which seems bound to create a conservative generation of offspring, biographers of Dorothy Whitney have puzzled over why she should have become so singularly socially active. Women of her time and place were supposed to join the Junior League and do good works to occupy their time before and after marriage. They were not supposed to allow the pursuit of good works to take the place of marriage. But Dorothy put her energy wholly into her good works for a time: she put off marriage and devoted herself instead to what she called her "social"—as opposed to her society—"obligations."[4]

As an early and constant member of the Junior League, Whitney belonged to a group of women who identified themselves chiefly as debutantes and who knew that so far as their families were concerned, they existed principally to ornament their fathers' and husbands' checkbooks. As one of her peers wrote anonymously in the *Junior League Bulletin*, the Leaguers' summer stream of consciousness probably sounded something like this:

> Three letters. Fine. Let's see—from Mary—she's going to Canada to go into camp is she? Oh! She says Laura's gone to California— I hate the train so. Poor thing I'm sorry for her—she'll miss the tournament. Hm—Oh! Well, Mary never did write anything interesting. Who's this? Jack Eustis, engaged, and to that little Irwin girl! She hates to dance and never goes out. Oh! Well, that's one more gone. Kitty does use the worst paper, I hate these passionate purple linings. Hm—hym—hm I don't believe it.[5]

They could only defend themselves against the triviality of these concerns with a plaintive credo: "That all the money and time which has been spent on us is not a lost investment to the world, that we are worth something in life . . . we want to be of some real use, no matter how small."[6] To make themselves really useful, they organized sewing circles and theatrical benefits and undertook home visits to the poor. The Junior League had originally been called the Junior League for Neighborhood Work, and the Leaguers voted themselves the principal duty of acting as teachers to the mothers among their poorer neighbors, not only through lectures and other group projects but through home visits. The Leaguer also

> visits for the teacher who through lack of time is unable to do this for herself the home of any child who has either been absent for any length of time or who in the schoolroom has seemed to be either mentally or physically below the standard, and discovers

whether or not the fault is due to home influence, ill-treatment, or perhaps lack of sufficient nourishment.[7]

To be sure, these visits might well, to their half-willing, harassed immigrant hosts, have felt more like home invasions, as a debutante Leaguer swept through the family tenement of a troubled child, censoriously seeking critical lacks in cleanliness, nourishment, or cultural environment. The Leaguers' adoption of this teacherly, parental role reflected their unflattering opinion of the immigrant poor—what one historian calls the inevitable "unexamined assumptions" of the reformer.[8] But this condescension was essential to the intellectual architecture of a reformer's imagination—if the poor of other cultures were not somehow deficient, then nothing could justify the intervention of an untrained debutante whose advantages came to her by virtue of her birth and upbringing, rather than by hard experience.

The most important way in which Dorothy Whitney differed from her fellow Leaguers was in her willingness to devote herself fully to a career of reform and not to worry about suitors. An advantage of misfortune permitted her this freedom: her mother, then her stepmother, and finally her father died while she was still a minor, leaving her in 1904, at the age of seventeen, legally in the loose care of her brother Harry and his wife Gertrude, which for all practical purposes meant she was left to herself: Harry and Gertrude had their own problems. William Whitney's will gave Dorothy an annual income of $50,000 a year (she would take full control of her capital on her majority at twenty-one) and, at least as important, he saw that she had a guardian, Beatrice Bend, whom the estate paid an additional $10,000 a year. When Dorothy looked back on her life from the vantage point of her old age, she wrote, "One event and one personal relationship were the determining factors of that period, and to a great extent, influenced the rest of my life." The death of her father gave her money, and also independence from parental concerns as to whom she might marry. The friendship of Bend gave her guidance "along a somewhat unorthodox road," as she wrote. She was dramatically, and awfully, free to do almost anything she liked.[9]

Bend was the daughter of a financier who improvidently died during a financial downturn. She helped Whitney to get a more serious education than she otherwise might, moving her from a socially prominent to a more intellectually rigorous school, and she accompanied her as she toured Europe, acquiring the American version of high culture (that is to say,

European culture). She helped Whitney to test herself safely against received opinion. Dealing intellectually with works of art, Whitney worried alternately that she was "unoriginal in her tastes" for conforming too much to canonical judgment and then "felt ashamed to admit that I don't care for Raphael's 'Transfiguration,'" and other presumably important pictures, artificial and natural alike: "I don't understand why it is called the blue Danube for it is really a dirty greenish color. Perhaps I haven't got an artistic eye!" As she saw more and thought more she grew surer in her judgment, and she dismissed masterpieces she did not like as "stupid."[10] Throughout her education, her relationship with Bend was the foremost fact of both their lives. She called Bend "Sister" and Bend called Whitney "Angel." When they parted, however briefly, Whitney missed her greatly: "I have never felt so lonely in all my life. What shall I do without her!" When they fought (over issues Whitney did not record), it depressed her. Bend was Whitney's closest early influence; she wanted to see her young charge do something useful with her moneyed life—and she had, in her own later words, "a prejudice against matrimony."[11]

Thus Dorothy Whitney spent her youth in a world of women that became for a while her whole world. Though she made her debut and did not lack for the standard range of importunate swains, she gave little serious thought to marriage. Instead, she spent her time taking the Junior League more seriously than the run of its members did. She became its president at the age of eighteen. On attaining her majority at twenty-one, she moved into a Manhattan apartment with Ruth Morgan, a like-minded woman of similar background. Both of them took classes at Columbia, seeking "the theory underlying social efforts." The problems of the poor, and the circle of women, comprised Whitney's world, and she delighted in it: "I'm living with Ruth!" she wrote in her diary, and recorded how, on snowy days, they stayed in bed to read together Maud Booth's *After Prison—What?* on the rehabilitation of criminals.[12]

As president of the Junior League and a reader of Thorstein Veblen and John Dewey (as well as Maud Booth), and as a student, too, of Jane Addams, Dorothy Whitney sought to turn the League toward closer engagement with urban problems—toward, as she later wrote, "social work of a more serious nature." Philanthropy supplied temporary, and needed, balms for social hurts, but Whitney wanted to change the terms of "neighborhood work" by changing the neighborhood. After consulting with the prominent settlement-house leaders Addams and Lillian Wald, she set the League a task even more ambitious than the settlement houses: to create for working women a clean, well-appointed apartment house they could eventually run themselves.

Whitney made the Junior League House her major project between 1908 and 1911. She dealt with the practical matters of funding, architecture, facilities, location, and staff. But "the fundamental idea" (as she wrote a friend) remained the same, irrespective of the details: "to build a tenement for working girls" and to be sure that whatever its structure or location it be made ultimately "to pay" for itself.[13] It turned out much as she hoped, opening its doors on 20 May 1911, in a handsome building in East Seventy-eighth Street, close by the East River. With a fund of $270,000, the Leaguers put up an impressive residential club, with a library, a series of reception rooms, a roof garden, tennis and basketball courts, and a room full of typewriters for the working women's common use. More than three hundred women could live in its rooms, whose windows looked either out of the building or over a well-ventilated courtyard. Its dining room could seat them all, plus the house superintendent (a position Whitney thought particularly important: she called the supervisor "the matron," and she herself interviewed the candidates for the job.)[14] The club succeeded as an independently funded operation: by 1922, the Junior League House was self-supporting, and in it, as the *Daily News* would self-righteously complain, "working girls now live like the 400 [Manhattan's supposedly most important four hundred citizens]. . . . The whole thing is virtually a sorority house built for self-supporting girls."[15]

Thus Dorothy Whitney proved to herself and her peers that the debutantes of the Junior League could address social concerns in concrete and philosophically significant terms. Women who worked and lived in the Junior League House would not require the cultural or charitable intervention of settlement-house workers or Leaguers. They enjoyed their own facilities for entertainment and exercise and lived in a house they could pay for themselves. They attained this independence after a period of minimal, matronly supervision. Whitney would repeat this pattern in her later ventures, encouraging the objects of her reform to take control of their own lives within cultural parameters she would set; she, and her reform-minded allies, determined what was worthwhile, and encouraged—and enabled—their charges to live up to that mark.

Through this phase of her career, Dorothy Whitney had much in common with many other women reform leaders. The first decades of the twentieth century were a grand time for women's organizations of all sorts, which together comprised the crest of a great wave of women's political activity that had been gathering force since the middle of the preceding century and would soon—though nobody yet knew it—break, leading to a calm, if not to a decided ebb. Many of these organizations acted similarly to Whitney's Junior League in that they pressed for social change indirectly rather than confronting controversial issues head-on. For example, though Whitney herself favored women's suffrage and joined parades and rallies and spoke publicly for it, she did not push the issue within the League, which divided into "suffs" and "antis" and could not have arrived at a common position on the question. Instead she worked within the League's existing framework of commitments, modifying its determination "to be of some real use" along lines she preferred. Whitney's League was also typical in establishing a women's separate world, ideally distinct from the political and financial world of men, in which women in fact held meetings, elected representatives, and raised, budgeted, and disbursed money. And the Junior League House, in its hands-on, local specificity, typified women's reform activities as well.[16]

But Whitney also innovated on the basic model of feminine benevolence, most importantly in her emphasis on the eventual independence of the objects of her reform, and in the planned gradualism of this approach to independence. Her study of Dewey gave her an interest in the meliorative effects of education, and her awareness of her own advantages gave her a yardstick by which to measure social and intellectual freedom. As she wrote, "my independent position enabled me to assume a position of leadership amongst my own contemporaries."[17] Even compared with her privileged peers, she was distinctly free, for she did not feel herself forced to make a correct marriage. She believed that all people (or at least, at first, all Americans) should enjoy similar freedoms, and she established the Junior League House with a conspicuous emphasis on its eventual independence.

Even as she succeeded within this world, she began to look beyond it. Junior Leaguers took their intellectual development seriously, though they took it occasionally, and through guest speakers they learned about issues of the day. Professionals addressed the Junior League on public policy; for example, Franklin Giddings spoke on economics and William McAdoo on the city police force. As Whitney attended these activities, she felt herself becoming, to use the word she began using in her diary, "interested." Where churches, harbors, paintings, and the weather were "lovely" or "beautiful" (or, otherwise, "stupid" or "horrid"), only political topics were "interesting": "Dr. Maxwell spoke most interestingly on

the Board of Education"; trips to Ellis Island with Bend were "very interesting!"; William Howard Taft's speech on the court system was "most
interesting"; lunch with Lillian Wald at Henry Street was an "interesting
time"; and Dr. Darlington's speech on the board of health was "most
interesting of all."[18] This pattern suggests that political matters interested
her as other things did not. And within her current purview, she could
not wield enough political influence to satisfy herself. As she noted when
she attended a conference on the New York City budget, she was the
"only woman, except Dr. Robbins."[19] Women—especially women without professional degrees—did not have much of a say in public meetings
on the budget and other similarly interesting subjects.

Whitney had led the Junior League to closer engagement with the conditions of the working poor. Within the limits of women's voluntary
work, she found she could create, on a small scale, the circumstances in
which representatives of a struggling class could learn to sustain themselves—under, of course, a measure of matronly and Junior League supervision. Ultimately the House tenants would run their own affairs while
enjoying excellent material and cultural conditions. But she wanted to
do more—to reach larger groups and make her voice heard, or if she
could not properly accomplish that then to make her influence felt.

In 1911, as she wrapped up her work on the Junior League House and
thus brought to a conclusion the first phase of her reform career, she
began to work on two projects that would take her further. One was an
alliance with former President Theodore Roosevelt that would take her
into the heart of Progressive reform movements.[20] The other was her
marriage, which she meant to do the same.

THE LIBERAL EMPIRE

Dorothy Whitney met Willard Straight over lunch at E. H. Harriman's
house in 1906. Even though at the time Straight was between jobs, he sufficiently impressed her that in her diary she mentioned him by nickname:
"Saw 'The Galloper' (Mr. Straight)."[21] Harriman was expanding his railroads through Asia and he wanted Straight's assistance. President Roosevelt would shortly make Straight the U.S. vice-consul in Manchuria, a
desirable market for American goods and a key area for railroad construction. He rose to this eminence principally on the strength of his per-

sonality, which (as Dorothy Whitney discovered) could leave a forcible impression in a short period of time.

Whatever political connections he had, he made for himself, for he had been born with none. He came from Oswego (way out west in New York State) and attended Cornell (a state university). His parents, who taught school, paid close attention to the Lockean theories of child rearing, by which precepts they brought him up from his birth in 1880. They taught him to think independently and establish good social relations with his toddler peers. He took to the instruction, asking them, "What John Locke say about Baby—so and so?" to get approval for an intended course of action.[22]

Straight lost both parents to tuberculosis, and thus, like Whitney, he depended on surrogates. For him there were two: his adoptive mother, Dr. Elvire Ranier (who took care of him while her housemate Laura Newkirk brought up his sister Hazel), and his mentor at Cornell, Professor Henry Morse Stephens, whom he called Foster Father.[23] Ranier encouraged him in his native artistic ability and he became a skilled portraitist and landscape painter, working chiefly with watercolors and pencil. Stephens helped him develop a guiding vision.

When asked about his vision, Straight always used the same language: "I am a borne [sic] imperialist," he would say; sometimes it would be a "rank Imperialist," or an "Imperialist confirmed and deep-dyed."[24] But by imperialism he meant something distinctive. His mentor Stephens promoted an ideal of the British Empire as a confederation, leading to the independence of its component states. He argued that the poetry of Rudyard Kipling gave voice to this ideal, though an ethic of "responsibility" accommodating both a sense of allegiance among states and also "the growth of national spirit in the protectorates."[25] Straight took these lessons to heart, modifying them in light of his own subsequent experience.

After his graduation in 1901, he took ship for China to serve in the Imperial Maritime Customs Service under Sir Robert Hart, whom he meant to imitate at Stephens's behest.[26] Hart was a model imperialist for Straight: though a British knight, he was legally an agent of the Chinese government, and insisted that he act accordingly even if it endangered British interests. His duty was, he believed, to the independent interests of Chinese institutions.[27] To Straight, Hart represented the idea of responsible imperialism, focusing on the mission and the result without representing any particular empire. But even though in Hart's customs service Straight learned Chinese and also the ins and outs of international trade, he felt himself constrained from real "character-making" in diplomatic circles.[28] He left the customs service to work as a journalist during the Russo-Japanese War, then joined the U.S. State Department at its mission in Seoul. He struggled to make clear his own ideas about a U.S. empire: it would have to be "a conquest of a different sort but it's the same old game of stretching out, mastering, not so much that nowadays, but leading, older civilizations. It is more peaceful and therefore less rude and more complex, it seems, but fine. I love it."[29]

He defined this ideal in contrast to the power politics he unhappily discovered were still always the business of empires. The principal example for him was Japan's military absorption of its Korean protectorate, while Theodore Roosevelt's U.S. administration stood quietly by. "Japan has appealed to the great interests of human progress, has boasted of her enlightenment, and the world has swallowed it all," he wrote, but "under the guise of waging a war for the preservation of her national existence, she has carried on a war of aggression." The solution, he believed, was for him to "unbluff the world," simply to reveal the facts.[30]

The most important element of Straight's ideal American imperialism was the emphasis on independence for China, which was now threatened principally by the old-style empires of Russia and Japan. Americans, Straight believed, had to make loans, conduct trade, and finance the construction of Chinese-owned railroads to help the Chinese recover control over their own territory and build up their strength against the incursion of their neighbors. This ideal derived from three sources: Straight's liberal prejudices, his adaptation of Stephens's imperialism, and the empathy for his subject that underlay his artistic talent. As one historian writes, "Unlike many Westerners who simply drew 'Europeans with oblique lines,' . . . Willard drew the Chinese with sympathy and understanding." In his youth he had toyed with the question of identity, posing "as a tramp," and in doing so he was disappointed that "people should not see under my disguise and welcome me as a friend and a brother." He continued to view the world in such terms, assuming the existence of common humanity in his fellows, and he described the process of Chinese independence in terms that deliberately employed comparisons to the story of U.S. independence: "Only when Alexander Hamilton had reorganized the finances of the country . . . were the United States able to borrow from foreign bankers on satisfactory terms." The imperial powers were supposed to assist China similarly to gain control of its affairs.

It would be in the interests of colonizers and colonized alike for China to stand on its own.[31]

There were, therefore, some similarities, but also, more importantly, significant differences between Straight's prescription for an ideal American empire and the narratives of masculine imperialism that one historian describes as "hegemonic" during this period.[32] Straight did emphasize an element of manly responsibility as a core tenet of his imperialism. But where the supposedly hegemonic discourse of masculinity emphasized the necessary barbarism of international competition, and the ruthlessness of the struggle, Straight's manliness was decidedly not of the primitive variety. He accepted tobacco as a vice, but beyond that would not countenance the liberties that generally accompanied life on the imperial frontier. When he heard "talk of the profession of Jezebel," he reported, "My heart shrivelled within me." Straight's idea of imperial competition had more to do with bat and ball than with tooth and claw.[33]

Indeed, Straight often took pains to set himself apart from whatever tendencies toward primitive masculinity might have characterized his peers. His classmates sensed this resistance in him and nicknamed him Izzy—as in the question, "Is-he-Straight?"—to which the answer was a rather grim Yes. Straight did not believe in sin or excess, especially sexual: he later told his son, "Save yourself . . . that you may go clean and unashamed to her who will be your wife." In this respect, as in others, the ideal of manhood to which he hewed was the Victorian one of civilized restraint rather than the new masculinity of primitive indulgence, in which he had little interest and for whose devotees he had no use. He was relieved to avoid them when at school and wanted no business with them afterward. When he wrote Stephens that as consul he would need a deputy, he said, "I want an active intelligent serious-minded fellow," not one who talked only of "wine, women, and Horse-flesh," but he despaired of finding one among college men: "There were few in my time who would have filled the bill."[34]

For Straight, as for other devotees of Morse Stephens, the principal parallel between right-thinking manliness and imperial behavior was the recognition of responsibility, and the corresponding avoidance of weakness and corruption. These were all keywords for Stephens's men. When Alfred Sze, a Chinese-born Cornell contemporary of Straight's, asked Stephens how his home country might gain its independence, Stephens recommended that China attack France in Indo-China, where they were "weak" and "especially corrupt"; for his own part, Sze wrote that "China is so weak and corrupt, I have grave fears for her future."[35] In the lexicon of Stephens's empire, weakness and corruption went hand-in-hand with the avoidance of responsibility. Instead of indulging themselves in "days of languor," worshipping the "gospel of the aesthetic," men of empire had to evince "a spirit of work."[36] Abjuring the languorous and the aesthetic did not mean giving up one's talent for painting (Stephens's favorite Kipling hero was the artist of *The Light that Failed*) but it did mean making artistry part of one's work in the world, rather than an end in itself. Straight followed these prescriptions right along. For him, the "rotten corruption" of common imperial agents and remittance men corresponded to all the varieties of self-indulgence common to men in power.[37] He determined himself instead to stick to an ideal of responsible behavior, denying his worse impulses, making his artistry do the work of empire, and keeping to a narrow path, "feeling like a clipping from Kipling . . . part of a great machine, of a service."[38]

This emphasis on the responsibility of men corresponded to the purpose of Straight's empire. He countenanced the practice of one nation leading another because it meant improving the chances of the other to gain its independence. At least one historian believes that the point of combining manliness and dollar diplomacy was to prop up the dollar diplomat's sense of purpose—that the point of the relation of powerful to powerless was the relationship itself, which was therefore "perpetual."[39] Powerful masculinity defined itself through continuing domination. Though there can be no doubt that Straight believed dollar diplomacy would benefit Americans, he was also as sure that it would benefit Americans even more if the Chinese grew richer and independent. For Straight, the only justification for the imperial relationship was its tendency toward its own dissolution. Indeed, he would ultimately part company with other dollar diplomats because (he was chagrined to find) they did not "care a cuss about Chinese finance" per se but were interested only in their own balance sheets.[40]

After Straight's conversations with Harriman, he returned to China as the U.S. vice-consul in Manchuria, where he set about implementing his ambition to unbluff the world. He had seen Japan take Korea, and now he watched the Russians and Japanese and British and Germans try to carve up pieces of Manchuria and China. Imperial nations professing good intentions instead indulged rapacious instincts. They were, in the language of Straight's world, corrupt, and their predatory hypocrisy needed exposure. So, on the assumption that if people knew what he knew then they would think as he did, he set out to disabuse them of their illusions. He established a network of resources and, in collaboration with elements within the Chinese government, began publishing information. As his deputy wrote, they put together "statements of fact, backed up by chapter and verse references and reinforced by exact figures and dates. Personalities . . . were scrupulously avoided, and we discarded everything which might appear to be merely sensational." Nothing more would be necessary if (like Straight) one believed he were spreading only the truth to ordinary honest readers.[41]

Despite his scrupulousness, his enthusiasm undid him, for in his idealism he was at odds not only with the Europeans and Japanese but with his own government. Although Theodore Roosevelt sometimes sounded as fantastically idealistic as Straight, he had a strong grounding in realpolitik and believed that Americans' interests lay in accommodating Japan's desires.[42] If the United States wanted to trade in Manchuria, it had at least (Roosevelt figured) to acknowledge that Japan wanted not only to trade there but to run political affairs. Twice Straight banged up against the U.S. administration's sense of prudence. In the first instance, he challenged the Japanese in Manchuria over the safe passage of the mails. Japanese soldiers carrying mail got into a tiff with the Chinese guard at Straight's consulate, ultimately carrying the fight into the grounds and thus onto U.S. territory. Straight drew a pistol, rounded up the insurgents, and took them to confront the Japanese consul over the small invasion. Straight's pistol was broken, not to mention unloaded— but when the story of his bravado got out (ironically, through the publicity machine he had built) it made him look a little like a cowboy and also, as he put it, "a cad." Consuls waving weapons and collaring Japanese nationals were a sufficiently peculiar species even when their own press agencies did not seek to glorify them. Shortly afterward, at the urging of Harriman, the State Department pulled him out of Manchuria and asked him to negotiate a plan for the funding of a Chinese railroad with American assistance. This plan in its turn met defeat owing to the Roosevelt administration's rapprochement with Japan as reached in the Root-Takahira agreement. Though the agreement did little more than affirm the status quo, it suggested that the Americans were not about to do anything—such as assist in the funding of a Chinese-owned railroad—that would irritate the Japanese by undermining their sense of primacy in such affairs. The U.S. administration had again left Straight high and dry.[43]

In both cases, the government under Roosevelt took the better part of diplomacy and deferred Straight's grand plans for assisting Chinese independence in favor of a closer alliance with Japan. Even so, Straight did not, and never would, give up on his belief that the just end of imperialism was the independence of colonized peoples. After 1909, Straight would return to China and pursue this ideal through an affiliation with the House of Morgan, the driving force among a consortium of banks seeking to make loans to China. If Roosevelt was too hardheaded for Straight's idealism, Morgan's head was concretized. But Straight would not realize it until he had to live among his employers in Wall Street. While he lived and worked in Asia, he could feel himself on the frontier of his imaginary empire, and it was in this ambitious frame of mind that he began to court Dorothy Whitney after their reacquaintance in 1909.

To expect of Roosevelt, Harriman, and (later in Straight's career) J. P. Morgan something more than an appreciation for the bottom line implied a certain naïveté. So did the belief that the Chinese were following a national story of independence that paralleled the American revolution. But however naive, they were Straight's beliefs, and they helped him impress Dorothy Whitney, who was looking for a visionary of sorts.

TWO SIDES OF THE SAME STORY

During one of her visits to Europe, Dorothy Whitney wrote herself a letter. She was trying to figure out whether she wanted to marry, and what she wanted out of it if she did. "If I demand so much in a man in the way of mental capacity and desire for work and accomplishment of what is worthwhile—doubtless that man will be far beyond me in every way, and after a few years I may drop out of his life having ceased to be of any help, and then each of us will go our own way," she worried. Still, she was quite sure she wanted to ally herself with "a man with a good mind and a feeling of living and being 'up and doing' "—but then, if he had so much character of his own, she wondered if he might not need her enough—and surely her husband should need her. In any case "I don't think I could fall in love with a man who had no ambition or no aim in life—because I feel a great longing to become a part of his life and help him when possible to do his work—and then besides if he lacked all ambition I couldn't admire him." Taking all qualifications and desires into consideration, there was, she wrote, one person who seemed to fit the bill: "I have only seen one man that came near to what I long for—only one man that I would really like to marry—at least I think I would! Sometimes I feel 'oh, no'—not even you—but altogether he fills up most of the holes and I know he is much too good for me." And there she stopped writing. Though the dating of the note is uncertain, it appears to have been written after she met Straight, so he could well have been the one man. Certainly nobody projected "a feeling of living and being 'up and doing' " so well as a man whom she could call "The Galloper."[44]

After they met again at a dinner, he wrote her to say he wanted to see her again and was "really quite serious."[45] They began a correspondence that became a courtship. He told her about his adventures (as he saw them) and implored her to come visit China: "We are all awaiting you with the red carpets and the brass bands straining at the leash."[46] So she went to see this man in a world for which metaphors failed him.

He encouraged her to see that world as he did, and she packed books that reflected his enthusiasms. She left behind her usual Henry James and took instead *The Light that Failed*, *Kim*, *Just So Stories*, and *Plain Tales from the Hills*.[47] The literature cast its spell, and she saw Asia through his eyes and with him at its center. When she visited Peking (Beijing), she let Straight take her "templing" (as they called it) around the countryside, and was quite sure, as she wrote a friend, that he was "a famous man all over China and up in Manchuria . . . we . . . hear words of praise of him on every side and people loved him as much as they admired him." She— with, of course, her friend Beatrice Bend—toured the temples, the cities, and the countryside with Straight and his deputy. The experience persuaded Whitney that "they are serving their country in a way that makes one proud."[48] It overwhelmed her, and even after she left Straight's presence, she still felt his influence as she traveled through India. Writing to a friend about a Kipling poem that began "Alone upon the Housetops," she confessed, "Willard Straight used to sing it often to us in Peking—but I never really felt the atmosphere of it until I came to India."[49]

It is well here to remember the truly mundane nature of Straight's everyday work, which consisted almost entirely of seeing to it that the American bankers he represented got a fair percentage—along with British, French, Russian, Japanese, and German bankers—of loans made to the Chinese government, which wanted to build railroads. In the basic business of it, there was little romance except what Straight put there. Thus when Whitney fell in love with him and admired him, it was for his "desire for work and accomplishment of what is worthwhile"—qualities she had said she hoped to find. She recognized in him a kindred sense of "what is worthwhile," and a willingness to pursue it.[50]

But though she acted as if he had quite succeeded in the romantic department, she meant to test him, to be sure of him. She had come too far in her own life to squander her resources in a conventional marriage. If he had made her see his point of view with the appropriate books, then she would do likewise. She dispatched him a copy of a recent novel on marriage, having marked especially important passages. Then she waited to see what he would say.

The book was *Open Country*, by Maurice Hewlett. In it, a visionary man woos and loses a young woman whose principal attraction is her "lovely mind."[51] In the end she chooses someone else—the wrong sort of man, but ultimately a safer husband than a visionary who sees only ideals and not real women. Straight got the point immediately: "I shall have to compress within the limits of a letter—an endorsement of the premises with a rebuttal of the conclusions."[52] He knew he bore a certain resemblance to the noble, idealistic loser: indeed, nobly and idealistically losing had become something of a specialty of his, as he tilted at imperialist windmills. But he understood, too, the noble loser's fault: he "was more in love with the garments of his own weaving that he hung upon Her" than he was with the lovely mind herself. At the same time, he approved of the idealist's view that marriage required a voluntary and equal assent: "The tie must be accepted . . . and not a shackle at all but a golden bond—that gives solemnity and sets a seal . . . for we are all subject more or less to the sentimental influence of tradition—upon the Greatest Thing in the World."[53]

In Hewlett's description of his heroine—"very much in earnest, using incisive phrases, surveying life as a whole with a calmness"—one sentence especially suggests a point of identification with Dorothy Whitney: "She had too much character to relinquish the habits in which she had been bred simply because she was being swept off her feet."[54] Throughout her Asian sojourn she kept her head, sustaining by correspondence the Junior League House project and considering what she might get out of a marriage. She needed to know on accepting a proposal that the union would give her room for the life she had and not require her to surrender or subordinate it. If she found Straight's courtship romantic—and she certainly did—she also knew the perils of too much romance, for people could not expect their lives to proceed according to the narratives of sentimental novels. So she tested Straight, pushing him to speak for himself on the matter of what marriage could be. He understood. The ideal of equal partnership had to apply, and had to accommodate not only the mythical roles of ideal men and women, but respect for the actual aspirations of real men and women. Hence his endorsement of the ideal premises and his rebuttal of the conclusions. Contrary to Hewlett, the lovely mind should marry the noble dreamer, loser though he might presently seem. Whitney agreed.

There remained in Straight's mind one excessively romantic notion: that he and Whitney might make their life in China. The idea reflected nothing so much as his naïveté, for he had climbed very far very fast and he had no concrete experience of her metropolitan life and so no idea of its roots in the American city that sustained it. When he wanted to press his suit, he could not take it to her parents, so he did the next best thing and broached the subject to the partners of the banking group who, though they might not have been of Whitney's circle, nevertheless knew that its circumference did not extend so far as Asia. One can well imagine the smile on the face of Mortimer Schiff (of Kuhn, Loeb) when Straight told him about his courtship of Whitney. "He laughed and asked me if I expected to support you on twelve thousand a year," Straight wrote. Schiff had continued: "We'll bring you home—you can't live in China with her—we'll find something in finance in New York that will enable you to support her—so that you need have no apprehension."[55]

Apart from Straight's naïveté, there was the matter of his history. Some people whispered that he was the sort who "wished to marry 'a very rich girl.' "[56] And it seemed there was more to it than whispering. An ally of Straight's had warned him, he wrote: "There have apparently been lots of stories about me—She said she was glad to know the facts—for she'd heard quite a lot—but that she'd always had faith in me—and . . . had always defended me. She told me that people were talking about us."[57] For himself, Straight had put all his cards on the table to Whitney, including the story that he "was supposed to have been engaged to Mary [Harriman]." But the community to which she belonged was apparently a little exercised on her behalf. After all, in the absence of parents, somebody had to look after a single woman's interests, they believed. Straight's sponsors—Morgan partners and diplomats—stood up for him, but some members of the community, and the newspapers, could not resist the chance to wallow in innuendo. In its profile of "Willard Straight, Who

Is to Marry Dorothy Whitney," the *New York Times* laid it on especially thick:

> Miss Whitney was seized with a desire to visit China. She crossed the Pacific Ocean, as Miss Harriman had crossed it. She visited Mukden, as Miss Harriman had visited it. She met the big, healthy looking, forcible American Consul General, just as Miss Harriman had met him, and, like Miss Harriman, she fell in love with him.[58]

And in the end, what if Straight did need to marry money? If he did, it was because he needed fuel for his ambition, not because he wanted to spend it on polo ponies. Dorothy Whitney, for her part, wanted to marry an ambition equal and parallel to her own. She had long been looking for someone who understood this wish, and she believed she had found him. They made one concession to the unsettled state of community opinion and chose to marry in Geneva, to avoid a New York "circus."[59] They were married in the Etat Civil on the morning of 7 September 1911 and had a church ceremony that afternoon. There were only six guests— the Bends, mother and daughter; Whitney's brothers Payne and Harry; and (representing Straight) two old China hands. That evening the newlyweds began a trip that would take them across Siberia to China.

Straight had loose ends to tie up in Peking and Manchuria, but the couple knew exactly where they would go after seeing to business in China. As Whitney wrote, "I had a long talk with T. R. on Sunday—and I felt afterwards that the best thing for a few years might be the staying-home game and getting into things here. . . . I am terribly excited over some work I am trying to do."[60] Straight had written, "We'll be in this game up to our necks one of these days,"—though he sometimes worried that Roosevelt was "a fanatic."[61] She would try to convince him otherwise. She packed a Rooseveltian text for her honeymoon trip—Herbert Croly's *The Promise of American Life*. But when they arrived in China she was reading Carlyle's *French Revolution*, an unhappy choice: a revolt then beginning in Hankow would somewhat delay their entry into the home game of Rooseveltian Progressivism.

Given her hardheaded expectations ("Of course," she had written, "the man one marries cannot be all one dreams of having him—and I am fully expectant of disappointments") it is unsurprising that she now wrote, "Married life seems almost too good sometimes."[62] Their life together was immediately exciting. With the revolt that began in Hankow, the

Manchu government suddenly lost its authority to negotiate, and Straight had to scramble to find out just who had power. It was all fascinating—and all of it was on his side of the household. Dorothy hosted teas, dinners, talks; Willard hosted hurried meetings, angry whisperings, and blind connivings. Dorothy remained sure that, especially in times of revolution, there were tremendously interesting things going on in men's sphere: "I had a very dull French lesson this morning while Willard had a very interesting interview with Alfred Sze" (his old friend from Cornell was maneuvering for a place among the shifting coalitions).[63] And so it went: standard diplomatic parties were "boring"; lunches with generals, colonels, members of the royal family, and other major players were much more "interesting."[64] But in this time of crisis, she had to let Willard play out his hand.

On 12 February 1912 the Qing emperor abdicated. By the end of March, the Straights had left Peking for England, where the various national banking groups would try to salvage their loan agreements. When she left, Dorothy Straight wrote in her diary that she felt sick. She was pregnant.[65]

While bearing a first baby it would have been normal for Dorothy to be home and among friends—the chief candidates were Beatrice Bend and her mother. When she married, her constant guardian had at last left her side. Bend's mother wrote that she "was as brave as you might expect and we talked about the last few days and the future, but it was hard hard hard."[66] Because Willard Straight was a natural diplomat, he knew what and who was important, and he had tried to get the Bends' approval the previous spring. He knew he was in trouble by December 1911, when because of professional complications he had not returned home with Dorothy. He wrote that the delays were not his fault, though "I'll reluctantly accept the stigma—for I assure you when I promised a speedy return I had no idea that we were going to arrive on the very day the Dogs of Revolt began to bark." By summer 1912 he knew he truly had some explaining to do, as he worried the Bends would think him a "gold brick artist . . . who had lured her away—and bamboozled you—with false pretences [sic]." He sensed he was getting the worst of it in a circle of feminine communication: "Dorothy showed me one of your letters in which you quoted Amy [Bend, Beatrice's sister] as saying that I had told her we might be here for a couple of months. I may have said that—but not wittingly . . . after past experience I always say 'I don't know—maybe two weeks maybe two months.' "[67]

In the end, Bend wrote Dorothy, "I fancy it will end in your having
the baby in England. Let me know as soon as you decide about it for in
that case I would go over." She gave Willard the benefit of the doubt:
"You are very fortunate to have married such a man and it gives me a
nice comfortable feeling for your future. Of course you deserve it but you
might have married other men who would not have been as satisfactory
as he is to you in every way."[68]

With Dorothy's involvement in Progressivism on hold, Bend served
as her proxy, reporting on the campaign. She watched as TR grew stronger
and Taft got "flabby"; the race of the conventional party candidates
seemed to her "rather a discouraging state of affairs."[69] In June she went
to Chicago for the Republican convention. She wrote that Dorothy should
get details from the papers, "but the papers can't give any idea of the
excitement the electrical atmosphere of it all." After she toured Hull
House and the city's playgrounds ("How I wish we had such things in
New York, also the open air schools etc") she went to the meetings. "We
get all the Roosevelt dope from Alice [Roosevelt] Longworth . . . and all
the Taft dope from [Nicholas Murray] Butler. . . . Oh Dorothy it is all
such fun. How I wish you were here you would love it." Alice Longworth
knew her father was going to bolt the party. When he did, the tension
rose. Delegates quarreled and occasionally punched one another. On 23
June, Bend wrote that she had sat on the stage while Roosevelt announced
the new party.

> It was packed with thousands of people clammering [*sic*] to get
> in. . . . Roosevelt was greeted with the greatest enthusiasm the del-
> egates from the national convention who had refused to vote
> marched in with their banners shouting their different slogans and
> there were deafening cries of we want Teddy and the song which
> every one is singing to the Turkey Trot music—Instead of "Every-
> body's doing it Turkey trot" it now runs "Everybody's yelling it
> Roosevelt Roosevelt." It is very catchy and when the bands play it
> in hotels or conventions everybody sings it. At the Roosevelt meet-
> ing we assisted at the birth of the new progressive party. We did
> not get back to the hotel until 2 A.M.[70]

All their people were there in Chicago—the Longworths, the Butlers, the
Griscoms, an assorted Vanderbilt or two. Roosevelt was in his element

and the excitement was high. And Dorothy was pregnant, in the Deep-dene, in Dorking, England, while her husband fretted over ways the bankers could agree with some Chinese of dubious authority on how to prop up the sinking tael. In August, the Straights boarded ship for New York.[71]

They moved into Dorothy's house on Long Island. She went to town as often as she could, but her doctor sent her to bed in early November. She and Willard read together and she helped him when she could, rehearsing with him a dinner speech on the Chinese loans he would give at Delmonico's. Beatrice Bend came out from the city to stay through the end of her pregnancy. She brought H. G. Wells's new book *Marriage* to read to Dorothy while they waited.

Bend's choice reflected once again the concerns Dorothy faced while trying to integrate her marriage into the world she knew. Wells's book relates the story of a young husband and wife who must discover that the world, and therefore marriage, are now different because women are emerging from the home to get their educations and take on new roles on the world. Like contemporary feminist Charlotte Perkins Gilman, Wells's characters argue that "Sex . . . has got hold of the women tighter than it has the men," and as "women begin to be released," marriage must become more an object of scrutiny, to be consciously redefined rather than accepted. Wells's reform-minded heroine has ultimately to pry her husband away from the world of business so they can realize their shared vision of a public partnership resulting from marriage.[72]

Dorothy Whitney Straight herself, despite her inheritance and her free-dom from parental scrutiny, despite having made her own decision whom to marry ("in spite of the comments of her friends," the *New York Press* remarked in an article of this period),[73] despite having negotiated a new perspective on marriage with her husband, still found herself in a tradi-tional predicament. She meant to bring her husband's ambition into her own world of reform, and through her partnership with him make her own mark on the political world that so held her interest. Instead her marriage had so far kept her in a domestic world away from what she liked: "Town!" as she wrote in her diary when she was able to return.[74] And meanw hile, her husband worked at what had, since the revolution in China, become a traditional desk job. When he was home, he sat close by her bed, sketching or painting while Beatrice Bend read. On 6 Novem-ber, Dorothy gave birth to a son, Whitney Willard Straight. Through the rest of the month, most evenings Willard Straight stayed in the city until 8:00.[75]

The courtship and early marriage of the Straights reveals the troublesome character of marriage and gender roles for self-conscious, educated men and women in these years. Both of them set themselves apart from the roles they were expected to play—she by deferring and redefining marriage, he by rejecting and redefining standardized masculine behavior. They struggled to arrive together at a version of marriage that would fulfill their expectations of working together and were almost overtaken by the weight of tradition.

They communicated with each other not only by telling one another their ambitions, but by comparing themselves with received notions of what they should be. Perhaps it was only natural that, as orphans, they should have resorted to texts: their parents had scarcely lived long enough to shape their lives, and to find out what others expected of them they looked to stories in the public sphere. Consequently, as he wrote to her, their desire for each other could be expressed as "I want to mark books with you—as well as for you."[76]

To have lived briefly, cozily together, far away from the demands of the world, would have made Dorothy happy—"just like Kipling's story 'A Habitation Deferred,'" as she wrote.[77] The romance of Kipling— Kipling as filtered through Morse Stephens and Straight—would suit her for the length of a honeymoon. But the sojourn lasted longer than they had planned, and kept her from the world she loved. Now an ordinary marriage loomed—a child, and a husband always away in Wall Street. As she wrote, "I don't find much joy in reading when I can't talk over my books with you."[78] In it there was little of the significant camaraderie Willard had expressed when he urged her to "walk with me—arm in arm child—through life and all that it means—between us we may be able to be of a little use in the world."[79] Now that their life together had commenced, he was often away, came home late and tired and wanting quiet, and she felt, by her own account, "injured."[80]

In Wells's novel *Marriage*, the ambitious couple concludes their reassessment of the institution by resolving to represent themselves to the world as a team dedicated to reform. They mean to accomplish it through producing social "criticism. But everything that matters is criticism!"[81] Throughout Dorothy's pregnancy, Beatrice Bend had kept her in touch with the larger world and the politics that interested her. At the close of her pregnancy, she brought to her, and read to her, this book that suggested what a marriage ought to be in a world of changing gender roles, and that implied once again a sense of the "social obligations" of her class. When Dorothy Straight emerged from bearing and nursing her first child, she set about reforming her marriage along these lines.

THE SHADOW OF A MARRIAGE

The proposed project of social criticism, to fulfill a mission of social leadership, developed from the shared elements of their ambitions. Both of them believed they must assume a position of superiority to the powerless of their world, and nurture and educate them to the point where they might control their own destinies. In both Straight's imperialism and in Whitney's social feminism, there lurked an implicit realization that their standards (of behavior, of citizenship, of educated intelligence) were the only standards. This assumption—rarely articulated, never interrogated—made reform a moral responsibility for men and women with the ability to undertake it.

Once Roosevelt had lost the election of 1912, making Woodrow Wilson the first Democratic president since Grover Cleveland, the various sources of reform energy that the Rough Rider had concentrated in his personal crusade found fresh channels to flood. The season of 1913–14 saw a profusion of reforms sprout on legislative and extragovernmental agendas. The new president also gave Dorothy Straight an opportunity: in a short-lived flush of anti-Hamiltonianism, Wilson withdrew U.S. support from the banking group for which Straight had so long labored. Willard Straight, out of a job, had lost his empire and now needed a new role. Dorothy Straight would see to it that they would together transform their marriage, and their society.

The *New Republic* was an institution that was the shadow of a marriage, not of a man. Dorothy had read Herbert Croly's *The Promise of American Life* to Willard as they sailed away from China the preceding spring. On 8 June 1913, Herbert Croly, who had been only a paper presence in the Straights' lives, showed up on Long Island for lunch with Willard and Beatrice Bend.[82] Dorothy was busy looking after the new baby; as when she was pregnant, Bend was her proxy in political matters. Dorothy wanted her husband to have something worthwhile to do, that she could share. Both had found Croly's *Promise* provocative: it was possible that the parallels between their agendas might emerge, filtered through Croly, and prove useful in establishing guidelines for a new project.

The *New Republic* grew out of Dorothy's understanding of her husband's imagination. She decided to pay for the magazine to realize her ambitions for a joint project, which meant that it had also to suit what she called Willard's "high minded devotion to the principle of Right" (which, she said, "has been a very wonderful inspiration to your wife").[83] This sense of Right was inextricable from his idea of empire, and Willard Straight's ideal empire was supposed to be an agency for fostering self-government. Croly's plans for home echoed Straight's plans abroad. Like Willard, Croly believed that self-rule came only with time and education, and that present-day elites had an obligation to hasten that process, without immediately surrendering any of their responsibilities or privileges. In Croly's reformist, the powerful would use centralized (Hamiltonian) means to achieve democratic (Jeffersonian) ends.[84] During one of Croly's habitual funks, Willard set out the symmetry between his imperialism and Croly's progressivism:

> Of course I myself am, at heart, a rank Imperialist. . . . it's only by having more responsibility than you can chew and trying to grow up to it that makes for progress with nations or individuals—there's no difference in the two problems. . . . The people—no matter what their defects—should be given an increasing power so that they may be sobered and educated by their responsibilities until they are able to live up to them. . . . Retraction and retirement and thumb sucking should never be the sermon of the author of the "Promise of American Life." When you feel or think that way you've lost your faith in Democracy.[85]

This passage sums up Willard's reconciliation of imperialism and democracy, of power and justice, which fit Croly's scheme of Hamiltonianism and Jeffersonianism. Willard and Croly recognized, in American society and the world, an existing inequality of power that made injustice inevitable. They both suggested therefore that the powerful had not only to wield their power wisely, but also to extend that power to the people at large. Peoples, just like individual people, needed proper education to take responsibility for themselves and solve their own problems—a notion that mirrored Dorothy Straight's conception of her social obligations. Through the appropriate medium, they could bring people like their peers into closer contact with social problems, make them more aware of their obligations, and give rise to new projects.

Croly and his wife hit it off with the Straights, and the couples soon spent mealtimes and weekends together. On 8 November 1913, at home on Long Island, the Straights held a conference about the *Republic*, as the project was then called; present, in addition to Dorothy and Willard, were the Crolys, the Learned Hands, lawyer George Rublee, journalist Philip Littell, and Felix Frankfurter.[86] During the next year, Croly accepted Dorothy's offer of financial assistance and quit his job editing the *Architectural Record*, and the venture got its headquarters at 419 and 421 West Twenty-first Street, which the Straights bought from a financially strapped Croly.[87]

If the philosophy of the magazine marked a conjunction that Dorothy perceived between Willard's and Croly's interests, so did the headquarters. Both men liked cigars, antiques, and the clubby atmosphere of New York men's society. The *New Republic*'s offices were furnished to these tastes.[88] The central feature was the round table, to which great names would be invited, served dinner cooked by the in-house staff, and where the guests were then themselves grilled by the editors and publishers. For the first few years of the journal's existence, that table was Willard Straight's territory. Felix Frankfurter remembered that Croly "could hardly open his mouth. Somebody else had to do the inciting and the interchanges that keep a dinner table going, if it goes. If it had depended on Croly, there would have been an eternal frost."[89] Willard could begin the talking and keep it going, as well as hold forth for himself and smooth over differences between others. Croly envied Willard his abilities and was grateful for the performance of services he could not himself provide: "You were in great form the night of our last dinner, and I thank you from the bottom of my heart."[90]

Willard, the natural and practiced diplomat, performed his role of publisher splendidly. Few of the editors knew, and fewer trusted, the others. Croly did not trust his brood of young "radicals," nor did they trust him—or each other: Francis Hackett did not trust Croly; Philip Littell did not trust Willard Straight; and nobody trusted the too-evidently-brilliant Walter Lippmann; but over the project's early months they learned to work with each other. Hackett did not like being published (as he saw it) by Wall Street, but soon found Willard "thoroughly satisfactory"; Littell found it striking that Willard "could unite such fighting force with such a deep-seated tolerance." Within a year of the journal's founding,

Straight resigned his post at J. P. Morgan. Eventually one of the editors would take the Straights for a model: Walter Lippmann wrote that Faye Albertson and he had decided they should end their bohemian romance and marry on account of the example of the Straights.[91]

If the structure of the journal resembled a men's club, it existed within a woman's philosophical and fiscal world, as Dorothy gave shape to the journal and its aims. Theodore Roosevelt liked *The Promise of American Life,* not only because it praised him, but because both progressive judge Learned Hand and conservative leader Henry Cabot Lodge recommended it to his attention.[92] Croly's first book had something for both: a Jeffersonian future, a Hamiltonian present—partly because he was trying to appeal to an upper-class patron, specifically the boyishly heroic Roosevelt. By the time he wrote *Progressive Democracy,*[93] he had given up on Roosevelt because he and the Straights had found each other. The later book reflects their joint hopes and beliefs; some of its key passages come from Croly's speech on the founding of the *New Republic,* and it probably originated in a report they commissioned from Croly on a plan for social education.[94] The reliance on Rooseveltian heroes vanished from the second book. Instead, Croly presented what the title suggested: a vision of American life growing gradually more egalitarian. In *Progressive Democracy,* the people led themselves to their destiny by appointing appropriate teachers and critics (presumably he and the Straights belonged to this category). "Formative criticism . . . cannot contribute anything to social amelioration which will dispense with the creative power of the democratic faith . . . but it may claim rightly that the social democratic faith is powerless without its assistance."

The popular will must discover an appropriate impulse. "The socially righteous expression of the popular will is to be brought about by frank and complete confidence in its own necessary and ultimate vehicle"— that vehicle being an organ of criticism such as the *New Republic,* which would purvey "education in the deepest and most fruitful meaning of the word."[95] Education was the only just, the only conceivable, role for a privileged class in a society dedicated to democratic ideals. Because only a few people could go to universities, those few incurred an obligation to use their learning for the benefit of society, by working to express articulately the popular will. The credo incorporated an ambivalence about that will, which, on the one hand, was the only legitimate source of authority, and, on the other, had to be prodded and taught.

Though Dorothy spoke her mind quietly at first, leaving her husband to do the public "holding forth,"[96] she considered the journal their shared responsibility, and "never made an outside engagement for a Friday"— the day the editorial board met. "She was absorbed in the events of the week and how to reflect them and comment on them in next week's paper," one of her friends remembered.[97] The Straights read over the issues together, compiled critiques, and when they were not together, she wrote him her impressions. Just as they had always loved to mark and critique books with each other, now they shaped their own critical narrative of society together.

Croly knew whom he must first please. He constantly communicated with the Straights. Before the journal appeared, he warned them humbly, "The Republic is not even borne. [*sic*] He may not prove to be all his proud parents hope and anticipate."[98] Once it began to appear, and he began to receive their critiques, he wrote Dorothy, "If you are not satisfied, nothing else in the way of success will be any compensation. It is my personal relation to you which dominates the whole business."[99]

She urged the journal toward social seriousness. She could not understand the point of an early piece on auction bridge. A piece on the horrors of the newly begun world war was "banal." She preferred by far Ray Stannard Baker's effort to encapsulate the spirit of the Progressive period as an effort to perfect "the art of living together." As she wrote, the journal must provide "a really deep, constructive foundation of thought."[100]

She generally preferred to exercise indirect influence, but she was quite willing to intervene directly in a matter with which she felt familiar. When New York State's commissioner of charities revealed poor living conditions in Roman Catholic orphanages, the church went on the offensive with an ad hominem attack. Dorothy "was surprised to find that The New Republic knew nothing about the situation. So I am planning to meet Herbert this afternoon and give him the facts."[101] The journal responded quickly, suggesting that even if Catholics did not believe "the history of civilization is the history of secularization," they ought not to declare that the commissioner of charities was a "former hobo or jockey" and bribe other officials not to testify in his behalf. More to the point, the journal cast the issue in terms that reflected Dorothy's primary interests. The problem with the orphanages "was not merely that filth of the most disgusting kind existed. . . . The failures on the educational side were conspicuous," and, they added, the church's position amounted in effect to "antagonism to public education as practised [*sic*] in the United States." Reformers, the *New Republic* said, wanted

> to formulate democracy as a positive ideal. . . . The community has certain positive ends to achieve, and if they are to be achieved the community must control the education of the young . . . [which] means the development of the independent powers of judgment in the young. . . . Democracy claims no right to interfere with worship or opinion, but it does claim the right to develop in every child the capacity for testing its own convictions . . . experimental naturalistic aptitudes shall constitute the true education.

Ultimately, the journal argued, to achieve these purposes all dependent children who were "not defective" might go to families for "less mechanical care."[102]

In this exemplary episode, the journal at Dorothy's prodding tackled an issue squarely within her concerns as a Junior Leaguer and a woman reformer at a point where these issues intersected the power politics of New York. It was precisely the sort of intervention she could not have made on her own, but now that she had created a sympathetic political journal within her compass, she could see to it that it confronted issues in which she took an interest, and that it put these issues into the world of men's politics. The recommendations it made at her suggestion once again recapitulated the basic thesis that underlay her and her husband's Progressivism: the importance of education for dependent classes and the essential notion that education must serve the ends of independence. She was happy with making this constructive criticism. And when Willard himself took a turn offering a (pseudonymous) opinion in the journal's pages, he struck the same note: "Paternalism in any form—no matter how beneficial its results—will not ultimately be acceptable," he wrote. "What has hitherto been termed philanthropy—like commerce and industry and politics—will tend gradually to conform to a more democratic ideal." Both Straights envisioned, through a process of social criticism, taking on a parental role that would end in the fulfillment of creating a more democratic society. They knew the journal had "really arrived" when (two months after its inception) teachers began using it in schools. Ultimately, as Willard's other work took him away from New York, her role and his became indistinguishable: as she wrote, if he were away, "well, I've got to be a man—that's all."[103]

In later years, Dorothy spelled out the journal's fulfillment of the Straights' hopes: "The paper is really extraordinary—and I believe it is going to do more for the education of this country than any other one force I know of. . . . I do believe that The New Republic is the best thing that you and I ever put over."[104]

Though both Straights influenced the *New Republic*'s character and contents, the journal was not their puppet. They agreed that together they would exercise only a single vote in the magazine's councils, and when disagreements arose they kept their peace or, as on the occasion of the editors' endorsement of Wilson in 1916, wrote a letter to the journal.[105] But, as Willard said in that letter, they and the editors were "in essential agreement, both as to our aspirations for *The New Republic* and as to the general cause which it should serve."[106] Indeed, that episode only increased public awareness of the journal's mission, increasing its popularity because it emphasized the paper's principled independence of opinion.[107]

Yet even if the Straights had no official veto, Dorothy had a real one: she paid for the journal's publication and could quit doing so at any time. The *New Republic* originally cost 10 cents an issue, or $4.00 for the year. In 1916, with 17,000 subscribers, it cost $7.00 to produce a one-year-subscription's worth of papers. The Straights paid the difference. In 1953, when their youngest son Michael Straight prepared to give up the journal, he revealed that the Straight family had given it an average of $95,000 per year for thirty-eight years. They never threatened to withdraw funding.[108]

The *New Republic* did two essential things for the reform career of the Straights. It brought Willard's imperialism home and harnessed it to a domestic agenda. He had constructed an imperial ideology that created a duty on the part of colonizer nations to see to the eventual independence of colonized nations. In advocating an end to paternalism in U.S. politics, he was recapitulating at home his imperial mission to end imperial relationships. It also gave Dorothy a way to take part in the world of politics she found so interesting. Through the meetings and the publications of the *New Republic,* she had access to a world from which she had been largely barred. In accomplishing these two ends, the journal allowed the Straights to redefine their marriage as the source of a collaborative reformism. The two of them together now had a text they could mark and shape to their purpose.

During its early years, the *New Republic* was the Straights' most important joint project. It allowed both of them to promulgate their beliefs in the meliorative power of education, broadly construed. Indeed, through its columns they could both teach and advocate more teaching. At the same time it allowed them each to abjure the standard prescribed spheres for men and women of their time. They had found a way they could work together in a way that suited their liberal convictions about the proper role of socially powerful people. They could promulgate their politics of an education that meant the end of paternalism and the beginning of true democracy: thus they defined progress. But they had scarcely begun their work before the world began changing under the influence of war.

Two

MARY RITTER AND CHARLES BEARD

The letter burners of biography . . . forget that there are other kinds of testimony, the memories of friends and bystanders, contents of letters written by other persons, . . . and the very fabric of an author's prose.

—Leon Edel[1]

To this day, every student of U.S. history has an idea about or by Mary Ritter and Charles Beard in his or her head, whether we know it or not. The Beards so deftly synthesized monographs, statistics, and anecdotes into consistently entertaining and enlightening stories that they became icons for scholars and popular readers alike. Unlike all but a very few historians of the United States, they possessed not only a sense of social justice and of narrative sweep but of humor as well: though in this they enjoyed the benefit of their era, when so much greatness lay before America and so little behind it. But like all icons, the Beards soon met their iconoclasts. In the late 1940s, with the impudent tribunes of the new American empire attacking their reputations and with Charles suffering from doctors who did not understand antibiotics, they took some measures to protect themselves by destroying their own historical records. Charles Beard died in 1948. Afterward, Mary Beard wrote a friend, "Charles destroyed some letters, indeed all his letters, a short time before he died. I did the same with all but current correspondence in my files about the same time. He had only kept confidential letters and he felt obligated not to release them. I shared that feeling."[2] But she did not tell quite the whole truth. Charles kept some of his letters—most conspicuously those that heralded his principled resignation from Columbia University in 1917. Furthermore, Mary not only preserved but also annotated what remained, signing her little slips of paper for the benefit of future readers. These exceptions tell us a great deal about how they wanted to be seen and remembered.[3]

As with other Progressives who married, the ideas of marriage, family, and their relation to ideal social bonds were much on the Beards' minds. Among the letters that did perish were most probably the Beards' correspondence with each other. None has been published or cited, and Mary expressed her annoyance with the public's prurient interest—"sexual curiosity"—in love letters.[4] Even so, there could have been few such letters. The Beards were scarcely ever apart. (This of course can be read as a datum in itself.) More important, they also made it clear in both publications and correspondence with other people that they believed familial relations affected larger social relations. And on this more public record they made their ideas quite clear. "One must somehow work from the family out to public activity," Charles wrote, expressing a belief they held so deeply that one historian describes it as a "prejudice."[5] The term is correct in its connotation of strength, but not entirely apt in its suggestion of unreflective bias. Though the Beards married early, they did not do so without examining the implications of their decision, nor did they refer to the implications of such decisions without careful thought.

The years around the two great wars mark critical and unfortunate periods in the Beards' lives. World War I saw both of them take themselves out of the public world of Progressive reform; World War II saw them take themselves out of the public record. But both times they left important parts of themselves behind. As their omissions, preservations, and later letters show, they were trying to restore their original story, to give back to themselves a sense of their optimistic youth, of what Charles called "golden and spacious days," echoing his friend Vachel Lindsay's description of the Theodore Roosevelt years. In those years they felt—they knew—themselves to be at the vanguard of a teeming generation of reformers preparing to make America a great civilization. "It was grand to be alive," he wrote, when "the world . . . [could] get enthused over some simple theory of history"—a theory that, drawing on one or more of the "Darwins . . . hidden in every clump of academic bushes," accounted for progress and the extension of democracy to people who had never had it.[6]

Like all conscientious historians, and perhaps therefore more so than other Progressive reformers, the Beards defined themselves by their involvement with the public record and the public sphere, where they created and re-created themselves and their projects. They had begun to think of themselves in this respect in their earliest years together, when as Midwesterners they had a special relationship with the public discourse of democracy.[7]

INDIANA IDYLL

The Beard and Ritter families comprised distinct, though related, species of Republicans. The Beards had been Unionist Southern Whigs who went North at the outbreak of civil war; the Ritters were German-descended burghers. The two families were distinct varieties of Quakers as well: the Beards pretty freely shone their inner lights over the general vicinity, while the Ritters less publicly followed the dictates of personal conscience. Charles's father, William Henry Harrison Beard, a farmer, rented his Indiana farmland to black citizens for a camp meeting when none of his neighbors would, and he bought his sons a printing press so they might air their opinions, the unfettered expression of which soon got them expelled from school. By contrast, Mary's father, Eli F. Ritter, made a private, conscientious decision to set aside the pacifist principle of his faith to fight "to save the Union," as he told his daughter, and then returned home to become an Indianapolis lawyer, urging zoning laws and municipal election reforms consistent with an urbane, liberal Republicanism. These familial traits—the willingness to set examples conspicuously, on the one hand, and more discreetly, on the other—passed to their respective offspring, Charles Beard, born in 1874, and Mary Ritter, born in 1876.[8]

Beard and Ritter met at DePauw University, where they distinguished themselves in the judgment of their peers both as a couple and as distinct, individual, public personalities. They appear repeatedly in their college yearbooks. With the cruel license characteristic of the undergraduate culture of the 1890s, the yearbook staff put the couple among those bound for the altar in the "Ministers' Aid Society," and listed Beard among the men who belonged to the "Shining Lights Club," whose rooms were the "Ladies' Dorm Parlors."[9] Mary Ritter won election as president of her class, voted into office by both men and women, and her peers judged her "both practical and good, well-fitted to command."[10] Charles Beard, by contrast, distinguished himself as a master of public rhetoric. DePauw's wits picked on him for his pet phrase ("By gracious!") and allowed him a measure of respect for resuscitating the school newspaper (which he did by putting its finances on a businesslike basis and, in a smart marketing move, changing its name from *Weekly* to *Palladium*), but marked him chiefly as a "Concoctor of Jove's Thunder" and a "Prohibo-populistic orator," and thus as one of the Big Five (men on campus).[11]

The mastery of debate had long been one of DePauw's specialties. After an unfortunate period of overambitious expansion inspired by "the verbal intimations of Mr. DePauw"—which later proved to have "discrepancies" with his will—the school retrenched and focused on its strengths: its liberal-arts college, in general, and its characteristically Methodist emphasis on public speaking, in particular.[12] Oratory and rhetoric had given the school its greatest heroes (among them, Senator Albert Beveridge); at DePauw, "he who won a [speaking] contest was as much a hero as he who was received into the Porcellian Club at Harvard, or one who made the crew or team at Yale."[13]

In a special summer course in 1896, Beard took "Recent English and American Orators" and went to Chicago to hear William Jennings Bryan's address to the Democratic convention.[14] The oratorical tradition held a special fascination for him. With it one could not only put the unspoken, commonly held beliefs of people into a story, but also use that story to inspire people to action. As one historian writes of the special place of oratory in Populist political culture, it "created its own symbols of politics and democracy in place of inherited hierarchical symbols, and it armed its participants against being intimidated by the corporate culture."[15] The symbolic language had much in common with the revivalist preaching that inflected the culture of the Plains and their Protestant colleges. Symbols had more power than close reasoning. It was more effective for Bryan to paint word-pictures of persecutors with crowns of thorns and crosses of gold than it would have been for him to argue monetary theory. Thus Protestant revivalism and Populism both presumed on the innate goodness of the people and also on their fallen, weakened state. People had it in them to see the good, but in this fallen world it might be acceptable and even preferable to lead them to the light by a path lit more vividly than truth would permit. Adherents of both movements therefore aimed to rouse believers from their lethargy by reminding them of what they intuitively knew but could not (or, possibly, dared not) make articulate. Both movements prized a plain style: in Indiana's oratorical contests, points went to the speaker who used the highest proportion of Anglo-Saxon-derived words—words that clarified complexities and thus gave listeners the courage to trust their own political suspicions.[16] Both used the story of the people to arouse the people in their own cause. Charles Beard mastered these techniques early in his life, learning early on that to reach large numbers of people he had to speak loudly and simply, and that such exaggeration had a moral justification. He made the most of these traditions and these biases on behalf of the people to win the state debating title by arguing for a progressive income tax.[17]

As the rhetorical bias in favor of Anglo-Saxonisms suggests, there was an element of ethnic ownership to this story of the people. Beard studied history with Andrew Stephenson, a devout exponent of the "germ theory" of U.S. institutions, which "commence[d] with Caesar's account of the Germans" and ran through to the present, "making our history complete from the time of Julius Caesar to President Cleveland, and pointing out each change in our institutions as it occurs, while, at the same time, preserving the continuity."[18] The notion of "race progress" gave an unpleasant tinge to Beard's populism in his early years, though the mark faded from his escutcheon.[19] But it was the Teutonicism common to histories of those years that brought Charles Beard and Mary Ritter together: Stephenson's lectures on European and American history were the only classes they shared.[20]

Mary Ritter's interest in her Germanic descent is obvious from her student record: she majored in German and took six semesters of the language and three of the literature in addition to her intake of Stephensonian history. In keeping with her heritage, she was thoroughly burgherlich and respectable, standing out to her classmates not for her style but for her substance. Not only did she fare exceptionally well in student elections and in the classroom, but she attained the height of social respectability by joining the oldest sorority on campus, Kappa Alpha Theta.[21] Thus, though she would later remark that the example of her more adventurous peers suggested to her that "even a young woman could really break the social conventions which called for pseudo-patrician or genuinely bourgeois manners and be guided in her human relations by a more creative sense of values," noting further that "probably I too was a 'sport' in that I responded to such innovators beyond the conventions of a clan," she did not show significantly innovative tendencies herself.[22] Her sympathetic response did not extend to emulatory innovations until later in her life. She graduated two years ahead of Beard and settled into a teaching job. He decided to follow his Anglo-Saxon enthusiasms backward through geographical history to England, to study at Oxford.

During the brief time they were apart, Beard discovered a society whose political ferment would prove sufficient to occupy them both. His academic studies took a back seat to his interest in discovering a thoroughly industrialized economy and to his personal interest in the life he had left behind. His adviser, Regius Professor Frederick York Powell (who, in an equivocal recommendation, thought Beard "the nicest American" he had met), encouraged him in his political and economic discoveries, but also noted he had other concerns. York Powell urged Beard to settle his personal and political affairs before he pushed his professional work further: "My dear Mr. Beard," he wrote, "Don't be a fool and overwork. There is plenty of time. . . . You must marry and set to your work without hurry and with time for meals."[23] Mary Ritter's students believed her to be similarly preoccupied. They made up a jingle about their education: "And now we come to Lit-tra-ture;/We'll tell you what we've heared:/All about Sir Walter Scott/And Mr. Charles Beard."[24] Beard returned to Indiana to marry Ritter in her father's house in March 1900. Eli Ritter kept a watchful eye on his new son-in-law, whose newly casual approach to temperance, inspired by his time in a beer-friendly culture, troubled him.[25] The newlyweds shortly afterward decamped for England.[26]

They brought distinct contributions to the marriage, which would from the start draw on both their strengths to give shape to their partnership. They had already developed complementary styles of dealing with the demands of the public: he spoke to it, about it, for it—sometimes whether it liked it or not, because after all he meant to persuade; she, on the other hand, outwardly heeded propriety and worked hard to earn exceptional honors, distinguishing herself within established institutions, if on mildly unorthodox paths. He had already become a manufacturer of public opinion, while she was still inwardly rebelling against it. Each of these styles corresponded to gendered notions of appropriate behavior. Great orators who swayed or represented crowds spoke in masculine voices; they could achieve dramatic effects in the course of a single afternoon with a sudden rhetorical coup. The approved path to success for women was, by contrast, quiet, dogged, and private. But as the Beards became a public team as well as a private partnership, Mary moved out of her quieter role and began sounding her voice in public forums. Indeed, the Beards' future as cooperating reformers depended on Mary's transcending the traditionally feminine sphere and finding a combative voice for use in the public arena. She found her justification in their new, English venture.

THE OXFORD AMERICANS

Charles and Mary Beard were one of two American couples responsible for the creation of Ruskin Hall at Oxford University; the other, Walter Vrooman and Amne Graflin, brought similar convictions and (what was much more important) Graflin's inheritance from a Baltimore fertilizer fortune. Though the college borrowed an English philosopher's name and sympathies, and it soon became part of the British Labour movement, it drew equally on the Americans' sense of the progress to be obtained through the education of the excluded and oppressed. In borrowing Ruskin's name, the Americans found allies among Labour and Tories alike, for whom the industrial order was equally to be abhorred. Ruskin's critique of British industry struck chords across the political spectrum, and his insistence that knowledge should serve man seemed innocuous enough. Where the Oxford movement parted from Ruskin's inspiration was in its distinctly American embrace of progress—which he disliked, to say the least—to which it sought to lay claim on behalf of the working class of England.

Charles Beard's stint in Oxford before his marriage impressed him deeply with the importance of the place. "For historic interest and architectural grandeur Oxford, England, has but one rival in the world, Rome," he said, and meant it. With his farmer's eye, he noticed even the earth. "The very ground should be of interest to an American. This is the soil pressed by the feet of our Saxon ancestors when they swept away the Britons, and laid the foundations for the most magnificent political structures the world has ever seen—the great British empire—'upon whose shores the sun never sets'—and the twin empire America." Characteristically, he followed this hymn to sacred soil with a note on Oxford's past of clay, citing Erasmus's remarks on the filth that collected in the university's medieval halls. He would always enjoy humanizing monuments in this way, and he did not mean it to make them less monumental, merely more comprehensible. Having done so in this case he set about comprehending, and transforming, the twin of his native empire.[27]

Ruskin Hall would bring workingmen to Oxford to learn what their upper-class countrymen knew about the politics and economics of Britain and the world. It would therefore give them an avenue into the political culture of their nation, not a method of subverting or supplanting that culture. The Progressive theory that the English working class required an Oxford education to understand their place in history and the values they represented suggested a considerable naïveté regarding a class that had, according to its principal historian, been self-made and self-aware since early in the nineteenth century.[28] But this naïveté made the reform effort possible and gave the ambitious American democrats a role they might, had they been better informed, not have been able to assume. As it was, they decided that (in Vrooman's words) "what Benjamin Franklin and Thomas A. Edison have done with the lightning Ruskin Hall seeks to do with scholarship and philosophy"—which is to say, bring it to earth and harness it to human service. As "citizens of the English-speaking empire" who enjoyed the advantage of excellent education, they believed it their duty to "bring numbers of working-men to Oxford to familiarize them with the educational wealth and beauty of the surroundings of the university and teach them to think intelligently on the social problems of the time without the inculcation of any 'isms.' "[29]

Beard was the project's principal proselytizer. As head and entire teaching staff of Ruskin's Extension Lectures department, he gave talks throughout working England on the history of humankind and the role played by the common folk in that history.[30] As with the oratory of his youth, these speeches both educated his audience and urged it to action. In a lecture he gave at Wigan, in northern England, in December 1900, he told the assembled workers they lived now "at the close of the most wonderful century in all the history of man." The power of industry to produce and distribute food and clothing was "practically unlimited"— a celebratory phrase that in various forms he repeated throughout these lectures. The advance of science, coupled with the shattering ramifications of the theory of evolution—"there was no established order by the decree of God, but a changing, developing society"—meant that the course for the future lay in the hands of the throng. "Democracy was winning, but it was stumbling blindly," he said. "And what must be done? Teach the public to think."[31] Teaching the public how to think was, Beard believed, something he already knew well how to do.

In its practical aspects, the Ruskin extension program brought something very like the Oxford method of education to the working public, without Oxford's discrimination as to sex. The study center was "open to men or women" and made it possible for them "to meet together to study portions of the history of their country, and to try to ascertain the reasons of those conditions that seemed to have been fatal to prosperity, as well as everything that had tended to increase the truest wealth of the nation." They would then write essays on the subjects they had studied "and hav[e] their essays criticised by capable critics." On this tutorial aspect of Ruskin Hall education, Beard was especially clear: "[The Ruskin extension program] laid special stress upon the essay work, which helped to make people think. A man might read a hundred books and yet never have a thought."[32]

As Beard talked his way through the history of industry, he forecast its future course. Through an extended disquisition on the history of fertilizers (almost certainly inspired by the familial, financial history of his ally Amne Graflin), he emphasized the limitless possibilities of production and urged his audience to "organis[e] industry." The educational program he prescribed would not supplant the values of progress or the process of innovation, but repossess them for the masses. Hence his history of invention that "explodes the 'great man theory' in the history of mechanical inventions." Progress and the institutions that had begot it must be perpetuated for the benefit of the people. "He belonged to no institution," Beard told the crowd at Wigan, describing his own independence, "not even to Ruskin Hall. He made the institution belong to him." And by learning to write about their own history they would be able to do the same for themselves.[33]

The picture of Ruskin Hall and its extension division that Beard painted included the use of a central, metropolitan institution—located in Oxford, which Beard had described as the center of an Anglo-American empire of education—to colonize the surrounding countryside. This process of colonization and education only justified itself because, Beard reasoned, it would lead to the independence of its subjects. Students of the Ruskin Hall process would learn to command institutions to do their bidding and become the masters of their history and their destiny. This creative, liberal, interpretation of the purpose of imperialism allowed Beard to enjoy immensely the pageantry of the British Empire while fostering a movement that aimed, if not at its end, certainly at its radical transformation. It also allowed him to remain securely within the manly,

Rooseveltian role of imperial advocate. But he was using manliness and the progress of civilization to press for the independence of subject peoples, rather than their continued subjection.[34]

All of Beard's Ruskin Hall lectures followed the same pattern. He developed a story of progress, which he then claimed belonged to the common people. Then he asserted that if the people were to shape their future (as they had not been able to shape their recent past) they must learn—at the hands of those "capable critics," their well-intentioned, better-educated fellows—the elements of this story. They had to comprehend the forces that shaped the narrative of history and make it their own by the simple process of telling what they knew in their own words. This same pattern shaped the earliest scholarly work of Mary Ritter Beard, who published her thoughts on the matter of history and progress in Ruskin Hall's magazine, *Young Oxford*.

One of the first sights that quiet Mary Ritter Beard saw on her inaugural tour through England changed her (she said) for good. In May 1900, British troops relieved their Boer-besieged fellows at Mafeking, bringing a small, bright spot to the story of a war that did not produce Britain's finest hours. The wild and public celebrations that followed this long-awaited victory would certainly have impressed anyone used to the genteel life of Indianapolis: they definitely affected Mary Beard. As she later recalled, on that night the strolling Beards found themselves "confronted with a crowd of girls, about sixteen years old, from the mills. The girls are drunk, in the gutter, singing something about 'We're the stuff that's made Old England great.' I was shocked." Mary Ritter Beard had been married only a couple of months, and this shock brought her to question her purpose as a bourgeois wife. "I knew I must try to do something for women. If the incident hadn't occurred, I suppose I would have gone on giggling my way through life."[35]

Mary Beard used Mafeking Night to explain why she had become a reformer. In this informal autobiographical anecdote, the episode converted her from an ordinary middle-class woman into a person of purpose. She knew now that she must give her time to the cause of improving working girls. Whether or not the episode had such a dramatic effect on that night is less important to students of Progressivism than is her conviction that the episode would satisfactorily explain her conversion when she related it later. Thus the elements of the picture she painted are important. First she invokes working girls of only sixteen, in itself a circumstance to arouse Progressive ire. Such young women ought to be in a house or school, enjoying the advantages that a young Mary Ritter enjoyed, preparing for university under the supervision of their parents, not working in mills or roaming the streets—or, as Beard had it, the gutter—in crowds. Second, these girls are drunk. Third, and worst of all, they are proud of their condition, evidently lacking the education to understand their shameful state. But just as important as Beard's horror at the working girls' state is her anger at herself as she was. As she tells the story, the episode shocked her out of her complacency—otherwise "I would have gone on giggling my way through life." In this short story, Beard does not question the bourgeois feminine propriety that informs her criticism of the drunken girls even while she refuses to allow it to limit her own actions. Like her husband, she was sure that she must teach the democracy of the masses to play its proper role—presumably, to behave in such a way as truly to make England, and the English-speaking empires, great—and she would not let her prescribed social role stand in her way. She thus adumbrated both objective and subjective motives for becoming a Progressive reformer—for the former, the plain and agreed—upon state of the working class; for the latter, her own desire to make herself of use.[36] She also justified evading gendered conventions of feminine propriety and speaking with more confidence than diffidence on matters of public import. The articles she wrote soon afterward for *Young Oxford* recapitulate her awareness of the class divide among women, her dissatisfaction with affairs on either side, and her strongly expressed determination that to repair the split, she and people like her must do something to alter the institutions that defined women's social roles.[37]

Mary Beard published twin essays, "The Twentieth Century Woman Looking Around and Backward" and "The Nineteenth Century Woman Looking Forward," in the numbers of *Young Oxford* that spanned the turn of the century, December 1900 and January 1901. The two pieces assess women's place and progress in civilization and focus on the institution of marriage both as it had trammeled women in the past and as it offered them hope for the future.[38] Mary Beard here discussed women's lives as ladies of leisure and as household drudges as well as—however rarely—as professionals. Though it may seem curious to us today that she should not have remarked on the settlement-house movement—of which she would have been aware not only because she was a university-educated woman who had read Charlotte Perkins Gilman and had lived near Chicago and now lived in England, but also because her husband had made a point of visiting Hull House in 1896—it is less strange in light of her own deep concerns of the time.[39] The essays closely examine the relation of various classes of women to marriage.

Mary Beard's Twentieth Century Woman looks glumly on the parade of great men that populate the pages of history and wonders where the women are. She looks about her and sees three basic types: idle ladies, middle-class wives ("they are reproved if 'strong-minded,' and are seldom deemed rational beings"), and working-class women, whose estate merited only the most miserable of summaries: they are single mothers, unskilled workers, bringing up "a race of criminal, imbecile and diseased beings," or else they are "straining every nerve and thought to make both ends meet and to keep both husband and children in a fit condition—to live?—no, simply to work another day. I am not censuring them, only stating conditions," she wrote. In any of the conditions that befell modern women, they were not "enlightened by the experience of the past and present"; they "grow up in total ignorance of everything past, present, and future"; they "all alike are socially unconscious."[40]

The Twentieth Century Woman then looked for an explanation of these conditions and, after dismissing the inadequacy of current social theory, she looked at the evidence of history, finding that the institution of marriage had begun to shackle women "as mere property" to the household. She concluded, "In the early history of the race we must agree that woman contributed little to the race life but children." Over time, though, "we find the domestic ideal broadening out somewhat to give freer play to woman's activities." More recently, marriage, which had begun as an institution to oppress women, had begun its "approach to voluntary co-operation." Despite the admitted example of "the Amazons, as much undersexed as the average woman of to-day is oversexed," Beard's Twentieth Century Woman placed her hopes in this development of the institution of marriage. "It is certainly the duty of man and woman to create a stronger generation, mentally, physically, and morally than the preceding one, and this can best be achieved when both parents are able to unite in one common ideal for the race."[41]

With the turn of the century, Mary Beard preserved her contrarian stance and changed her title to the Nineteenth Century Woman, continuing her critique of women's present places in society. She recapitulated her descriptions of "the 'lady,'" the "companion to the cat," and "the household drudge," and then offered "some practical remedies." These included the progress of science to relieve the burden of household work, the use of sanitary standards in furnishing and maintaining houses, and the use of other labor-saving arrangements including "communal cooking." "All we need," she wrote in an echo of Charles's Ruskin lectures, "is . . . to organise our industry," and further to offer "purposeful education, having for its goal the development and expansion of the race." Once "every avenue of usefulness" had been opened to women, "marriage will then no longer become a one-sided arrangement, a boredom, a farce; but a life-long comradeship with community of interest in humanity, and the ideal of propagating a healthy, happy, conscious, aspiring race."[42]

Mary Beard here argued something quite unlike Charlotte Perkins Gilman or Florence Kelley or Jane Addams, who despite their commitment to certain ideal relationships did not seem particularly to believe that marriage must, for the future of the "aspiring race"—or society or civilization—adapt itself to women's condition rather than be gracefully shunned in favor of more serious pursuits. By comparison, Beard stuck firmly to the notion that marriage must be both preserved and expanded, propounding with an assumption of rectitude the thesis that the institution of family supplied essential experiences for men and women alike and must remain at the center of social endeavor. But even as she did so, she avoided making the case that women should draw on their presumably innate domestic virtues, and insisted instead that they should enjoy the same opportunity to fulfill their social potential as their husbands did: "It is the struggle for liberty to develop his individuality and native powers which makes a man great. Why does not the same principle apply to a woman?" This belief that the ultimate goal of education must be the independence of pupils paralleled the theses of Charles Beard's extension lectures throughout industrial Britain and drew specifically on a liberal ethos of individual development. So, too, did her belief that the conditions of women—especially materially deprived women—could best be addressed by education, so that their industry might be organized and their burdens relieved. The overlay of Teutonicism and the idea of race progress in her writing also echoed Charles's concerns of that period, but these ideas ultimately proved to be the disposable vocabulary of an imperial ideology (like that of Willard Straight) whose version of progress meant offering the advantages of society to progressively larger populations, and whose core was a specific link between the essential teacherly role and the role of a good parent: "Home," she said, must be "the means to a social end. Sooner or later the child must leave the home and become a part of the world."[43]

This insistence on the importance of the home and of family life as an instrument for producing independent, self-governing children gave the Progressive ideal of the family its distinctive character. On the one hand, the family must remain a social mainstay: as an agency of education it was a bulwark against chaos. On the other hand, the order it provided must undermine itself: it had to turn its dependent children into independent citizens. Otherwise the family had no meaningful social role. This idea gave life to the Beards' reform activities in whatever sphere they occurred.

During their years in England, the Beards lived in Manchester, across the street from suffragist Emmeline Pankhurst. Mary Beard later said that Pankhurst had persuaded her that the political project that would most benefit from better public education was the issue of votes for women, pressed uncompromisingly and publicly upon the party in power. Pankhurst was a plausible portrait of an older Mary Beard: she had married a liberal and politically sympathetic husband whom she thought representative of a few trustworthy political men; she had children; and she had an exceedingly active public life. The Beards' children later wrote that their parents often visited the Pankhursts during their time in England, and Mary Beard told her son that "it was she who spurred me to work for woman suffrage." It may have been so, but for the next few years—the years in which she bore and began to bring up her own children in keeping with her stated ideals—Mary Beard's pen lay idle.[44]

FIXING A HOME

Although Ramsay MacDonald is supposed to have wanted Charles Beard to run for office for Labour, and Keir Hardie offered a favorable assessment of the young man's political prospects based on his rhetorical skill, the Beards decided early in the new century to return to the United States.[45] As Charles Beard later wrote, "We came to the conclusion in the Spring of 1902 that it was 'now or never,' that we 'belonged' at home."[46] They took their daughter Miriam, born in 1901, back to the United States with them, and they settled in New York. Charles would finish his Ph.D. at Columbia and then become a professor there.

Despite the Beards' conviction that the household must serve as a plat-
form for the launching of social reform, the basic rearing of children
appeared to take up most of Mary Beard's time during her children's
youngest years. Charles later wrote to a friend, "I know how you feel
about the restrictions of young motherhood as well as any mere man can
know, for Mrs. Beard had everything fall on her young shoulders simultaneously. . . . But in spite of all its limitations I find her believing that
one must somehow work from the family out to public activity."[47] Mary's
comments were sometimes more terse: "Had to make the boy some
suits—no suffrage."[48]

If the mundane business of bringing up children sometimes over-
shadowed political activism, its importance as the basis for political ideals
remained clear to the Beards. They brought up their children in keeping
with their own theories about the ideal relations between citizens and
society—which meant their children grew up and got their education in
their house, not in a New York school. In keeping with Mary Beard's proposals in her early articles on women's condition, the Beards meant to
extend their politics outward from their family, which they knew to be
wholesome, to society, which they knew to require their assistance. As
Charles became a respected member of the Columbia faculty, and before
he had yet got himself a reputation as a radical, the unorthodox lives of
his children drew the attention of a reporter from the *New York Times*,
who made an expedition to the Beard farm to discover their condition.

The farm and its ways were part of the Beards' plans. Though both
Beards made themselves experts on modern cities and involved themselves
in the campaigns to improve them, they believed that until the metropoles became the thriving democracies they envisioned, they would take their
children elsewhere—though not too far. As William Beard, their son and
second child (born in 1907) recalled, his father had picked a site for their
homestead by getting on a train in Grand Central Terminal and staying on
only just until the hills were high enough to obscure the town.[49] The establishment of the homestead in New Milford, Connecticut, authorized
Beard to play, with a considerable sense of fun, what a friend described as
"your role as a Connecticut farmer."[50] More importantly, it gave the
Beards an environment they could design for the proper education of their
children. They planted trees around the house to screen the nearby village
from their view. They put in an extensive library (which eventually
included, by Mary's count, nearly six thousand books) and a tennis court;

and they banned the telephone. Their thirty-two acres gave them a place "to house our books, have privacy for living, and be out of New York." But the Beards were surely the only Connecticut farmers who maintained suites in the Hotel des Artistes in West Sixty-seventh Street, from which they could travel to uptown literary parties.[51] Both the impression of bucolic isolation and its barely hidden proximity to urban culture were important to the Beards. The duality suited their lives and politics, giving them (to use Mary Beard's language) a home whose circumstances they could control as they used it to work toward a social end.

Charles Beard put on his farmer hat to disarm the *New York Times*. "It is absolutely impossible to give a child a right bring-up in the city," he told the reporter visiting New Milford in 1909. Then he launched into a serious speech, mixing Deweyan theories of education with a critique of modern urban conditions. He endorsed the notion current among Progressive reformers of education that children must learn to master their environment from the experiences and texts in it. "Of course," he said, "there must be the right environment . . . given a home where there are books and where the child hears intelligent conversation, I feel that there is little necessity for holding a child down to learning a certain number of tasks." But to rear a child in the city meant putting one's young indiscriminately in the path of factories and commerce, which city governments seemed to serve before they served their human constituents. "The modern city is fatal to the child," he said. Unless "the race" saw to it that city planning, land use and taxation, and education all counted in the city's councils, the city would continue its deadly way. The *Times* gave them an informal report card:

> The little Beards compare favorably in respect of knowledge with children who have been taught in the regular way, and none can doubt the soundness of their small bodies. It is true that their information is not in all points like that of the school children, but if they know rather less about fractions they are informed as to the things of the country to an extent that is bewildering. Also on such topics as history and geography they have accumulated a store of knowledge.

Miriam and William Beard would later attend school with other children, once their basic development had been assured.[52] Meanwhile, the parental Beards saw to their children's extracurricular education, and with the invention of the automobile they went " 'to see America first,' " and later "varied motoring in this fascinating region with foreign travels."[53]

As for moving from the family out to other causes, the junior Beards began to learn from their parents' politics as well. Mary Beard involved herself almost exclusively in the development of her children until her second child had reached the age of two or three, when she begins to appear once more in historical records, campaigning vigorously for the vote. In this activity she enlisted both her children and her husband, who marched with her as she pushed for women's suffrage.

PROGRESSIVE DEMONSTRATIONS

Both Beards later resisted identification as Progressives (with capital *P*). But in the early 1910s, they enjoyed the emergence of the Progressive Party, under the aegis of Theodore Roosevelt, and the consequent popular interest in reform politics. Charles used the favorite Rooseveltian slang *bully* as a term of approbation, and during the heat of the 1912 campaign wrote, "The spirit of the Holy Ghost seems to be upon the Bull Moose!" Mary Beard took advantage of Roosevelt's celebrity reformism to cite him in her first U.S.-published article, where she used him to make her case for the influence of women on their own history.[54] When Roosevelt lost and Wilson won, the Beards set themselves firmly in the opposition. Wilson stood, they believed, for a blinkered theory of states' rights that prohibited federal involvement in women's suffrage or in child labor, and also for a naive Jeffersonianism that, Charles believed, had become "unreal and unattainable."[55] Charles heard Wilson deliver a speech in which he condemned federal labor legislation for its violation of states' rights, and wrote, "I cannot associate him or anything he ever said before about 1910 with a humane or liberal idea," and that "If Woodrow Wilson . . . [is] among the righteous then I stand not in favor with the rain god."[56] Both Beards allied themselves with the Progressives among their fathers' party—the Republicans—and fell in with the *New Republic* as it put pressure on the party in power. Mary Beard especially focused her ire on the Democrats, whose leader (as she later recalled) "was utterly hostile to the proposed federal amendment for enfranchising women." Consequently "I was engaged in opposing Wilson myself on that issue, and how."[57]

The Beards' emphasis on their role as educators of the public presumed a certain ignorance among that public; they spoke in what one historian calls "an earnest and unconsciously condescending tone."[58] The condescension, however dissonant to the modern ear, was necessary to their social role: they would not have tried to teach anyone who did not apparently need education to assume their independent roles as citizens. Consequently, as a good rhetorician must, Charles Beard relied on the manipulation of what one listener called "silly symbols" to whip up enthusiasm before he proceeded to more sober argumentation.[59] He urged the simplification of public discourse, and simplified his own public discourse to set an example. He had been used to this method of political activity since his university days. Now Mary Beard began working in much the same vein, and the two of them worked to create popular enthusiasm for their causes in language and symbols they would not have used in their books or professional articles. So long as they believed in the innate virtue of the people, they could be sure that this tactic would do no harm.

Charles Beard's professional academic writings from this period reflect this paradoxical attitude toward the public: on the one hand, this public was the source of legitimate authority; on the other, it was sorely in need of enlightenment. Two articles of 1909 nicely illustrate the contrast. In his appreciation of the Oklahoma state constitution, Beard praised the people of the territory for their sagacity. "The American people are not given . . . to deducing rules of law from abstract notions; and every important clause of the Oklahoma constitution has been tried out in the experience of one or more of the older commonwealths," he wrote, chiding unnamed nay-sayers who believed the new instrument of government a risky experiment. The people had weighed complex alternative choices and made sound—because conservative—decisions. By contrast, in an article entitled "The Ballot's Burden," he flatly stated, "The real failure of the democratic theory, however, is due to the fact that it is absolutely impossible for any considerable number of voters to exercise any discrimination among candidates for a large number of offices." If the people were to make intelligent decisions they must make fewer of them and make them after a clearly framed public debate.[60] In a letter of the period, Beard corrected Robert La Follette, who had argued that the people of the United States had once governed themselves and then had lost their government to the powerful private elements of society whom Progressives simply called the interests. "I believe we did not have 'a government of the people' to begin with," he wrote, and added, "Whether the people were ready for self government then, is another matter."[61] If La Follette had read Beard's recent book *The Supreme Court and the Constitution*, he would know that Beard regarded the "propertyless masses" of the early republic—who exhibited "leveling tendencies"—as, at the least, premature in pressing for democracy; he also implied that they had an unhealthy enthusiasm for stoning judges. In this matter, Beard made himself clear: self-government had to be learned.[62] And, as his career at Ruskin Hall suggested, he meant himself to be one of the teachers.

In the summer of 1911, Charles Beard joined the *National Municipal Review* and began observing the strenuous efforts at municipal reform already under way in New York.[63] Two years later, he produced his book *American City Government*, into which he wrote his approval of two trends: simplification of government and increased efforts to educate voters. Regarding the former, he outlined innovations in commission government and strong mayoralties, which streamlined the city's legislative and executive processes, making them not only more efficient but more comprehensible to the public. For the latter, he noted the advent of official city newspapers that documented public facts. Both sets of innovations had their drawbacks; commission government tended to destroy the deliberative and representative roles of government, and official newspapers too easily became the instruments of ruling parties. Beard altogether preferred solving political problems by methods that did not rely specifically on the government at all. He gave over large parts of the book to an appreciation of the New York Bureau of Municipal Research, whose training school he would himself take over in 1915. The nongovernmental bureau undertook a variety of educational tasks to explain city government to citizens. Beard especially admired the bureau's public-budget exhibit and he remarked specifically on its more theatrical devices. The bureau used searchlights to illuminate placards showing examples of waste and corruption exposed by the commissioner of accounts. It modeled the budget using a series of large cubes—gold to represent current expenditures and purple for proposed increases. Beard reported that eight hundred thousand New Yorkers came to get their political education and learn about their tax dollars from the bureau.[64]

For his own part, Beard meant *American City Government* to be an instrument of progress itself. It would reach a large public and encourage participation in municipal politics, in part by colorful language and avoiding scholarly apparatus: "I have studiously avoided the use of footnotes on account of the popular aversion for them," he wrote. Despite his extensive recitation of the American city's problems (workers were "dependent upon conditions . . . beyond the control of the individual worker," and among immigrants there was "a natural tendency . . . to retain their own customs and traditions in a manner that prevents their taking a large and generous view of city government") and despite his gloomy remark on the "almost pathetic confidence in education as . . . a solution of all social problems," he believed the American city might yet "prove to be 'the hope of democracy' " if the work of educating the citizenry proceeded honestly. And to this task he contributed his book.[65]

At the same time as Charles was writing this appraisal of the uses of public education in creating an urban democracy, Mary Beard was pursuing a similar strategy in lobbying for the suffrage. She tended to join the avant-garde of the suffrage movement and to focus on efforts to organize working-class women, working for the Wage-Earner's League and the Women's Trade Union League. She had joined the Equality League for Self-Supporting Women, the organization begun in 1907 by Harriot Stanton Blatch, who admired the Beards' British neighbor Emmeline Pankhurst, and when Alice Paul and Lucy Burns decided to revive the congressional committee of the National American Woman Suffrage Association, whose purpose was to win suffrage nationally and all at once by constitutional amendment, they sought out Mary Beard right away to join them. Their first project was a suffrage parade in Washington, D.C., on 3 March 1913, the day before Wilson's inauguration.[66]

The parade borrowed the Pankhurst strategy of pushing the party in power. It drew attention to the obstacle that Wilsonian states' rights posed to gaining the suffrage for women and justice for working women generally. It also used effective theatrical symbols to give it its tenor. Mary Beard had a hand especially in sketching these symbols, which illustrated her intentions to enlist her family in the political effort to lead dependent classes in a charge for their own freedom. She wore bright colors— a green cape with gold tassels—and marshaled a section of black women "whom she had insisted on including," over the objection of Alice Paul.[67] She also deployed her family, marching with her husband and her children, who remembered the jeers of bystanders, which included aspersions on Charles's masculinity: "Hey, Professor, your petticoat is showing!"[68] This episode educated the public and her family alike, and what was just as important, used a theatrical representation of her family and its open, inclusive attitude to make a political point. The Beards were married; they had children; and they deemed it important that those children get an education in political realities by seeing how the world out-

side their family operated. Charles appeared as a distinguished and publicly known man unafraid to identify himself with women's causes. Mary
appeared as a mother and a self-consciously beautiful woman unafraid
to take a political stand in public. Together they appeared as white parents unafraid to identify themselves and their children with black political liberation.

That year saw her march in further parades and ultimately testify
before Congress on behalf of a federal suffrage amendment. Under pressure from the suffrage association's congressional committee, the House
Committee on Rules agreed to hear testimony on the question of whether
to establish a suffrage committee. Mary Beard testified not only on her
own behalf but also, as she said when she began, "I always represent my
husband when I speak on suffrage." The majority of the committee were
Democrats—five of them Southerners. Beard invoked Civil War nationalism ("take a national point of view and help us obliterate sectional feeling"); she named the suffrage movement's strengths, citing the already-
franchised women of more advanced states ("we have free women who
propose to work for the unfree"); and the political pressure of the Progressives ("the party that stood second in 1912 is with us"). She felt confident therefore in saying, "We come not as suppliants . . . we stand pat.
It is your move."[69] But the House committee moved to report with only
eight members present, creating a tie. The Democratic Party caucus later
voted to respect states' rights and trouble themselves no further on the
matter of women's suffrage.[70]

The Beards continued aggressively to campaign for the suffrage, to the
point of personally haranguing their Progressive friends and allies. In its
first year, the New Republic seemed to criticize the federal suffragist strategy of Alice Paul and support the gradualist approach (New Republic publisher Dorothy Straight supported Carrie Chapman Catt), and it tended
moreover to disapprove urbanely of the tactical theatrics that the Beards
believed essential. The family of Progressive reformers was small enough
that, when the journal printed a piece remarking that Mary Beard had
overstated the case in saying Woodrow Wilson's history of the United
States included no women (he had mentioned "by name . . . Anne
Hutchinson, Anne Bradstreet, Harriet Beecher Stowe and several English
queens," they said) Charles went down to the journal's headquarters to
give his intellectual neighbors a piece of his mind. He upbraided them
for being "hostile" to the immediatist suffrage position. He "explained
and argued" his case until they agreed to publish an article by him in the

next issue ("I know that one signed by him would carry more weight than one by me," Mary wrote).[71] In the article, Charles justified overstating the case for women's suffrage because "agitators" required "more than poetic license" for a good cause.[72]

Charles Beard's own work had taken him even further in the direction of overstatement. When Mary Beard invoked him during her testimony before the House, she could be sure the representatives knew who he was: the "Scavenger" (to quote one of his critics) who had "Desecrate[d] the Graves of the Dead Patriots We Revere." That was how the *Marion (Ohio) Star* had described him in a review of his new *An Economic Interpretation of the Constitution* (a book that the *Star* admitted it had not actually read).[73] In the book, Beard had adopted the agitator's strategy he described in the *New Republic*, saying privately, "I was more belligerent than was necessary and overemphasized a number of matters in order to get a hearing that might not have been accorded a milder statement."[74] Beard wanted to take the founders down a peg and make them human, their actions accessible, and thus subject to amendment as society progressed. He depicted them as thinking more of money than of Montesquieu, as being ordinary men like his father—"People ask me . . . why I emphasize economic questions so much. They should have been present in the family parlor, when my father and his friends gathered to discuss public affairs."[75] By explicitly departing from George Bancroft's depiction of the founders as divinely inspired, Beard put the power to shape society in the hands of his contemporaries, including, especially, the successors of "the disfranchised[:] . . . the slaves, the indented [*sic*] servants, the mass of men who could not qualify for voting under the property tests . . . and women, disfranchised and subject to the discriminations of the common law," who, if they could treat the founders as mortal men, might feel capable of controlling their own destiny. The book marked, as Beard wrote Robert La Follette, an important step toward securing for the people the ability to govern themselves.[76]

An Economic Interpretation also satisfied Beard's desire to win himself a place in the limelight. His correspondence about the book not only acknowledges his deliberate exaggeration and its political purpose but also reveals his glee in it. Itching for a fight—"I have hit the tradition a body blow with the truth for a sword"—he was ready to see the almighty Constitution and its merely human (though undeniably intelligent) framers brought down to earth and isolated in a historical past with its own distant concerns, and therefore susceptible of correction. It worked:

where his milder books *American City Government* and *The Supreme Court and the Constitution* had won him professional respect, *An Economic Interpretation* won him notoriety. As one historian writes, we may have forgotten how astounding this episode was: "Beard's book, perhaps the first truly exciting monograph in the history of American historiography, achieved its excitement solely through the force and provocation of its argument." The book served as its own publicity department. Beard had accomplished this by treating the public—perhaps the first time a professional historian had done so—as if it were ready to grow up and take care of itself, as if it had "an adult mind." The impact staggered his audience, who at first tended to remark on how offensive this assault on myth truly was and then, afterward, remarked on how refreshing and honest the book had seemed.[77] The effect transformed Charles Beard—indeed, both Beards. When in the year of its publication Mary Beard appeared before Congress and identified herself as her husband's representative on the matter of suffrage, she claimed his authority and his perceived radicalism as weapons in the fray.

"Everything has to go with such a rush," Mary Beard wrote to Belle Case La Follette's secretary in 1914.[78] She and her husband wrote letters to editors, organized and marched in parades, offered testimony, sought votes, and continued the education of their children. In addition, Mary that year returned to writing women's history. In an ironic twist for an adamant suffragist, she discovered "the legislative influence of unenfranchised women" and wrote an essay with that title.[79] In her Ruskin Hall essays she had lamented the absence of women's voices from the pages of history; she had concluded that women had been imprisoned within marriage and required a reformation of that institution to attain their freedom. Now she was listening for quiet voices in that official silence. She discovered in them a weighty influence to whose importance she had been alerted by the rhetoric of Progressive critiques of capitalism. "If it is true"—and Progressives, top to bottom, believed that it was true—"that powerful economic interests, organized and always alert, have often written their will into law, through popular representatives and in spite of popular will, what can we say of the weight of beneficent influences, and particularly the influence of voteless women?" She concluded that voteless women had accomplished a great deal, much of it in the form of pushing for their own enfranchisement. "Representative government is, to some extent at least, a government by petition," she wrote, and women's petitions, both public and private, had ensured the passage of pure-food laws, housing legislation, and labor legislation. Women had organized themselves and made themselves into competent politicians and had done so not only by importuning and shaming legislators, but also by joining male reformers: "much of women's effective legislative work is done in connection with those organizations which draw no sex lines. . . . Women are more and more loath to accept all the credit for social legislation today, and men seem actuated by the same spirit." Naturally she concluded by remarking that, as effective as unenfranchised women had been to date, "it is interesting to note that those women most actively using indirect influence are coming to prefer direct action on their own account" and pushing for the suffrage where they did not have it. Taken all together, the varied involvement of women in Progressive reform efforts "marks a long journey from women's old spheres," as they began to involve themselves with men in the public arena rather than remaining by their own hearths in their own homes.[80]

The essay marked a new dimension to Mary Beard's thinking. In it, she made women the agents of their own destinies and important actors in history for the first time. Where thirteen years before she had seen women as historical victims who needed to educate themselves that they might cast off their chains, she now saw women as influential historical actors who, though they could not speak on the official record, had nevertheless spoken eloquently and worked hard for their interests: their work "was not passive and moral, merely expressed . . . privately." In so doing, women had moved progressively away from their moral, religious, and domestic spheres toward public, civic responsibility and appeared ready to take on their proper independent role as full citizens with votes of their own. They had done it—as in her earlier work she had predicted they must—by working on an equal basis with like-minded men. And most importantly, in writing this new version of women's history, Mary Beard clearly intended to influence women to make more of it. Women's public activity "has grown, is growing, and will grow," she wrote.[81]

In all, the prospects for the Beards' ideal American civilization looked good in the early years of the Progressive movement. It made little difference that Wilson rather than Roosevelt had won the presidency; after all, there had been an unusual election. Roosevelt still looked strong and the movements he inspired looked even stronger. Wilson was a coward, and weak to boot (or so Mary Beard believed), and after the president began moving toward a cautious advocacy of suffrage, Charles believed Wilson would convert swiftly to whatever Progressive measures appeared sufficiently popular: "This President saw a great light on the road to Damascus in 1916," he wrote mockingly of the president's attention to the election returns, "and I am reliably informed that before that he would not even let his daughter mention the subject in his house."[82] Together the Beards employed the tactics that Charles had always enjoyed: the use of a certain poetic license to make a point, presuming confidently that the common sense of the public accorded with their sense of the political situation, and that this exaggeration could therefore have no ill effect.

Mary continued to single out romantic Jeffersonianism as the principal obstacle to progress, assailing the "tatterdemalion of a States Rights scarecrow" and arguing in a piece coauthored with Florence Kelley that "the state method is slow, cumbersome, and in many states, hopeless."[83] Charles, though more wistful ("To-day nearly half of us belong to the 'mobs of the great cities'—sores on the body politic. What message has the sage of Monticello for us?") was just as ready to see the end of the Jeffersonian ideal.[84] In its place there would come an ideal of society that the Beards had been nurturing together and in parallel since they married.

TOWARD THE MONUMENTAL

When, in 1913, Charles Beard published *An Economic Interpretation of the Constitution*, he had already begun to think of it as a step toward a wholesale reconsideration of the framework of U.S. history. He had swept away the cobwebs from the dusty Treasury archives ("The present writer was able to use some of the records only after a vacuum cleaner had been brought in to excavate the ruins")[85] and had (he claimed) discovered an "Ethiopian in the scholarly woodpile," much to his delight and to his opponents' displeasure.[86] But the book did more to demolish a myth than it did to work out the implications of giving historians broader scope. Beard was gestating something he called "the 'monumental,'" a synthetic history of U.S. society that would push "Battles to the background. Mere talkee-talk fests in Congress ditto. I want also to put the ordinary political history in the back place." When he emerged a year later with *Contemporary American History*, he again addressed himself to a wide public engaged with politics. Covering the period from 1877 to 1913, he had "sought . . . to furnish a background for the leading issues of current politics," writing a history designed to inspire social action. In this case, the plainly correct conclusion was that President Wilson's "opposition to all attempts at government regulation" was wrong and stood in the path of all recent progress, especially that gained as a result of Roosevelt's administration and his 1912 campaign. *Contemporary American History* put yet another notch in Beard's gun and marked another step toward a comprehensive history of American civilization that would inspire political and social progress.[87]

In *American City Government*, Beard wrote, "Any evaluation of popular movements in cities to-day must take into account the remarkable activities of women as private citizens, electors, and public officers."[88] Mary Beard expanded her essay on unenfranchised women into a companion volume to *American City Government* under the title *Women's Work in Municipalities*.[89] Amplifying her thesis, she documented the activities of individual women and women's organizations as they took on social problems of all kinds, including education, health, housing, and "the assimilation of races." She also pushed further the article's implication that women's influence on history had been as extensive as the undiscovered story of business, saying that her findings "warrant a new interpretation of that age-worn slogan, 'Cherchez la femme.'" Women were not absent from history, just differently present. And she repeated also her belief that women's progress tended toward an equal citizenship with men: "The logical outcome of the deep and intelligent interest in public affairs shown by women, the suffragists say, is the possession of . . . the ballot."[90] As both Beards had previously done, she intended to claim history for the unenfranchised and the otherwise dispossessed, thus giving them a stake in the future progress of society's story.

Ever since their Ruskin Hall days, the Beards had worked with each other on their separately authored projects, and their practice of combining their home and work life shows itself in their commonly held categories of analysis: the forward advance of democratic civilization, the need first to arouse and then to enlighten the populace so they might attain their independence. When either of them planned to give a speech, one "rehearsed" it over and over with the other, preparing the performance to do just what they hoped.[91] Now they were prepared to carry their work forward together.

From writing similarly focused works and working together privately, as well as speaking out publicly on the same issues, it was a short step to writing together. Thus in 1914 the Beards came to the inevitable practice of coauthorship.[92] Together they wrote *American Citizenship*, a high-school civics textbook in which they restated their theses for the benefit of the next generation. "The changed and special condition of modern women in the family, in industry, before the law, and in the intellectual life of the community" warranted a new conception of citizenship and of American society, they wrote, and began urging that conception on their pupils and readers.[93]

The purpose of an education in civics was, the Beards wrote, to encourage the use of "private virtues in public service," and they made sure the reader would know the principal source of such virtues. In their discussion of human needs, their discussion of the family came only after their discussion of food, clothing, and shelter. "The family represents the first little group where the young and the old, the clever and the dull, the strong and the weak, learn to work together and to work together in harmony and affection. Here the virtues of good citizenship are discovered." At its best, the family produced excellent citizens. "How deep and important are the ideals of fatherhood, motherhood, child life, affection, loyalty, care for the helpless, and unselfishness which develop wherever there is a wholesome family life!" they wrote. Moreover, they remarked that these ideals did not remain within the home, but rather immediately extended outward through the most important of familial virtues, empathy.

> It is through the family that women who first loved only their own little children have grown to care for the welfare of all little children; that women who have sacrificed and worked for their own children have learned to be interested in the struggles of all women to rear their children properly; and that men with families of their own to work for have understood and respected the struggles of other men to maintain proper homes. The community which the government serves is in many respects simply an enlarged family.

The Beards did not limit the structure of the ideal family to the presumably normal kind. They cited families with single breadwinners, male or female, families with two breadwinners, and families in which children worked, noting of the stereotype, "Whether this is the best type of family we need not stop to discuss . . . there are so many variations from this type . . . that it is scarcely to be regarded as typical any longer."[94]

The Beards also broached, however delicately, the question of changes in the family wrought by evolution of law and custom. "In the old days . . . the idea of giving women generally an education at public expense was deemed absurd, and the thought that women would ever have any share of making the laws through the acquisition of the right to vote was deemed preposterous beyond measure. The system of subjection prevails in China still"—which though it may now sound a non sequitur, revealed then their definite bias in favor of the shift away from that system. The resulting families in which women had rights and legal standing of their own—families that were "reasonable and refined"—stood a better chance of providing children with the proper education and inducing parents to expand their empathy beyond the little circle of the household.[95]

Once they did so, they might find themselves taking on further parental responsibilities toward those outside their homes: "Instead of denying the ballot to persons of foreign birth," the Beards suggested, "it is better to educate them, to improve the conditions under which they work and labor, and to give them a fair chance to become valuable American citizens." This task of education and improvement belonged to all who already understood enough of citizenship, who bore a responsibility for the sound development of public opinion: "We are therefore all makers of opinion, men, women, and children of a school age."[96]

In *American Citizenship*, the Beards wrote together for the first time and made explicit much of what had already driven their political life. They believed in the equitable relationship of citizens, men and women, to each other; they believed in the obligation of the strong to help the weak, the clever to help the dull, the knowledgeable to help the ignorant. As parents assisted in the upbringing of children, so should every citizen assist in the development of dependent classes, who like children needed to learn the necessary virtues and proceedings of self-government.

By 1916 the Beards had established for themselves a niche among Progressive reformers. They advocated using the federal government and extragovernmental agencies alike to educate the public, on the theory that a fragmented populace comprising a variety of groups shut out from the processes of government required education so that they might take their government into their own hands. Depending as they did on a philosophy of mass mobilization, and speaking as they did both to and for the democracy, they did not hesitate to use, and to praise others for using, symbolic (and not wholly accurate) speech in the interest of getting attention and making a point. The occasional suggestion that this strategy might under unfortunate conditions engender equally symbolic and strong resistance—a remark from the crowd about masculinity, a remark from a caucus about the sanctity of state sovereignty—did not yet appear to amount to a considerable phenomenon. So they proceeded joyfully to assail the enemy on all fronts.

More important, not only did they wage their campaign together, they made this companionship in struggle the very cause for which they fought. They could scarcely write about the idea of progress toward a better society without invoking the best elements of family culture: the equal relations, both public and private, between men and women; the unequal, but beneficent, relations between parents and the children they educated; the similar relations between the educated of all classes and the uneducated in their society. Their ability to live confidently in keeping with these ideals, and to embody the theories they propounded, depended first of all on their financial success, which underwrote their establishment of an ideal environment for their children, but second and more importantly on their intellectual success. They had identified problems—the institution of marriage that in its nineteenth-century, American varieties prevented women from taking part in the common life of society; the conditions of industry and urban life that likewise prevented immigrants from doing the same—and they had focused their energies on changing them. The principal obstacles were obvious to them: not only the economic conditions that put working-class and immigrant men, women, and children in factories for unconscionable hours and swaddled their bourgeois counterparts in comfortable ignorance, but also the cultural conditions that shaped expectations for men and women. The essential development of society toward better conditions for its workers, toward the political involvement of its citizens, toward the making of women into citizens, depended on the creation of a civic life in which men and women worked together on an equal footing, free to state their convictions on any topic, irrespective of its presumed propriety for one gender or another. So Charles spoke and marched for the cause of suffrage; so Mary spoke on the constitutional implications of a federal or state-centered strategy for securing the vote; so together they worked on a more inclusive and purposeful narrative of U.S. history that would both depict and usher onward the creation of an active and educated citizenry.

Their political success depended on their ability to play their roles as educators publicly as well as privately, and to remain secure in the knowledge that their audience approved of them. And their audience did approve: they bought the Beards' books, and wrote the Beards letters, and some even joined them in their reform projects. In 1914 Mary Beard noted the disintegration of boundaries between women's and men's political issues, writing that committees promoting social legislation increasingly told her, "All our work is done through committees of men and women."[97] In 1915 Charles Beard wrote the *New York Times* to ridicule a doctor's assertions as to what comprised the essentially feminine; along the way, he attacked the very ideas of masculinity and femininity as they applied to identifiable virtues and vices. "Pray, what is their [women's] sphere? Who shall set the metes and bounds to it?" Beard asked. Then, as he so often found it useful to do, he treated the *Times* to an illustrative example from his rural past:

> It makes me laugh to hear a comfortable, protected New York citizen speak of 'courage' as a masculine virtue, when I recall my own pioneer grandmother, who often drove howling wolves away from the front door with flaming firebrands and on more than one stormy, black night rode on horseback ten or twenty miles along blazed forest trails to do errands of mercy for distant neighbors—and incidentally bore fourteen children.

He remarked, too, on the pernicious generalizations of the historical past (with respect to Jews or blacks or peasants) and condemned them all, writing, "The great qualities of human nature—courage, industry, patience, wisdom, endurance, virtue, honor, originality, and sympathy—are not the monopoly or even the 'distinct characteristics' of any race or sex or class," concluding, "That is why those of us who sympathize with the modern woman movement—even 'blatant feminism'—have confidence in its essential soundness." Like his wife, he believed the effectiveness of the women's movement derived from its insistence on the use of common sense to debunk cultural myths, however precious they might seem. And in the years before World War I he could still believe that the accumulated common experience of the American people ran so nearly parallel to his own as to justify the belief that his sense was common sense, too; that "our experiences, our sympathies, our associations, our interests, our lines of reading and thought, our notions of justice" would ultimately lead all Americans to begin the creation of an equitable, cooperative common life based on liberal familial relations and the ultimate independence of all presently dependent classes of people. Only when the war began to wring its effects in the fabric of American life did the Beards begin to doubt these assumptions.[98]

Three

LUCY SPRAGUE AND WESLEY CLAIR MITCHELL

Properly speaking, *a man has as many social selves as there are individuals who recognize him and carry an image of him in their mind....* The most peculiar social self which one is apt to have is in the mind of the person one is in love with.

—William James[1]

Wesley Clair Mitchell was Wesley to his economist colleagues, Clair to his friends, Robin to his wife, and Dr. Mitchell to those who knew him only through his work. These many names signified many social roles, and they bespeak the difficulty of integrating social selves, of making personal convictions drive professional research, of making political purpose out of statistical severity. In our own time, scholars have both praised and blamed Mitchell for keeping these roles separate, and some date this separation from the start of his career. But during the decades between 1900 and 1920, Mitchell tried hard to integrate the professional and personal, the social and familial, claims on his time, and so did his wife-to-be, Lucy Sprague. Mitchell, though a scholar of money and of business, hated the damage that modern commerce did to human relations. Sprague, though herself a beneficiary of new money, felt similarly. Both hoped their own new family might resist the effects of the crass new economy and become the source of transformative energies that would begin to heal social relations. Both needed to work as reformers, and to have this work spring from their ideas of themselves, rather than from what others expected them to be. Their construction of projects based on the model of the liberal family—projects that included, of course, their own family—allowed them to make their private concerns their professional ones.[2]

Sprague and Mitchell began their careers in new universities, where they believed they would be able to undertake projects that would provoke social reform. They both found basic academic behavior insufficiently integrated with ordinary life and began moving toward more worldly pursuits. At the same time, they began considering the prospect of marrying. The two concerns became intertwined: how could they design their marriage to allow them to pursue their commitment to reform? After a few false starts, they settled on a configuration of social selves that would satisfy them and permit them to pursue their goals for a time. Ultimately they discovered a common basis for their two missions, a shared vision of a society in which everyone could have what they had, in which (Mitchell wrote) "every girl shall have as full an opportunity to blossom as you have had, in which every boy shall be as free to find his work and his love as I have been."[3] They established together a household that became the foundation for these ambitions and the heart of a series of reform efforts. Though we might find it tempting to talk about the Mitchells' marriage as an emotional solution to an intellectual problem—using love to blot out the contradiction between family and social claims—the Mitchells themselves used intellect to solve this problem, drawing out the intellectual compatibilities between their reform agendas, and furthermore to rooting these compatibilities in their idea of what families were supposed to do in society.

PUBLIC EDUCATION

The movement of young Wesley Clair Mitchell's family tended toward cities. This was for reasons of educational eminence and cosmopolitanism: the former would supply necessary resources for the precocious Wesley, whose interests in disputation, calculation, and lepidopterology marked him early in life as belonging outside the farming community norm; the latter would make room for the Mitchell family's history, for though Wesley's father John Mitchell had all his life loved only Lucy Medora McClellan, when she rejected his first offer of marriage he married another woman, then soon divorced her so he could marry Lucy. In their small-town, Methodist congregation, this stain, once discovered, marked them for ostracism, so they moved on to a bigger city and greater tolerance. A doctor, John Mitchell had an office in Decatur. The family lived nearby on their fruit farm.[4]

All of these elements shaped young Wesley's outlook. He rebelled against uncompromising dogmatism; he always retained a respect for manual labor; and he also yearned for cosmopolitan occupations. The environment he first found that was conducive to this varied temperament was Chicago. Because Chicago had barely begun its life as an American city but already challenged New York for financial and cultural importance, it contained educational and business enterprises of worldly scope that clashed and meshed not only with labor movements but also with farming communities. When Mitchell was older, he would write with sympathy of the economist Thorstein Veblen that a "boy brought up in such a family, largely sufficient unto itself, acquires an outlook on life unlike that of the son of thoroughly acclimated parents." Thrust afterward into U.S. business centers, such a boy would become "a sceptic by force of circumstances over which he had no control." The description of Veblen could also be applied to Mitchell himself.[5]

Wesley Clair Mitchell was born in 1874, the eldest of seven children. Dr. Mitchell had sustained a leg injury while assigned as an officer to the Fourth U.S. Colored Infantry in the Civil War. This chronic physical debility combined with a "rashness" in business affairs made the parents rely heavily on their first child. As Wesley later wrote, "they could not help resting a part of family responsibilities on me, as the eldest son, far too early. I had to think about money matters, to learn the hard side of life, when most children are free from care." Among the hard responsibilities he undertook was the collection of rent from the poor tenants who occupied small, unplumbed houses that the doctor had built on his property. Thus Wesley got an early sense of how economic circumstances could constrain individual freedom.[6]

Early on, intellectual life allowed him an escape from some of the unpleasant aspects of worldly responsibility. He collected butterflies and their Latin names. He learned to make points in debate, a skill he claimed to have learned from needling a Baptist grand-aunt: "I suppose there is nothing better as a teething ring for a child who likes logic than the garden variety of Christian theology. . . . I developed an impish delight in dressing up logical difficulties which my grandaunt could not dispose of."[7] But as he became an expert in argumentation, he became more concerned with the life of the world. He turned his guns on the usual target for young people of his generation: political corruption. One of his sisters remembered hearing him practicing his orating in another room. Through the wall she could hear only the essential, damning phrases "ward heeler" and "election crooks."[8]

The founding of the University of Chicago in 1890 presented the gifted young man with a chance to better his lot. He switched schools so he could prepare himself and he crammed for entrance exams. The new university, like the city itself, sprang to eminence almost overnight, acquiring a world-class endowment, faculty, and campus within a few short years. The instantaneous eminence of the school reflected civic ambition. Chicago businessmen had given it being to complement their wealth with erudition, and the university's faculty returned this attention by seeking to speak to the city's public. To serve as the head atop the city of big shoulders turned out to be more difficult than the professors had thought, but they were determined to do so. This was the moment that Mitchell arrived as one of the first class of students.[9]

A new university in a new city had a different role from those that had evolved more slowly. The school imported outsiders who had no organic connection to the local culture. These professors had therefore a difficult relationship to the populace among whom they lived and whose children they taught. The troubles of the faculty need not have affected a student; the university's students had immediately created a full-blown undergraduate culture, and within their first year established in abundance the fraternities, social, literary, theatrical, and drinking clubs that formed the standard landscape of the American university scene.[10] But for Mitchell these student activities had nothing to do with college: "to a boy of my experience and temperament college was a shining opportunity, not a dull duty. The life was so free from care, the course so full of interest, the tasks so easy!"[11] By abjuring the ordinary social career of the college man, Mitchell made himself what one historian of campus life calls a characteristic "outsider."[12] The culture he was outside was the culture that defined masculinity for men of his class, and he would later pay the price for ignoring it. Meantime, his decision made him the protégé of his professors and involved him more deeply than the ordinary student with the intellectual life of the faculty.

Looking back, Mitchell would remember John Dewey as a great influence on his youthful thinking. But we should take care with this observation. Mitchell's Dewey was a philosopher who understood the cultural

significance of habits and institutions and whose import he could easily
absorb as he "went on to ethnology."[13] It was this Dewey who, in Lucy
Sprague Mitchell's later words, "has become so much a part of our culture in countless ways that we *no longer distinguish him* within our culture."[14] Most importantly, Mitchell's Dewey was politically bland. As
Dewey's biographer writes, while at Chicago he "vented his radical spleen
only in his private correspondence."[15] Thus Mitchell got from Dewey
only a sense of the importance of cultural momentum in determining
human behavior, not a sense of the meliorative and even radical power
of education—the thesis for which Dewey is more importantly known
and the thesis that underwrote Mitchell's own later reform efforts.

The second important influence on Mitchell was Thorstein Veblen,
for whose personal history he had empathy and whose rhetorical skill he
observed with uncomfortable admiration. Mitchell wrote:

> Veblen, of course, was a . . . disturbing character. He did not con-
> trovert the classical doctrines. . . . Instead he explained why the
> classical masters believed what they did and why our contempo-
> raries thought as they did. What upset our intellectual complacency
> was that his explanations of current habits of thought applied to us
> personally . . . a student had to be dull indeed not to see that he
> shared the pitiful respectabilities writhing under Veblen's scalpel,
> and most of the economic preconceptions we were accepting
> uncritically. To a well-brought-up scion of American culture, tak-
> ing one of Veblen's courses meant undergoing vivisection without
> an anesthetic.[16]

For Mitchell, though, the probing of the scalpel followed lines with which
he himself was familiar, having already begun to enjoy the task of taking
apart rigid dogmas. Veblen's technique also fitted with Dewey's and with
the ethnological approach: they all looked at ideas within their social and
historical milieu. Veblen's principal shortcoming, in Mitchell's estima-
tion, was that his critical words worked, sociologically, like a purgative
jeremiad: having listened to an angry, godless prophet, his students could
leave and feel themselves shriven. They did not have to do anything.
Veblen never developed a "systematic treatise" of his own to replace conventional wisdom; nor did he particularly enjoy speaking to large audiences. Thus his teaching could not foster social change, only create social
discomfort. Mitchell learned from Veblen the vulnerability of a moneyed

civilization to critique, but to learn how to construct an alternative and how to argue its case he had to look elsewhere for instruction.[17]

In fact, the only systematic thinker Mitchell knew at Chicago was his principal adviser, J. Laurence Laughlin. Laughlin's system was the traditional one of classical economics: as Charles Beard would later say, he spread the doctrine of laissez-faire "as wide as the silver dollar bearing the motto 'In God We Trust.'"[18] Moreover, his method of argumentation consisted essentially of a "logical scheme" like the ones through which Mitchell had long enjoyed poking holes, and it was Laughlin's scheme that was Veblen's principal target.

But for his own part, Laughlin thought of himself as a goad to public thought, and in this role he inspired Mitchell. Laughlin admired his own teacher, Henry Adams, for his "desire to shake up established complacency, to start others to think," and he himself adopted the same attitude.[19] His handbook *The Study of Political Economy* argued that the general public needed to understand the new discipline if it wished to control its affairs. The Civil War, the end of slavery, income taxation, railroads, telegraphs, and the effects of federally-issued paper money had created a new national economy that affected all citizens. Laughlin argued, therefore, that everyone should take up the discipline sufficiently to comprehend these issues, and he encouraged his readers to become evangelists themselves. He even gave technical instructions on how to build charts for public display.[20] For himself, Laughlin took his role as public teacher seriously enough to challenge the popular apostle of cheap money, William "Coin" Harvey, to a public debate, and prepared charts, jokes, and other simple explanations to win public opinion.[21]

Mitchell wrote:

> Laughlin was a most effective teacher. He owed this success to his firm faith in the laws of economics, to the zeal with which he sought to make his students accept his faith as he saw it, to his genuine interest in our personal fortunes, and most of all to the fact that we could not accept his hard and fast doctrine.... We had somewhat to justify our dissent.[22]

Just as Adams pushed Laughlin, Laughlin pushed Mitchell. Mitchell followed Laughlin's lead in attacking the advocates of cheap money, though he did so for reasons of his own. More important, he wanted, like Laughlin, to address a wider public than an academic might. Laughlin had written, "Since it is absolutely certain that there will be economic ideas of some kind in the minds of the public, it is evident that we can make these ideas good ones, only by working at the purveyors of such writing in the journals of the land."[23] Thus, after finishing his Ph.D. under Laughlin and following an unhappy—because inconsequential—stint compiling statistics for the U.S. Census Bureau, Mitchell got himself hired by Robert W. Patterson Jr., of the *Chicago Tribune*. He went on the *Tribune*'s behalf to cover the strike of the Amalgamated Association of Iron, Steel, and Tin Workers against the newly incorporated, billion-dollar U.S. Steel Corporation.[24]

Mitchell had written his graduate thesis, at Laughlin's behest, on the dangers of cheap money, focusing on the use of paper currency—greenbacks—to pay for the Civil War. A standard, doctrinally classical economic argument about the dangers of greenbacks—the kind of argument Laughlin would make—might have offered an essentially religious opposition, referring to the vicious habits of borrowing encouraged by paper money. Mitchell employed instead a statistically based argument that showed that, virtue and vice aside, cheap money cost the common worker dear. Intent on precision, he figured the effect of greenbacks on the cost of the war by enumerating wartime expenditures for commodities and securities, by discussing the influence on government receipts in terms of increased willingness to pay taxes with depreciated currency, and by figuring the augmentation of the federal debt by currency depreciation and the cost of interest on the increased debt. In the end, the adoption of greenbacks increased the federal debt by $589 million, out of a total debt of $2.9 billion. More important to Mitchell's argument, the average laborer and the common soldier bore the brunt of this increased debt because wages rose more slowly than rents or prices, making their share of the debt burden heavier than it should, by rights, have been. Consequently, the average American had a personal, rather than an ideological, interest in supporting sound money.[25]

Mitchell noted more in sorrow than in anger that arguments over the merit of soft money were traditionally "crude." And though his own work was by contrast a conscientious appeal to economic interest, leaving passion out of the argument, he nevertheless made it clear where his sympathies lay. In the politically charged atmosphere of the 1890s, when every argument for hard currency opened an academic to the charge of serving as a tool for the interests, Mitchell instead made himself the instrument of public interest, focusing on the material cost of cheap money to laborers, rather than on the vicious habits it might inspire among them. He appealed therefore to the working classes as rational actors with a quantifiable stake in "the interest of the community in a stable monetary standard."[26] To appeal to the emotions, like Coin Harvey, might have been more satisfying, but Mitchell sought instead to educate people to see their real interests.

His work for the *Tribune* demonstrated the same sympathies, though here he hoped to reach a wider audience. He sided in principle with the Amalgamated Association, but disapproved of the union's strategy. The Amalgamated members' finest hour had been their strike against the Carnegie mills at Homestead in 1892, when in battle with the company's hired thugs they established their virtue beyond a shadow of a doubt, and at a considerable cost in lives. Since then the Carnegie mills had joined the companies that turned steel into finished products, creating the mammoth U.S. Steel Corporation. The Amalgamated struck, hoping to unionize the new trust. The union's strike had a visceral appeal to its leadership, but it went so plainly against workers' immediate economic interests that it was doomed to fail. Thus Mitchell's story was that the story was over. "It was the declared purpose of the Amalgamated association to get up a parade today, march to the Duquesne plant, and then return with the entire force," he wrote. "The parade did not appear, as there was no one to parade, and the open-hearth mill is running full blast." Though there was sporadic violence, the strike fizzled. Other chapters of the union, rather than join in, requested that the strike end, as did the union's executive board. The *Tribune* editorialized that the union could better spend its time looking after the interests of its members than the pride of its leaders.[27]

Though, as before, Mitchell sided with the working classes—U.S. Steel president Charles Schwab came off poorly in his reportage—he found that the union, relying like Coin Harvey on an old faith, could not effectively galvanize labor to defend its interests. Workingmen needed to elect representatives that better comprehended the new American economy.

Mitchell's contributions to the *Tribune*'s editorial page continued, but he grew frustrated with newspaper work. If the Census Bureau had been too precise to matter to the public, the *Tribune* was too involved with its public to attain the precision he cherished. He had swung from one extreme to another in his effort to balance his desire for intellectual honesty with his desire to address the public. Thus when Adolph Miller, his colleague in economics at Chicago, asked him if he would like to go with him out to the University of California, he said he would, and he returned to his starting point, in academia.

Despite these oscillations, Mitchell remained throughout his youth persuaded of his overriding purpose: to educate the U.S. public about the new industrial economy that currently rocked the populace with booms and busts, infused the political system with cash and corruption, and seemed immune to virtuous opposition. It yielded only to painstaking analysis of its inner works. Mitchell believed that such analysis would enable ordinary Americans to run their own affairs. He had only to find the right way to address his audience. While he was seeking to balance his social roles as academic and as public man, Lucy Sprague (who had launched herself on a similar mission) challenged him instead to fuse these concerns.

THE GROCER'S DAUGHTER

Lucy Sprague was born in 1878 to Lucia Atwood and Otho Sprague, the fourth of six children and the youngest daughter. Sprague was a partner in Sprague Warner, a successful wholesale grocer. He had not gone to college but had bought—and read—a first-class library. He was determined to consolidate his material and intellectual gains in and for his posterity. When he built his family a house in Chicago, he insulated and protected them, installing buttons labeled, respectively, *Fire* and *Mob* to call the appropriate municipal services in the event of either. He established for himself the role of paterfamilias, treating his wife like a daughter and his youngest daughter like his dedicated servant. He was the central fact of Lucy Sprague's early life, both goading her onward and reining her in. He would first stifle and then underwrite her independence.[28]

Otho Sprague served under General Ben Butler in the U.S. Army during the Civil War; he was invalided out with what turned out to be tuberculosis. Consequently, despite his vigor as a businessman, he succumbed to bouts of weakness that worsened with age. His wife suffered sick-headaches (migraines) and often retired to her darkened bedroom to recover. These parental sicknesses left Lucy the job of "family nurse and receiving so little education, except such as I grabbed by myself."[29] The children had been in public school until one got into a scuffle with a working-class child. After that they went to private school, but even that environment was too much for Lucy, who whenever she went to school "twitched constantly and uncontrollably and had those terrible pains in my legs which were then called 'growing pains.' At any rate, I was always taken out of school."[30] Thus little Lucy had two lives, as nurse and as entrepreneurial student. She lived both of them within the walls of one house, but the latter life took her mind out to the wider world.

The resources for her self-education easily matched what she could have found in school. She read right around her father's library, subjecting herself to the same discipline and curriculum he had used to teach himself. She talked over the books with her father—"that was a part, of course, of the urge to do it [i.e., to read his books]. Because I got attention and I got praise because I was able to bring into our conversation unexpected kinds of information."[31]

In addition to Otho Sprague's books, there were Otho Sprague's visitors. Like his friends Marshall Field and George Pullman, Sprague took a proprietary interest in the city and the cultural institutions he had helped pay for, including the new university, whose faculty often came over to dine. John and Alice Dewey came to dinner. So did Adolph Miller, a professor of economics who married Lucy's sister Mary, and Miller brought with him a young graduate student named Mitchell, who made a poor impression on Lucy: she did not like his mustache.[32] Most important of the university connections was Alice Freeman Palmer, who came to be the first dean of women at Chicago. She lived in the Sprague house when she first took up her new job and she impressed Lucy deeply: "Mrs. Palmer was to me one of the great women of the world. Here I was, this nervous, high-strung, lonely fifteen-year-old, and she used to talk a great deal with me."[33]

Perhaps most impressive to Lucy Sprague was her father's patronage of Jane Addams's Hull House. Her first trip there gave her a glimpse of what she called "the real world," and she continued to visit afterward.[34] Addams became for her the voice of reform and ultimately the cause of a crisis in her relationship with her father, an experience she afterward cited as critical to her conversion to Progressive reformism. It happened because of the strike Eugene V. Debs led against the Pullman company in its eponymous town. "In the town of Pullman, Mr. Pullman built houses for all the workers, and he built morals right along with them. He handed out his code of conduct and he expected it to be followed. Father was very proud of that," Lucy remembered. Indeed, not only was he proud: he contributed to it, serving on Pullman's board of directors. He thought of the model town as a useful way of helping the working class

and saw no necessary contradiction between supporting Pullman and
supporting Hull House.

> Then, when Jane Addams came out for the strikers, and to this
> insult was added the fact that she was a woman, Father felt strongly
> about it. . . . He was very proud of the paternalistic town of Pull-
> man which Jane Addams resented. I took the side of Jane Addams.
> Not verbally, I assure you. I never said anything. But at that time
> I felt my father had something wrong with his standards and I never
> got over it.[35]

Though the Pullman strike and the choice of Jane Addams over Otho
Sprague marked an important point in Lucy Sprague's intellectual development, it did not give her the confidence she needed to use her own
voice. That would come later.

As tuberculosis consumed his tissues, Otho Sprague had finally to leave
Chicago. He built for himself, his wife, and a consumptive niece a house
in Pasadena, California, that would serve as a private sanatorium staffed
by a single nurse—Lucy. She cooked, kept track of medication and the
weather, and each morning cleaned spittoons full of infected expectorate.
"I knew cleaning the cuspidors was dangerous work, for no maid was
ever allowed to touch one. Father was scrupulous about protecting anyone in his employ," she dryly noted. The split in her life between her
family duties and her educational imperatives became more evident. She
could now stand going to school—perhaps because her home life was
now less bearable—and developed what she called a "split personality"
during this time: "gay and happy and studious during the week, and a
trained nurse over the weekend." The absence of adjectives in her description of the familial role is as eloquent as the omission of overt comment
on her father's willingness to protect his employees over his daughter.[36]

When Lucy reached the end of high school, she wrote her sister (who
had married Adolph Miller, the economist with the mustached friend) to
ask if she could possibly help her get out of the house and into college.
Mary replied that, though she understood, she believed Lucy's family duty
to be paramount. But she also passed Lucy's plea on to the Sprague's former boarder, Alice Freeman Palmer, now living with her husband George
while he taught in Harvard's Philosophy Department. Alice Palmer wrote
back "inviting me to live with them," Lucy recalled, and she further "said
she would not allow me to break down, she would supervise me. So I went

under those conditions and at once became healthy!" As for her family, "Mother was glad. Father did not oppose my decision."[37]

For the remainder of her formal education, Radcliffe, Harvard, and the Palmers did wonders for Lucy. Though she fared indifferently in most of her classes, she excelled in philosophy during a time when the Harvard (and thus the Radcliffe) Philosophy Department contained an unequaled collection of intellects—George Santayana, Josiah Royce, and William James principal among them.[38] The William James of the 1890s had put his own invalidism behind him and was busily "amusing himself with himself and his students," as one of his Radcliffe students of the period wrote.[39] He impressed Lucy with his confident freedom, both physical—his lengthy stride and swinging arms—and intellectual, which struck her as whimsical and delightful as he let himself and his mind fly off at odd tangents: "Palmer [i.e., George Palmer, Alice's husband], I've raised the last cent for the psychological laboratory," she remembered him crying as he burst into a room. "Come along now and we'll clean out our chimney flues."[40] James, who traditionally discouraged students from enrolling for graduate study in philosophy ("Don't do it," he would say, "you will be filling your belly with the east wind"),[41] nevertheless accepted Lucy as a graduate student after she earned her bachelor's degree. Royce told her that her work was good enough to warrant pursuit of a doctorate. She had found her metier and her voice: "I never talked much until I went to college," she wrote.[42]

Even so, the rift between her social selves persisted. She had developed a chronic cough as a result of her nursing work for her family and had to write her examinations in a separate room to avoid disturbing other students. A doctor told her that if she returned to her familial service, she could expect only to die of tuberculosis herself. Even with this warning, and despite the freedom and the examples that Alice Palmer, William James, and Jane Addams had given her, she acknowledged once again the family claim on her life. After the death from consumption of her mother and the nervous breakdown of her sister Nancy, she returned to Pasadena to act as nurse once more.

Now it seemed even her rescuers would betray her liberty: after the Palmers again pulled her from Pasadena, this time to take her to Europe— "once more I stepped into a new world," she wrote—Alice Freeman Palmer suddenly died and George Herbert Palmer became her new charge. "Am I," she recalled herself wondering, "always to lead a vicarious life?" But once more—and finally—the world of education opened up to her, freeing her from the role of helpmeet. In the spring of 1903, Benjamin Ide Wheeler, president of the University of California, visited the Palmer house in Cambridge, and after talking with Lucy he suggested she move to California to take charge of the women students at Berkeley. "Can't you," she asked, "give me any idea what you want that job to do?" He said, "Yes. I want you to find out what needs to be done and do it." Palmer advised her that if she should take the job, she must insist that Wheeler make her a member of the faculty. "Well, this would never have entered my timid mind, but Mr. Palmer insisted. Mr. Palmer, like my father, was a person to be obeyed." Wheeler agreed. Lucy once more packed her bags for California, but this time as a professional woman and head of a household of her own.[43]

It was not until she had a job offer that she could extricate herself from her extended family's claim on her life. She had until then oscillated between her perceived duties to her relatives and her duties to herself and the community of intellect. Even now, when she was a full-fledged teacher and innovator, she would find herself unable entirely to choose one role over the other.

PROGRESS IN CALIFORNIA

Lucy Sprague became a member of Berkeley's faculty in 1903 and, after a period of settling in, officially became dean of women in 1906, a position she held until 1912. Throughout these years she enjoyed Wheeler's support in looking after the women students of the University of California. She did not merely represent women students to the administration: thinking the students insufficiently ambitious (90 percent of them wanted only to become teachers), she set out to transform them into citizens engaged in their political and commercial society. She fulfilled this mission, first by making her own household the center of a community of women students concerned with public affairs, and eventually by seeking to alter the students' living arrangements so they could manage their own affairs as they learned the complex details of their lives in modern America. The leading obstacle to her project was the university's requirement that she deal with her young women specifically as women—as sexual beings subject to physical demands as well as to the dictates of their own will.

Lucy met with perceptible bias from some portion of the male professors. She was one of only two women on the Berkeley faculty, and at first she roomed with the other, Jessica Peixotto. The pair of them agreed to skip faculty meetings and keep a low profile. Lucy herself set about making sure that the men knew "they had nothing to fear from me." Nevertheless, Wheeler wanted her to have authority to innovate, so her "promotion was put forward at an abnormal pace because Mr. Wheeler wanted me to get on with the job of being dean."[44]

As she settled in as dean, Wheeler asked her to look into the question of whether the women students at Berkeley were tending toward a "natural segregation" from the men and whether something ought to be done to integrate the student body.[45] But she spent more time corresponding with him on the terribly mundane business of meeting women's needs on a university campus: "machines containing sanitary serviettes." This matter dragged out for five months, with Sprague diplomatically prodding the university to order what Wheeler delicately called "the articles." At first, the purchasing agents maintained that the equipment did not exist; then, having finally found it, billed the women's undergraduate society for its installation. Sprague objected and finally secured the university's cooperation, but such extended negotiations over such basic business took time and energy away from her real interests.[46] So did the school's immediate requirement that she teach "prophylaxis." She faced a student populace suffering in the usual proportion from the results of (as the university's physician put it) "too ardent love-making."[47] The crash course in sexually transmitted diseases that she first took and then conveyed without a blush to the students earned her a querulous letter from Wheeler for interfering with the normal schedule of the first day of classes. But it became a necessary part of her repertoire as a woman educator. Responsibility for women meant responsibility for their sexuality. As her sister Mary told her, "If you're going to be modern, you have to say the word 'syphilis' at least once a day."[48]

She balanced these required maternal duties with her own true interests. She bought a parcel of land in the Berkeley hills next door to the university's architect, whom she commissioned to build her house, which was her own and was glorious:

> When I opened my eyes in the morning, I looked directly through the Golden Gate. . . . The view of San Francisco Bay was . . . spectacularly dramatic. To the north and to the south, the Bay stretches as far as the eye can see, and immediately opposite opens the Golden Gate. Beyond, the opalescent Farallon Islands seem to float on the

western horizon, and steamers bound for China slowly disappear over the curve of the earth.[49]

The house was a resource for teaching, the view both a text and also the backdrop for (as she put it) "a stage. I needed a place where I could do what I wanted, and I tried to get the students to be as free as possible."[50] She opened her doors every Wednesday evening, first only to freshmen women, then, in response to demand, to all women students. Hundreds came, many simply drifting through in the lovely evening, to see the view that this young dean, hardly older than they, enjoyed daily; to tour her gardens; to listen to music from her piano. She hauled out her poetry books—Coventry Patmore, Rudyard Kipling, Matthew Arnold, Robert Browning, and a collection of Romanian folk songs entitled *The Bard of the Dimbovitza*. She read, the students read, and many more sat and listened. Her students came from families entirely unlike her own. Many of them were daughters of farmers or miners, attending the university for "the prescribed dull course for a teacher's certificate," but she thought it "preposterous" that even modest farmers' daughters should return home "without ever touching the big human problems." To them, education meant access to a better job. To Sprague this vocational idea of education awfully confined a person, so she tried to give them the benefits that she had: a beautiful house, an open library, a civilized life.[51]

She also gave them the practical knowledge she had. She led students on field trips around the San Francisco Bay Area, where they could see settlement houses, poor houses, leper houses. She took them to the wharves, where they received a crash course in disease control: rats bearing bubonic plague had shipped in from overseas, transmitting the germs through fleas to the local gopher population. But she had really taken them there because she wanted them to learn how a port ordinarily worked, how it channeled commerce, bringing trade to the cities of the Bay Area. As her father's daughter she knew these things, though somehow this marvelous new political economy managed to cast faint shadows in the groves of academe, particularly in the courses women took. She did not think that teaching her women students about the larger world made her a radical, or even political: "We did have a few feminists, but they represented a special group that I never joined . . . that was a kind of a militant thing; it wasn't that kind of thing I was trying to do. I was trying to have students understand how the community works, which really had nothing to do with women's rights as such."[52] Despite this disclaimer, she did innovate by urging her students to look beyond their roles as potential teachers and consider their roles as citizens.

Even though President Wheeler had a personal stake in Dean Sprague's success, the university as a whole still considered women's programs less important than men's. As Henry Morse Stephens (who had moved to Berkeley from Cornell) said, "At present the men students are a majority, and in America the majority rules."[53] Though Lucy Sprague tried to get the university to fund the construction of a women's dormitory, somehow the men students got the money and the location the women wanted.[54] She lobbied Wheeler to get the tutors she wanted and got some of them, but had to pay part of their salary herself, which she gave anonymously.[55]

She could not have accomplished what she did without the help of her father, with whose authority she made a "dramatic—perhaps melodramatic—compromise." She had nominal independence: her own income, job, and residence. In Berkeley she was far enough from Pasadena that she did not have to visit too often, but close enough to spend summers with him. Her own income could not, by itself, have supported her innovations. She could now see that despite the felt indignity of a salaried daughter, her self-taught father who loved to have professors visit for dinner took great pride in his daughter the dean. Indeed, he wrote Wheeler that he could not give more money to charitable causes in part because of the "inroads on my bank account" he allowed her to make.[56]

As dean, Sprague began to work toward a synthesis of the demands on her as a women's dean and of her desire to innovate as an educator per se. As the official chaperone of chaperones, she learned all the ways even a well-meaning student could discover corrupting influences in an ordinary urban environment. Single women students had to live somewhere and they could not afford to live like their dean. So, she found, she had to police the Bay Area's boardinghouses and residential hotels, having to suspend students who, while living in the wrong areas, had engaged in "unsuitable conduct."[57] But even while she was trimming the excesses of their liberties, she did not want to see her students become her wards. It ran against all she was teaching them about learning to make their own way in the larger world. So she began lobbying Wheeler for authority to begin an experiment in community living for self-supporting women students. Self-governing houses for such women, with a certain amount of supervision from a "matron," would ensure that they had a "nutritious diet and wholesome companionship instead of the dreary and unwholesome isolation of housekeeping suites." And, she argued to

Wheeler, it would also provide "a basis, not for experimentalism, but for illustration, in Domestic Economy courses." It would therefore relieve Sprague of some of her chores as monitor, while giving her students an excellent opportunity to establish their independence—within acceptable guidelines. To ensure the success of the enterprise, she would need from Wheeler the authority to withhold registration from women who persisted keeping up unsuitable housing arrangements.[58]

Wheeler gave the go-ahead, saying "I approve very decidedly of your plan." She scouted locations, found an ideal place, and secured a roundabout way of getting the university to pay for part of it. When it opened, under the scheme she suggested, it became a self-supporting, self-governing success as College House, which thrived and did for its inhabitants what collectively they would have been unable to do for themselves—at the price of $20.00 a month. The house gave body to her desire to see her students run their own affairs and attain their independence while living within and learning about the larger community, rather than simply pass through their university years on their way to a teaching career. In its concern for the need that self-supporting students had to learn to govern themselves, it reflected the parental ethos of contemporary Progressive efforts, including, of course, Dorothy Whitney's Junior League House.[59]

Despite Sprague's undeniable success in bringing together her professional and personal concerns, and her certain delight in creating for herself a household of her own and a circle of relationships with her colleagues and her students, she felt a lack in herself during her years as dean of women. Her father died in 1909, leaving her free of both his censure and his praise. But she was not yet able to say what she wanted for herself. In 1911–12, she addressed these felt absences by taking two trips away: one to New York, to study new innovations in reform work, and one to the Sierra Nevada, to determine the course of her personal life. Not all her understanding of economics had come from her life at home: she had enrolled in economics classes at Berkeley taught by Wesley Clair Mitchell, who had been trying to reconcile his own personal and professional interests.

AN ANTICOURTSHIP COURTSHIP

Mitchell's academic career rested securely on the basis of his work on paper money. But he wanted his work to have greater social relevance, and through the years between the turn of the century and his marriage to Lucy Sprague he struggled with a problem that economists cannot resolve with statistics: the problem (that is sometimes the blessing) of irrational human behavior.[60]

Like Veblen, Mitchell understood that the modern specialization of economic activity did not proceed simply in terms of manufacturing products and rendering services in exchange for other products and services. The creation of money to ease transactions had changed economic activity qualitatively, not merely quantitatively. To be sure, exchanges of value could, owing to the new medium of exchange, occur more fluidly and more swiftly and thus in greater number. But the existence of a tangible medium representing value did more than make it possible to trade vast amounts of (for example) grain. The medium of exchange representing value—money—became desirable in itself. It superseded grain as the raison d'être for economic activity. People, following their competitive instincts, hungered after money where before they had only hungered after bread. The appetite for food could easily be sated, but the appetite for money appeared to know no bounds.

Moreover, Mitchell believed that the way people behaved when they sought to accumulate money was, plainly, morally inferior to the way they behaved when they answered other, perhaps less obviously logical, imperatives—when they sought to make something of intrinsic value, or when they sought to assist members of their family or their community. During this critical period in his intellectual development, Mitchell struggled to apply his moral insights to a field that he believed ought really to proceed on the basis of science. He had seen in the adversarial clash of capital and labor a dramatization of the effects of an economic ignorance that he believed he had to rectify, but he found that as a journalist he could not make sufficiently respectable arguments for his cause. Having returned to academia, he began work on a project that he hoped would combine moral force and scientific authority.

The principal embodiment of Mitchell's struggle lies in the unpublished "pile of MS" he called "The Money Economy," a history of how money transformed social relations.[61] There were three essential steps to his argument. First, by offering a history of economic behaviors that political economists (like Laughlin) defended as simply rational, Mitchell meant to undermine their otherwise absolute authority to describe desirable economic actions. In this respect he followed Veblen, though he offered considerably better-researched illustrations of his thesis. Second, he meant to show that the apparently rational behavior of modern economic actors subverted traditional institutions like families and values like craftsmanship. In the name of freedom of contract and the allegedly sober pursuit of profit, modern societies were destroying what they professed to hold dear. Third, he hoped to inspire the conscientious evaluation of industrial progress in the light of traditional values and thus to motivate organized, mindful social change—the creation of a society whose members governed themselves instead of subjecting themselves to perceived laws of behavior.

In establishing the first point—that pecuniary institutions developed in response to changing human desires, rather than deriving from natural law—he was on his solidest ground. His colleagues at Berkeley shared his interests and they frequently gave and critiqued papers on the evolution of social institutions. Throughout 1905, one of Mitchell's clubs, the Kosmos, dedicated every one of its monthly meetings to a different aspect of sociologist Herbert Spencer's application of evolutionary theory to human society, and Mitchell himself gave a paper on Spencer's sociological theory. In pursuit of the idea, Mitchell assigned himself to read Spencer's autobiography.[62]

During a year studying at Harvard in 1908–9, Mitchell took advantage of that university's propensity to value "erudition over production" and read more deeply in history, studying the Renaissance. The period struck a chord in him, because out of that chaos of ambitious and competing princes something very like a capitalist system had come. The parallel to his own time, when princes like Rockefeller and Carnegie made mischief, gave Mitchell license to hope.[63]

He began lining up the proofs of his thesis when he looked forward to teaching again at Berkeley in the fall, writing:

My plan is to provide a descriptive analysis of the present economic organization of society, and its workings. . . . It is a simple straightforward survey of the present situation—unencumbered by metaphysical concepts and unsound psychology. . . . The class is to be so trained that a text-book of theory will seem like a wrongheaded mystification of sun-lit truths when they get into Economics 2. . . . Does it amount to willful malfeasance in office?[64]

He supplemented this plan with a 1910 article, "The Rationality of Economic Activity," in which he argued by citing modern psychological treatises that "it is superficial to call the use of money superficial."[65] He praised Jane Addams and Graham Wallas for applying to their theories an understanding of humankind as social organisms, and proposed that economists do the same, rather than rely on the traditional, abstractly rational actor who followed logically deducible rules—and who probably never existed. He concluded by posing the questions that troubled him: "Why is pecuniary rationality so difficult for men to learn; why is its rule firmer in making than in spending incomes; what is the relation of this rationality to the elder traits of human nature; and how far do the latter maintain themselves in the struggle for domination with their younger rival?"[66] Throughout this first and easiest phase of his assault on tradition, Mitchell demonstrated that the pecuniary calculus threatened traditional institutions, but he did not go into detail as to what effects this conflict had on society. He meant to take that up in "The Money Economy," elements of which he adumbrated in his talks of the period.

In a speech titled "Money Economy and Modern Civilization," Mitchell made clearer the cost of behaving as if one believed in pecuniary rationality. "Instead of making the goods their families require men 'make money,' and with their money incomes buy for their own use goods made by unknown hands," he began, noting that money thus displaced "an earlier form of economic organization in which families relied chiefly upon goods produced by their own efforts and were bound together by economic ties more personal than the cash nexus." His principal concern, he remarked, was "the significance for human life" of this shift. Throughout the talk, Mitchell highlighted the moral ambivalence of this significance. The advent of the cash nexus liberated laborers from their feudal masters and freed the medieval "lady" to use her "money income and buy foreign luxuries" as well as move about freely. At the same time, medieval conceptions like fairness and justice in economic affairs had gone: "While we talk freely enough of unfair prices when we deem ourselves injured we find it exceedingly difficult to state any practicable principle upon which evenhanded justice can be done between the seller and the buyer."[67]

Ultimately, Mitchell made clear his unease over the effects of the money economy: "We are not yet sufficiently under the domination of the money economy to feel confidently proud of the new standards of beauty, truth, and goodness which are gaining sway over our secret selves." Though we have learned to calculate social worth in money, it is "an aptitude which . . . is not altogether a part of our selves—at least of our nobler selves." He left his hopeful conclusion as a challenge to the audience: "It may be . . . that we are to work out a definite conception of human welfare which will serve as a standard by which pecuniary values will themselves be habitually judged, and will turn our daily thoughts from concern with money to concern with other things."[68]

Mitchell's identification of what society was losing and what it needed to make an effort to preserve—the more personal relationships between workers and even between family members—found further expression in his published disquisition on the preservation of families in a consumer economy. Here he began to move toward the third element of his agenda—the suggestion of what might be done in the light of industrial organization. In "The Backward Art of Spending Money," he once again argued that though it might be rational to organize economic consumption along lines parallel to those of economic production, it would mean the dissolution of the family as an institution, and thus the abolition of personal ties that remained "precious."[69]

Mitchell belonged to the California Consumers' League and so dealt with the problem of consumption as an activist as well as an economist. To him, both the problem and solution of consumption in a modern industrial economy were clear. The producers of manufactured goods had an unfair advantage over their putative clients: they enjoyed economies of scale, the benefits of centralization, and command over channels of distribution. Consumers, meanwhile, remained organized along the old-fashioned lines of the agricultural household, as if they were still subsistence producers buying only the occasional, exceptional, item, when in fact they relied on the market for nearly everything. They therefore had neither the economies of scale nor the resources and information that producers did. A purely rational, straightforward solution was obvious: abolish the household as a unit of consumption and commit the care and feeding of families to business organization:

> It would be subdivided into several departments, and each department would have its own minute division of labor. Then there would be the commissariat with its trained corps of purchasing agents and chemists, each giving his whole working day to the buying or testing of meats, or vegetables, or groceries. Then there would be the departments of building and grounds, of furnishing, of fuel and lighting, of the laundry, of clothing, of the nursery and the like—all bringing specialized knowledge to the solution of their problems, all having time and opportunity to test qualities and find the lowest prices. The single family can no more secure the

advantage of such division of labor in caring for its wants as consumers than the frontier family could develop division of labor in production.

This modest proposal amounted to little more than fantasy, Mitchell believed. Americans knew full well the advantages that they might gain by such rational organization, and they had not adopted them "because," Mitchell wrote, "we have not wanted to. . . . Our race-old instincts of love between the sexes and parental affection, long since standardized in the institution of monogamy, are at once so precious and so respectable that we have looked askance at every relaxation of the family bond, whatever material advantages it has promised." No matter how rational an improvement on social arrangements might prove, it also had to preserve the bonds that made families desirable, bonds in which "the human part" of a relationship "ranks higher than the business part."[70]

The solution as he saw it was the progressive expansion outward of these bonds, creating networks of common interest, from encouraging communities in apartment buildings and cooperatives to "providing with a larger liberality playgrounds, parks, library stations, day nurseries—a socialized spending of money with a neighborhood instead of a family as the unit." Mitchell was sure that by conscientiously overseeing the progressive expansion and adaptation of older institutions, people could preserve those elements of their nobler selves that the pecuniary calculus—more commonly known as moneygrubbing—threatened to replace. He believed that by expanding on such survivals as existed (specifically the personal ties of the family) citizens could regain control of their lives, and society's evolution might take a more desirable course.

Throughout Mitchell's work on his "Money Economy" manuscript and its accessory arguments, he hoped to impress Lucy Sprague. She had been in on the theory's development from the beginning: she took Mitchell's "Economic Origins" course at Berkeley in 1904, when he laid out the bases for the historical critique of the modern economy. But she thought of him then and continued to think of him afterward as a cloistered academic. In wooing her, Mitchell highlighted the elements of his work that reflected his social and political involvement. But he had to do more to win her.[71]

Mitchell and Sprague's on-and-off acquaintance went on and on through the first years they were in Berkeley, until one night in 1906 she astonished herself and him and all their friends with a passionate dance at a faculty party. The next day Mitchell sent her a poem and a proposal of marriage. She said no, and he withdrew his attentions. He nearly followed his father's course and married someone else. But after the year in Harvard, he returned to Berkeley to take up his habitual walks in the Sierra Nevada, to which he now invited Lucy Sprague, along with other friends. Over the course of the summer of 1911, they took more such walks, and she gave him the name Robin (of the woods, perhaps?) to signify her affection for his sierra self.

Despite their companionability, Sprague could easily put her finger on Mitchell's principal problem, perhaps because it paralleled her own. There was more than one man in Wesley Clair Mitchell, just as there was more than one woman in Lucy Sprague. He wanted scientific authority as well as moral certitude, academic precision as well as manly vigor. She wanted a professional life and a family life; she felt a responsibility to society and a responsibility to her own, as yet nonexistent, family. Their courtship became a struggle to reconcile these divergent desires. Sprague's correspondence with Mitchell while she was in New York reflects her awareness of these differing tendencies in their tempers. It also reflects her uncertainty as to what she might want to do with her life. Though over the course of these months she became more or less persuaded that she and Mitchell might strike a balance in their political and social ambitions, she remained unsure of what they might do about their personal relations. The letters, though constant and concerned with the possibility of marriage, are not love letters. If anything, they represent a persistent effort to cast the whole enterprise of courtship in doubt.

In New York, Sprague studied and admired Lillian Wald's settlement-house work at Henry Street, where she was doing work similar to Jane Addams's at Hull House.

> I do not think I am a Lillian Wald but I think I am of her tribe. . . .
> And if I do not marry you I shall break with the academic world and train myself under someone like Miss Wald or Miss Addams. . . .
> Would this side of me make marriage with you more or less worth while both for you and for me? . . . If I marry you, your work and your standards shall prevail. I don't mean, of course, that I would become a mere Haus-frau. But I do mean that unless I consider the things I gain for myself and the things I am able to make you gain through me, of more value than the things I could gain without you, I shall not marry you.[72]

Mitchell replied gamely,

> A wife's interest in some constructive work outside the home, far
> from being a source of dissatisfaction to the husband, ought to be
> a source of stability and wholesomeness in the marriage relation-
> ship. . . . It is true that we know few married couples who attempt
> and still fewer who succeed in living thus. . . . The chief circum-
> stance [in our favor] is that while our specific tasks are different on
> the surface, they have a common basis. If you wanted to decorate
> china and I wanted to make money in steel we might find a chasm
> difficult to bridge. But the further you develop your philanthropic
> plan, and the more I can make of economic theory, the nearer we
> shall come together.[73]

As a step in that direction, he asked her to critique his current manuscript. "To feel that we are working together will be a joy to me. And
won't it be to you?"[74]

Perhaps it was, though she remained unsure. If there were obvious
intellectual compatibilities between their ambitions—at least, obvious
once Mitchell developed them—she had worries about other matters.
Mitchell had appealed to an old-fashioned version of femininity and of
the appropriate relations between besotted members of opposite sexes
while wooing, and she had to be sure he was not serious about that. "I
say I am unworthy of you," Mitchell wrote. "Oh my dear—don't you
know me—don't you know men—better than that? Do you suppose that
any decent man ever asked a woman whom he loved to marry him without saying exactly that to her? Why—it is as much a part of the old old
story as kisses are."[75] Even as she urged him to take her off her conventionally feminine pedestal, she herself compared her vision of him with
conventionally masculine imagery. In reply, he admitted, "Perhaps I do
put you on a pedestal, dear one," adding, "but don't you perform that
same questionable service for me?"[76] She rather brutally wrote back, "The
fact remains that your masculinity does not compel me. . . . I do not bow
before you in that intangible time-honored way which does not contra-
dict a companionable equality."[77]

Here she hit on a point that especially bothered him. Mitchell had long
ago decided to go his own way in matters of his responsibilities as a man,
devoting himself to his own muse rather than to the demands of his peers.

He had his intellectual integrity and his moral courage, and he could not bear what passed for masculinity among society at large. "I get so out of patience with our men of place and consequence whom the crowd hails as leaders, who pass for strong men . . . they lack vision. They lack courage too, or insight. . . . For years I have been troubled by the fact that most men—even most leaders among men—share exactly the view of men and my kind which you express with such efforts to be kind in your letter." He argued by way of analogy that he was really an explorer, a pioneer in his way: "His own generation will not follow him and the generations which do follow better his surveys and remember him at most by some name on the map. How can a man who has no company of followers be a leader? And yet, dear one, is he not a leader?"[78] He thus claimed for himself the privileges of manhood without the indulgences of primitivist masculinity, making courage and leadership into intellectual, rather than physical, attributes.

Irresolute, at the end of her stint in New York and staying now with her family in Chicago, Sprague wrote, "Don't take me too seriously, dear. I'm writing foolishly just because I feel like it. And I don't want my words thrown back at me. I'm trying to get rid of them!" That same day she composed a poem expressing her hopes and fears alike: she knew herself to be

> Free, for I'm neither daughter, mother, wife.
> (But oh, this treasured freedom costs me dear)
> And I, who've feared no other burden fear
> To bear the burden of this unbound life.
> Beloved of my heart, and can it be
> You've come to free me from my liberty?[79]

Here she showed her compatibility with Mitchell not only in mind but in spirit. For he, too, believed the only remaining bases for social morality were those institutions that, however irrationally, limited human freedom in the interest of developing social morality.

Neither Sprague nor Mitchell wanted to play the conventional roles prescribed for them by their peers. Sprague wanted to avoid housewifery, to assert her prerogatives as one of Lillian Wald's tribe. At the same time she could not dedicate herself wholly to social claims on her life, but needed to admit familial claims as well. Mitchell wanted to keep clear of assertive masculinity, to substitute for mere physical courage and strength his intellectual integrity and innovation. If they were to marry, they would have to make accommodations for their ambitions as reformers. They would also have to preserve those elements of tradition they held dear—"love between the sexes" and "parental affection," as Mitchell wrote, those bases of personal bonds more important than merely rational organization.

In an excellent biography of Sprague, Joyce Antler writes, "Marriage was an integral part of Lucy Sprague's maturation into womanhood: it was the key to the reconciliation of her passion and her intellect."[80] It was more, too: as she negotiated it over the course of those months in 1911 with her prospective husband, it comprised an intellectual and political partnership linked to a vision of ideal personal and social relations. During their correspondence, Mitchell and Sprague settled three important issues. The first, that marriage must make accommodations for a woman's public ambitions as well as a man's, was the easiest to cover. Both agreed on it immediately. The second, that they must not expect of each other what conventional, gendered discourses required, took longer for them to discover, but they quickly dispatched it once they realized its presence. The third, reconciling their similar visions of their role in changing their world, was the most important and took the longest to settle. It was not until the end of Lucy's stay in New York that she hit on a plan for reform that made her happy.

Though she admired Lillian Wald and Florence Kelley, she could not envision herself making the personal sacrifices they made of their lives and their time to the cause of reform. When she went from the settlement house to a statistical laboratory to watch Pauline Goldmark, she again found work that she could admire but could not envision herself doing. It was not until she shadowed educator Julia Richman that she began to imagine a new future for herself in reform. It was, she later believed, a moment of revelation.

> Public education is the most constructive attack on social problems, for it deals with children and the future. It requires endless research concerning children and what they need to make them grow wholesomely. It requires experimentation in curriculum for the children and in teacher education. It requires an understanding of our culture. It is the synthesis of all my interests, all my hopes for humanity.[81]

She began drawing up a plan for a new program of education for children, working from what she had already done to what she hoped next to achieve. "Aim: to stimulate, crystallize, explain and justify the ideals which have to do with all sex relationships which manifest themselves in the civilized world in conventions (manners founded upon sense of privacy and responsibility) and institution of the family (including courtship, marriage, child-bearing and child rearing)."

In her focus on the development of traditional human institutions and in her focus specifically on the family as the central such institution, she paralleled Mitchell's work, down to her conviction that these bonds, once putatively instinctive, now required explanation and innovation to preserve them. Her evidence for this need—from "slackening in sense of personal dignity (kissing etc.)" to "perverted sexual desires (women's colleges and army etc.)"—revealed, too, her bias in favor of what she regarded as normal human society. And in keeping with the conviction she shared with her husband that the ultimate result of such education ought to be its pupils' independence, she regarded the project as akin to contemporary "experiments in self-government."[82] Mitchell immediately remarked on the parallels and approved. "It shows the part of you which I believe to be not only the best but also the most real and abiding part of your whole complex personality—the part of which I feel most proud and which I love the best . . . ah, my dear, they are your great qualities."[83]

The marriage between Sprague and Mitchell put together not only two people who plainly loved each other but also two people whose visions of the relations between family and society were the same. Both believed that the relations between husbands and wives and parents and children were the core of an institution poorly suited to modern industrial and political developments. Both also believed that the traditional family too closely confined its members. At the same time they considered its emphasis on mutual responsibility too valuable to surrender, even in the interest of personal freedom. Therefore they both believed that innovation on these old personal bonds would be the only bearable reform of society. Their personal relationship to each other and to their future children shaded smoothly into their relationships with their friends, their colleagues, and the objects of their reform activities. Thus when Sprague returned to California and went again to the mountains with Mitchell, she confirmed the immateriality of her worries over the business of masculinity and femininity and agreed to marry him, which she did soon after, on 8 May 1912, in a Swedenborgian church in San Francisco. After a honeymoon in Europe, they settled into a new house facing Washington Square in New York.[84]

THE FAMILY SCHOOL

A few years later, the Mitchells' oldest son John would surprise them by telling his elementary school teacher about his father's occupation: he worked, John said, as a carpenter. The teacher gently corrected him: his father—as everyone knew—was an eminent professor of economics at Columbia University. "Yes," John allowed. "He goes out there to talk. But he's really a carpenter."[85] John's description had more than a kernel of truth. The root of the Mitchells' reformist convictions was their scientifically unjustifiable faith in the noble quality of family bonds, of work done for the benefit of another or for its own sake rather than for money. Mitchell highly regarded the bond created between people when they did work with their hands rather than purchase work done by an unknown manufacturer. He himself worked with his hands to support the Mitchells' reform world: their family household became quite literally the center of their reform projects, providing the building and grounds and personnel of an experimental school that Lucy ran and where Wesley built equipment, partitions, and such elements of the school as he could.

They adopted John in 1914, making the front page of the *New York Times*. Perhaps with eugenics in the air, it seemed unusual for two so evidently fit people to take a foundling into their household.[86] The Mitchells, who considered all kinds of innovations on the traditional arts of living, would have preferred eugenicists to Christians—at least, Wesley wrote, the former wanted "to make social institutions serve the purposes of living men"[87]—but they knew enough about themselves and believed enough in the power of education to have no worries about John's genes. "If Jack does not form a good character," Wesley wrote, "as disciples of Dewey we shall have to blame ourselves."[88] Shortly after Jack's adoption, Lucy became pregnant with another child, born their second son, Sprague Mitchell. In 1917 they adopted again, a daughter named Marian, nicknamed Marni, and then as before, Lucy found herself pregnant, bearing a third son, Arnold.

Wesley's reference to Dewey was no casual comment. The Mitchell family house at 15 Washington Square North became the Deweyan experimental school Lucy had outlined after shadowing Julia Richman. The official name of the project, the Bureau of Educational Experiments (BEE)—which smacked to Wesley of "polysyllabic intimidation"—mellowed into the label of Bank Street Schools (which has stuck to this day, despite the schools' relocation).[89] Some of the upper rooms of the Mitchells' house became the offices for one of the schools' projects. A building out back that had been a stable became the laboratory school, and the yard a playground. Lucy chaired the project's working council, on which Wesley and the two Deweys also served, and Wesley chaired committees on research and statistics and also one on toys.[90]

The Mitchells' bureau first sponsored the extensive research that Lucy identified as necessary (and possibly "endless"), putting out a survey of psychological tests to assay developmental progress.[91] But its most important early publication was Lucy's own *Here and Now Story Book: Two- to Seven-Year Olds*, which (not coincidentally) she put together during the period when her first son was between two and seven years old. In it she treated her children and the children of the BEE's schools in the way Progressives generally treated the objects of their reform: as the newly arrived inhabitants of another culture—with, as she wrote, its own "native art form"—who needed an education that would bring them into the existing American world so they might master it for themselves.[92]

In an extended introductory essay, she explained that her anthropological investigation of children's culture led her to believe that most traditional children's stories merely confused them with arcane and archaic information. The world of a child consisted naturally of the here and now—the immediately sensed world. Proper education required building bridges between immediate experience and the larger world so that children could assimilate its complexities into their understanding.[93] Thus her stories took children from the things they knew to the things they needed to know-from the plumbing in their houses to the steel mills and factories that put the pipes and joints together; from girls' dresses to their sources-to storekeepers, clothiers, weavers, and finally to "negroes," singing as they pick cotton in the sun. The stories begin with the child's own language and move outward—for Lucy (as for John Dewey) it was essential that the teacher move beyond the limits of the existing culture to encompass what lay beyond.[94] Otherwise there could be neither maturation nor assimilation: as Lucy remarked to a colleague, "I am not interested in creating a world of secure morons."[95] She would not spend her time reinforcing the boundaries that defined the children's culture as she found it. Rather, as she had earlier suggested she should, her experimental education focused on stimulating, explaining, and extending the personal bonds that underlay the essential social institutions that she (and her husband) believed the root of personal dignity in society.

The Mitchell household thus became a model of what both Mitchells had identified as the ideal source of social relations: an extending family, expanding into its community. The Mitchell children (themselves descended from various parents) lived in a house that was also a school where the children of other parents came to learn and play. In the schoolhouse, parents and parental figures came and went on business that looked very much like their ordinary family life. The Mitchells deliberately blurred the boundary between private and public—the Mitchell children appear under their own names and sometimes embarrassing nicknames in *Here and Now*—because they believed the private family required an innovative expansion outward of its boundaries.

In this new environment, Wesley Mitchell did economic work that exemplified the values he had been suggesting ought to triumph over pecuniary logic. *Business Cycles* emerged "part and parcel" from the defunct "Money Economy" manuscript.[96] The larger thesis, Mitchell decided, did not admit of proof. But a smaller component of it—the effect of money-making thought on human lives in the modern economy— would submit to statistical analysis. In "The Money Economy" manuscript he made what were essentially philosophical arguments: that pecuniary logic "permits e.g. wasteful exploitation of others" and the "injury of self in stunting other than money-making aptitudes."[97] In *Business Cycles* he could marshal statistics to prove (to the satisfaction of businessmen, economists, and others moved by figures) that a focus on the making of money, rather than on the making of products, created the very cycles of boom and bust that caused so much pain. Because in a liquid economy businessmen focusing on profit tended to overcommit their enterprises, they begot recessions; because in a stagnant economy businessmen focusing on cash reserves tended to refuse even probably profitable ventures, they prolonged the slump. Wesley relied on comparative, historical, quantitative analysis of business cycles in France, Britain, Germany, and the United States to show that the pernicious cycles had arisen with the creation of national business economies, and moreover that they had abated in those other countries with the establishment of central banks.[98] For Mitchell, the point of the exercise was to educate the populace to support a similar, U.S. effort to govern economic and social relations. He believed himself addressing a broad audience, and included instructions to businessmen in his introduction. He remarked in his conclusion on the grounds for making such a case:

> Subject as men are to the sway of pecuniary concepts and ideals they can still judge the workings of the money economy by more intimate and more vital standards. To make these latter standards clear, to show in what definite ways the quest of profits transgresses them, and to devise feasible methods of remedying these ill results, is a large part of the task of social reform. Economic theory will not prove of much use in this work unless it grasps the relationship between the pecuniary institutions which civilized man is perfecting, the human nature which he inherits from savage ancestors, and the new forces which science lends him.

He concluded the book by condemning the "superficiality" of "treating money-making as the ultimate goal of effort."[99] He had made his moral judgment and normative standards clear, and the source of his critique—intimate and vital standards—was the same here as it had been in his previous essays. *Business Cycles* emerged from Lucy's critique bearing a dedication to her. And it bore the hallmark of Wesley's dedication to craft over profit: he wanted it to be quarto size to accommodate the charts he had made.[100]

The Mitchells' marriage put them at the center of Progressive reform thought and activities. The common vision they pressed each other to articulate during their courtship paralleled various contemporary efforts (as Lucy wrote) to encourage a greater measure of self-government among dependent classes of Americans by teaching them to comprehend the changes the preceding few decades had wrought in economics and politics. Wesley's philosophic and economic lessons urging Americans to control their money rather than be controlled by it built on and improved the National Monetary Commission's studies, lending force to the movement for the establishment and active use of the Federal Reserve System, and made Mitchell's name a shibboleth for other Progressives who wanted to trammel the excesses of business.[101] Lucy's educational reform ventures put her in the midst of a variety of similar efforts, and as the BEE began to publish its work it became the voice of an applied Deweyan philosophy, advocating the use of education to resolve social and political problems by encouraging an informed and active democracy. These efforts, combined with their new location in the heart of Manhattan, put them in close contact with like-minded reformers—the Deweys, the Lipp-manns, the Straights, the Beards, and others—and as the campaign ener-gies of the Progressive Party diffused through the city and country, they believed themselves working happily in a humming hive of constructive change.

Thus the Mitchells had created in their family and in their household an environment in which they could together pursue the social reform they wanted. They lived and worked in their schoolhouse household on Washington Square with a brood of children and a network of allies that reached out across the city and the country. They worked together to propound their belief in the reforming influence of education, and they themselves acted on it. They urged their charges—children and busi-nessmen, economists and laborers alike—to learn what they must to rule their circumstances. In so doing they were able to fulfill the various claims they felt on themselves—familial, social, professional—without feeling they had slighted any. They did their best and most innovative work in these years together, work that only changed when the war changed their lives.

Four

WAR AND THE PROGRESSIVE FAMILY

The penalty the realist pays for accepting war is to see disappear one by one the justifications for accepting it.... His would be the manlier position, but then where would be his realistic philosophy of intelligence and choice?

—Randolph Bourne[1]

Over and over in the winter of 1917–18, Wesley Clair Mitchell stepped off a train in Washington's Union Station. The economist was going to war. The reformers' new era had hardly dawned when the light began to go out. Roosevelt's 1912 campaign had encouraged all manner of Progressive efforts, and in 1913–14 much that was good seemed in the offing. When the *New Republic* put out its first issue in November 1914, the Mitchells immediately recognized a collection of kindred spirits and read the weekly aloud together. But only three months later, Wesley wrote Graham Wallas, "The war ... has in a shocking way diverted interest in this country from the constructive problems of trying to make civilization what we should like it and thrown us back into a muddle of feeling strongly about issues which we have not the capacity to think out clearly."[2] In seeking to make civilization what they should have liked, the Mitchells had both been busily working on their familial, liberal, assimilative models of reform, urging responsible political control of the industrial economy, campaigning for women's suffrage, and improving the character of education—issues that for them remained linked. As Wesley Mitchell told an audience just after his gloomy letter to Wallas, "Our civilization faces grave problems that cannot be solved successfully without the cooperation of women voters," and he outlined the continuing problems of providing decent housing, clothing, education, and fuel for the bulk of the city population, suggesting solutions like those he had offered in "The Backward Art of Spending Money." As the war drew closer, he tried to separate his argument from "propagandist" ones, but he came to believe the propagandists had the upper hand, and he began to consider a new approach.[3]

He started thinking about leaving Columbia University in October 1917, in what soon turned out to be a season of principled resignations. His colleague Beard quit the university altogether over a matter of free speech, and his mentor Dewey gave up, in disgust, the chairmanship of the committee meant to defend intellectual freedom. Mitchell, always quieter than Beard, started to entertain proposals from Washington without making public comment. He turned down a commission as a major, on the ground that he preferred to keep the civilian's right to disagree with superiors (or, to put it another way, he, too, wanted to keep his intellectual freedom). By February he had an offer he could accept: an invitation to join Harvard Professor Edwin F. Gay at the wartime Division of Planning and Statistics, to which Gay himself had just been appointed.[4] Since "The Backward Art of Spending Money" and *Business Cycles*, Mitchell had maintained that the relations between the consuming and the producing players in the economy had really to be harmonized, if not altogether rationalized; now the war was giving him his chance to work at that problem from the top.

The City of Washington, like the City of New York, had its ambitions as a world capital. The differences between the two metropoles' approaches to their physical appearances provides a parable on two approaches to Hamiltonian Progressivism. Both cities had, at their heart, late-Georgian villages whose architecture reminded their inhabitants of early republican virtues. Indeed, the Mitchells lived in Washington Square, the center of such architectural sentiments; and when the Straights built themselves a new house up Fifth Avenue, they copied the modest Georgian style. By the early twentieth century, each of the two hamlets had grown into a city that was deciding conscientiously to plan its future shape. But here they diverged.

In New York, in 1916 the administration of progressive Democratic mayor John Purroy Mitchel, a friend and ally of the Straights, put through zoning laws meant to end boxy buildings. The code prescribed an allow-able envelope for buildings based on the width of adjoining streets but made no specifications as to style. When architect Hugh Ferriss set him-self the task of discovering the shape that made the most efficient use of allowable space, a style implicit in the law and within the constraints of materials and money, he sketched out a stepped, three-towered concrete and steel ziggurat. This archetype, Ferriss wrote, was simply "a form which results from legal specifications"; it would be endlessly varied in the most famous New York skyscrapers of the 1920s.[5] The social and mate-rial limits on construction gave builders outlines within which they could work infinite variations; their creativity, within boundaries set by these laws, resulted in a distinctive metropolitan style.[6]

By contrast, Washington's appearance was dictated by the Commis-sion of Fine Arts. In 1913, the progressive Democratic administration of President Woodrow Wilson gave the commission jurisdiction over all buildings "which affect in any important way the appearance of the City."[7] The commission was the creature of the late Daniel Burnham, whose eye had foreseen the bright, white Roman colonnades, ovals, and obelisks of the city that was to come. When Mitchell stepped off the train into Burnham's Union Station, he walked into a hallucination of a neo-classical imperial American future that he had seen before: the massive marble station's columns, oval drive, and statue of Columbus repeated Burnham's plaster and chicken-wire Court of Honor at the 1893 World's Columbian Exposition, whose construction and celebration loomed over Mitchell's rooms in his days at the University of Chicago. Washington's planners, unlike New York's, explicitly demanded the invocation of ancient imperial government.

Both metropoles wanted to demonstrate their power, and both wanted to restrain power in their citizens' interests. New York set limits on growth, encouraging a distinctive American style born of ambition, money, and regard for the people's interest. Washington mandated a style born of the same concerns. Both cities zoned, as cities do, by top-down reform. But New York worked in keeping with the parental principles of Progressives—setting limits and stepping aside to permit independent growth. Washington never stepped aside, but made an agent of the state into a permanent overseer.

Progressive reformers aspired to what they called social leadership. They belonged to a class of a fortunate few: educated, moneyed, com-fortable. But their prejudices in favor of democracy would not allow them to interpret their privileges as entitlements of upper-class status. So they dedicated themselves to a politics of reform that would diminish the gap between their advantages and the condition of the average citizen. The experience of the war would suggest to them that the educational methods they had chosen for this project might do more harm than good and forced them to consider that not everyone in the United States—and indeed, perhaps, hardly anyone therein—enjoyed the same sense of freedom and potential they did. Perhaps, they came unwillingly to believe, the lessons of their own experience could not so easily be shared with an entire citizenry.

A short way from the unfinished Lincoln Memorial (which in its desolate state could as easily have been half-destroyed, resembling the imperial ruins that inspired it), the wartime government went about its business in long rows of undistinguished temporary buildings. A warren of these huts sprang up on the Mall to house economists, businessmen, strategists, marketers, and other promising planners. There Mitchell and other reformers who went to Washington tried to define the proper limits of the government's activities. The government needed new powers to meet the crisis of the war. Would it act according to Mitchell's, and Mayor Mitchel's, parental principles and foster the creativity and independence of its subjects, or more in keeping with the prescriptive rules of Burnham's capital?

It has for a long time—indeed, since the start of World War I itself—been a commonplace notion that the war was bad for the cause of Progressivism. But in respect of Progressive families and the idea of the Progressive family as an engine of reform, the war was especially injurious. During wartime, society's promulgation of gender roles that define men and women specifically in relation to their duty to the military state becomes an effective means of socializing labor along gender lines. It also breaks up familial structures such as those the Progressives created, and during World War I the project of making men and women useful to the state at war directly interfered with the progress of familial reform toward democracy.

As Mitchell would discover, advocates of the authoritarian approach benefited from wartime discipline and the opportunity it brought to reassert the need for traditional social roles for men and women. War split up, however temporarily, the partnership that the Mitchells had put together. While he was in Washington, Wesley could not do his part to educate and bring up the children of his family and of New York, no matter how much he tried to keep up his end through the mail. The Straights, too, were put asunder by the war, which had different uses for men than for women. In the case of the Beards, the war did not separate man from wife, but it did bring to an end their ongoing joint projects and force them to reconsider their approaches to reform.

PROPAGANDA

The war came early to the Straights. The early stages of Wilsonian foreign policy, combined with the Chinese revolution that overthrew the ruling Manchurian Qings, spelled the end of the Morgan Company's China venture just as the European war began—which meant that Willard Straight became one of the first Americans to begin worrying how to meet its demands. With Morgan partner Henry P. Davison, he negotiated the Allies' relations with the House of Morgan in 1914 and 1915, and on that account went to England in early 1915.[8] He became a proponent of U.S. military and business preparedness for the war. He went to the Plattsburg training camp with Henry Stimson, Mayor Mitchel, and other preparedness advocates, to provide an example of readiness for soldiering.[9] He spoke to business and trade associations on the need to consider the effects of the war on commercial strategies and tariff policies.[10] In his spare time he published the *New Republic*, presided over the traders' club India House, and served as a trustee of Cornell University.[11] The Straights had two more children, Beatrice and Michael, and their letters (Willard being often away) were full of mutual consultation about the children's welfare. Willard thought particularly of his first son: when Morgan sent him on the *Lusitania* to England through waters that hid German submarines, Willard began directing his diary entries to Whitney, because he thought his son should know what sort of man his father had been if he, Willard, were to be killed.[12]

In April 1917, President Wilson prevailed on Congress to declare the United States at war on the side of the Allies. Straight took an army commission as a major, thinking it would mean going to the front. Instead, somebody gave him a project better suited to his talents, if not to his ambitions. In October 1917, he took over the War Risk Insurance Bureau, which by act of Congress offered to each soldier up to $10,000 life insurance. The legislation for the act emerged from a coalition between political Progressives and settlement-house workers and represented, in the words of one historian, "a climax to the social insurance movement." The bill, drafted by Judge Julian Mack in consultation with Hull House alumna and Children's Bureau head Julia Lathrop, set and offered to provide "a minimum standard of subsistence" in the event of a claim.[13] In a typically Progressive accommodation between authority and voluntarism, war-risk insurance would not cover soldiers unless they signed themselves up, but it simultaneously established a program of education to make sure they understood it was in their interest to do so. It was Straight's job to find, enumerate, and encourage to register all the doughboys, which he did well before his deadline, probably humming to himself the Kiplingesque "Ballad of the W.R.I." that he had written for the occasion.[14]

Although Straight joined the army out of a sense of his manly duty, he did not at all like the manly posturing of his onetime hero Theodore Roosevelt and of Roosevelt's sidekick from Rough Rider days, General Leonard Wood. Straight thought Roosevelt a "darn fool" for his belligerent speeches at Plattsburg; both TR and Wood "have built a lot of fairy stories about themselves. . . . They dramatize themselves." He supposed they were useful as "pace makers"; and maybe they inspired the men: "When General Wood gets on preparedness, he is mad—and on politics, ridiculous—but as a soldier, talking to the officers and the men, he is admirable."[15] He thought Wood a "real man" and a "great personality," but he confessed to Dorothy he could not bring himself finally to accept the man's view of the war. "It's terribly unintelligent and unreasonable— the whole thing. I hate unfairness and greed and stupidity—and war is all that—and it is not redeemed by the fact that it brings out many heroic qualities in individuals and in peoples. It must in the end brutalize."[16] The war forced him to confront the soldierly imperial masculinity he had rejected during his China days. He did not like it in 1917 any more than he had when he was younger, but he was in the army now. The government awarded Willard Dickerman Straight the Distinguished Service Medal for putting together the War Risk Insurance Bureau efficiently and compassionately.[17] He was a hero for the right sorts of reasons, but his forebodings about the stupid and brutal nature of men in war were the truer augury of his future. He was not going to have a good war.

Willard Straight and Charles Beard were cut from the same bolt. Both came from small towns; both grew up loving the idea of manly Roosevelt men but half-hating the real item; both married women as intelligent and steadier than they; both enjoyed cutting a public figure; and both had a

streak of romantic enthusiasm that sometimes got the better of their intel-
lection. Moreover, they shared a friend: Dorothy Straight admired them
both, and after Willard went off to war, Charles Beard took over his role
as debate arbiter at the *New Republic*'s table.[18] Beard, too, was having a
bad war, and he began going to the *New Republic* in part to decide what
he should do to improve his circumstances.

Both Beard and Straight developed wartime hatred of Germany. "I
detest the German, personally, politically, socially," Straight wrote. "I
have never been able to walk down the Unter den Linden without a terrible desire to commit manslaughter, nor can I hear that guttural tongue
without inward revolt. . . . Although for sausage and beer I am grateful."[19]
Beard hated Prussianism, the "merciless military dictatorship" that
threatened Western civilization.[20] And if Straight were already a self-made
and imperialist entrepreneur, easily conscripted to organize for the government when the war came, Beard was a self-made propagandist for
reform, easily recruited to the official job; so when George Creel's Committee on Public Information (CPI) appointed Guy Stanton Ford head
of a project employing professional historians, Beard, along with Carl
Becker, John R. Commons, and other well-known members of the profession, joined. Ford asked Beard to write a history of the United States
for distribution to the people of Russia and Latin America because he
figured Beard's radical tone would engage citizens of those revolutionary
nations. Beard agreed and even suggested that Ford arrange for the book
to appear under a private imprint, so it would seem more credible than
an official government publication.[21]

Beard's piece for the Russians and Latin Americans never appeared,
but he did contribute to the formidable *War Cyclopedia* put out by Creel's
CPI. The cyclopedia was supposed to provide an arsenal of facts for those
considering the war; as President Wilson inelegantly said in the book's
epigraph, "I find that the particular thing you have to surrender to is
facts."[22] Beard was assigned a set of pieces mostly meant to point out the
Germans' particular evil. He wrote articles under "Atrocities," "Belgian
Violations," "*Schrechlichkeit*" (Frightfulness), and "*Notwendigkeit*"
(Necessity).[23] The German chancellor had justified the violation of Belgian neutrality, which he recognized as an international crime, on
grounds of necessity , and the troops there had waged a war of terror in
order to control the population. "German junker 'necessity' knows no
right, no law, no mercy, no limit except that imposed by a superior force,"
Beard wrote, noting that in Belgium "villages and towns were burned,

wounded soldiers massacred, non-combatants shot or maimed, women outraged, and children tortured by the soldiery." The entry under Belgian violations consisted of a long quotation from the chancellor's speech on necessity followed by, "Nothing more need be said."[24] The brutal Prussian in the *War Cyclopedia* was purely Kipling's "lesser breed without the law," appearing opposite the law-abiding Americans, who had a written constitution that protected their liberties, and the allied British, who, even though they lacked a constitution, played fair—or so the entry under "Blockade" maintained.[25] Beard and his colleagues painted a plain picture of American civilization as law-abiding and superior to its enemies and even its friends.

By the time the United States entered the war in 1917, Beard was already beginning to wonder if he might not have put too much faith in the government of the people, and if perhaps those who would live by excitements might not suffer unduly by them. He was himself a solid interventionist and a patriot, but he was also keen to defend the rights of those who were not. Those rights were after all distinctive features of American civilization. In April 1917 (the month the Americans entered the war), Beard defended a man who shouted "to hell with the flag," by saying such insults were better heard in public than kept private to fester, and noted that the price of liberty was a willingness to suffer fools. The *New York Times* criticized him for defending an unpatriotic citizen.[26] A committee of Columbia trustees called him on the carpet. He stood his ground on the flag matter, but then had to stay to be questioned on the subject of his historical scholarship, and was warned not to say things "likely to inculcate disrespect for American institutions."[27] Of course, Beard was furious. Nobody was a more fiercely loyal American than he; nobody had favored the Allied cause against the Hun longer than he; yet now these newly born-again jingoes were questioning his loyalty and integrity. Beard had long known that agitation and propaganda worked best when they were made simplest, starkly separating the world into goods and evils, us and them. Now the war's simple propaganda was putting him on the reverse of the medal.

War propaganda had also taken over the major project of Charles and Mary Beard's political lives-the agitation for women's suffrage. Propaganda's effects were as damaging there as they were generally. As an ally of both the national, immediatist-suffragist Alice Paul and the New York State, gradualist-activist Carrie Chapman Catt, Mary Ritter Beard had to strain her diplomatic abilities. She warned Paul in 1914 that moving the

Women's Party headquarters to New York City would make trouble with Catt, who looked askance at Paul's less-than-delicate tactics.[28] On the other hand, Beard told Catt in 1915 that Catt should decry Woodrow Wilson's attitude as loudly and strongly as she did that of the militant suffragists.[29] Neither side seemed wholly to see things Mary Beard's way. And when the war came, bringing with it the chance to enlist patriotism in behalf of suffrage, she grew even more uncomfortable with the split in the movement.

After a temporary defeat for suffrage in New York State in 1915, the moderates' position held little excitement for her. She wrote to Paul that she was unenthusiastic about campaigning for Charles Evans Hughes—which is what Catt, and her powerful allies like Dorothy Straight, would do—in the 1916 presidential campaign, though she would of course gladly campaign against Wilson.[30] Hughes announced himself for a national women's suffrage amendment in August, only a week after she wrote the letter, so perhaps that changed her mind; in any case, Charles Beard, along with Willard Straight and other habitual Republicans, voted for Hughes.[31] But as troublesome as presidential politics were, Mary would find the notion of campaigning for war and suffrage together even more difficult.

Perhaps Dorothy Straight had something to do with Hughes's August announcement on suffrage. In early July, Dorothy led Women for Hughes by donating $5,000 to his campaign.[32] And then in 1917, as the war came to New York City and to the suffrage campaign, she embraced the opportunity that Mary Beard shunned: she unashamedly combined appeals to patriotism with appeals for suffrage. As Willard headed Mayor Mitchel's Men's Committee for National Defense, she headed the corresponding Women's Committee. In October 1917 she appeared on the stage at Carnegie Hall along with Catt to take advantage of war fever by holding a "Patriotic Suffrage Meeting."[33] Like many Progressives, Dorothy hoped to make the war into a political opportunity.

Mary Beard could not make herself cheerful about wartime opportunism. In November 1917 she made her last public appearance with the suffrage militants. She went with a contingent to Washington to protest the arrests and mistreatment of White House picketers. The president left for Buffalo, and Mary accused him of "fleeing." She also repeated her habitual threat: "We can take care of him and his party politically," referring to the large numbers of already enfranchised women in Western states who could vote against the Democrats.[34] The day after her speech, more pickets were arrested. Catt spoke up to say "the pickets . . . make the psychological mistake of injecting into this stage of the suffrage campaign tactics which are not of accord with it." She believed the time for agitation had passed, that the enemy had surrendered, and the time for negotiation had come.[35] Maybe Mary agreed with her. It also seems that Mary decided, on seeing and hearing so much actual picketing, she did not like all the shouting after all. In any case, on 17 November, only a few days after her return, she wrote to a National Woman's Party correspondent, "I can't fight the battle the picketing way even to win any more than I can use war work as a cudgel even to win. So please, let me depart quietly."[36] After November 1917 she was finished with the business of militant agitation. She left the field, effectively, to Catt's moderates and Dorothy Straight, who saw the New York State campaign through to its war-linked conclusion. Dorothy stood symbolically by while the absentee soldier vote was counted and New York women were awarded the right to vote by their male peers.[37]

Mary Beard's resignation from the militant wing of the suffrage group, if taken by itself, appears only to be the product of disillusionment with the picketers' tactics or their political associations. But its timing shows it was part of a larger problem. True, the proximate cause of her resignation from the National Woman's Party was her unhappiness with her trip to Washington, but she quit only a month after her husband resigned from Columbia University, with which he had been affiliated exactly as long as she had been part of the U.S. woman suffrage movement. His resignation, too, had an evident proximate cause, but, again like hers, it was more truly the result of an accumulation of episodes, and, if considered in conjunction with hers, reveals more about their shared strategies of political activity than it does about his particular circumstances.

Charles Beard told his class at Columbia he was resigning on 9 October 1917. The university trustees had just fired professors James McKeen Cattell and Henry Wadsworth Longfellow Dana. Neither was a political ally of Beard's, or even a particular friend. But he saw their firings as the latest episode in a long story of Columbia's failings. Beard's letter of resignation blamed the university for allowing the institution to fall "under the control of a small and active group of trustees who have no standing in the world of education, who are reactionary and visionless in politics, narrow and medieval in religion."[38]

Like Willard Straight, who discovered in the army the crushing stupid brutality of military lives, Charles Beard felt himself suddenly subject to a slave's discipline after years of proclaiming his freedom. Peacetime Columbia was willing to sustain him and even Cattell, to whom Dean Frederick Keppel pointed in 1914 as living proof of the existence of academic freedom.[39] But the war required soldierly obedience. Men had to line up behind the flag. They had to give up their independence, or, as Beard saw it, their manhood. Dewey, who resigned as head of the faculty committee, lost the chance to organize the professors, Beard thought. "If scholars ever had a chance to work out a code [of integrity] they did and they were utterly unequal to the occasion," he wrote; "the good men," instead of standing up for their rights, had "scurried around like bewildered rabbits. . . . So I just jumped out and told Butler to go to the devil."[40]

The resignation of Charles A. Beard from Columbia University was public theater. Beard wrote the script, rehearsed it (in the spring, when he told the faculty the story of his interrogation about the flag episode), and acted it out as the drama of a man fighting for his independence. Afterward, he even reviewed and analyzed it in the *New Republic*.[41] His peers immediately understood the import of his action. The responses must have rung in his ears as gratifying echoes of his major theme: "Bully for you!" they said, and "Bully for you!" again, or, as one correspondent wrote, requiring no interpretation, "Dear Beard: You're a man."[42] Even after Beard burned much of his correspondence, he left intact a huge mass of these congratulatory letters, all of them tribute to his magnificent gesture. His resignation was a public act of self-creation, or self-rescue, imprinting on the retinas of the community the brilliant image of the honorable professor—or, what was more important, man of honor. Beard had (however temporarily and partially) reclaimed manliness from the proponents of wartime discipline.

Beard left Columbia because like his political ally Harriot Stanton Blatch he could not stand the "over-bearing methods of new-born patriots."[43] He and his wife both resigned from their long associations because neither could stomach the zeal of the latecomers, who rallied to the van of militancy for its own sake, not having earned their ways there as the Beards had. Both of them had grown weary of the excesses to which propaganda was put, and neither could any longer feel comfortable with their fellow exciters of public enthusiasms. The effects of state propaganda hit the Beards hard precisely because they themselves had long relied on similar methods of overstatement to make their political points. But war propaganda advocated roles for men and women inconsistent with their visions of themselves as independent thinkers and educators of other independent thinkers. For the purposes of wartime patriotism, men were supposed to be good soldiers, women their loyal supporters. The older association of manliness with independence made it possible for Charles to wrest control of his own public role from institutional control, but Mary could find no satisfactory equivalent. She mistrusted both militancy and acquiescence and could find no support for a medium position. She later suggested that even Charles's resignation drama played too much upon public passions. She put a note in with his collected letters of congratulations recalling a friend of theirs at Barnard, Henry Mussey. After Charles left Columbia, Mussey tried to get the faculty to pass a resolution at least appreciating Charles's contributions as a teacher. When he could not get even that, Mary wrote, "He resigned—but quietly."[44]

By leaving their current organizations behind, the Beards were neither giving up on the ideals they cherished nor the roles they enjoyed playing; they were simply sloughing impure allies. When she withdrew from the militant suffrage organization she helped to found, Mary Ritter Beard believed that she, unlike the new leaders, was a suffragist "who cares about means to an end," and that she was therefore "anathema" to the National Woman's Party; she supposed, she wrote, that her beliefs made her a mere "doctrinaire."[45] As her language plainly shows, she compared the episode to a theological split. The Beards were by nature and by family history come-outers; they held their ideals more precious than the company of their coreligionists. If it made them doctrinaire, then so be it. They would come out of the flock and seek the society of those who saw the light. In each of their withdrawals of autumn 1917, a Beard was moving away from the most vocal elements of masculine or feminine politics; Charles stepped away from the newly warlike men and Mary from the newly warlike women. Like other progressive marriages, theirs had become a partnership rooted in their willingness to apply a line-item veto to the gender agendas of their time. Charles would be masculine and belligerent, but not to the point of losing his intellectual integrity, which he would nevertheless try hard not to mention, preferring instead to pose as an undeniably manly farmer, sleeves up and brow sweaty. Mary would be feminine, wifely, but not submissively so; also militantly feminist, but not to the point of intellectual dishonesty. Her rejection of militant suffragism was built on the same foundation as her lifelong quarrel with the main body of feminist dogma. She would not give up her independence of thought to the cause. When they both resigned in 1917, they had not decided to retreat to their farm in Connecticut, but rather to regroup in order to pursue the same idea, that of reform through education, from a different angle. To begin, they went, as perhaps seemed natural, to the *New Republic*.

LIBERAL EFFICIENCY

When Wesley Clair Mitchell first went to Washington, he worked under the aegis of the Council of National Defense, an organization appointed by President Wilson with the idea of coordinating business, labor, and government under the supervision of Bernard M. Baruch, a financier with a catholic knowledge of U.S. industry and no special interest in any part.[46] For his part, Mitchell was supposed to begin collecting data on the supply of and demand for commodities relating to the war effort. Eventually he and his divisions would isolate and consider fifty-seven commodities.[47]

The *New Republic* had long been pushing for a more efficient organization of the war effort. This push intensified when Willard Straight joined the army, for Major Straight began accumulating evidence and experience of military ineptitude—ineptitude that not only made a terrible war longer but cost lives as well as money. He contributed notes and stories and ideas to the journal, some of which ended up in the columns of William Hard, a stringer from *Metropolitan* who contributed articles on mobilization to the *New Republic*. Hard's columns deplored the government's practice of assigning career military men (such as a general who said he hated trade unions) to run the military's purchasing divisions and other operations that had to deal with the civilian sector. The war effort required military minds for managing troop movements and fighting, but it needed a collective "industrial brain" for purchasing and businesslike coordination.[48] Like his patron (and like Beard and Mitchell), Hard saw the debate in terms of manliness questioned; he wrote a piece called "Efficiency and the 'He-man,'" in which he told the superpatriots to back down, that the United States needed a "liberal efficiency," not rigid social organization on a German model.[49] Hard's model was one of cooperation or coordination, not of authoritarian organization. Dorothy wrote Willard that seeing Hard's pieces, when she "thought back to origins," was "like seeing an egg hatch out into a chicken."[50] Willard Straight pushed Hard to call for better coordination of industry and pushed Croly to keep Hard at it, even though he was a smart-mouth and a difficult employee.[51] Eventually Hard, too, came over to the *New Republic* full-time and became a regular at the all-important Friday night editorial dinners.[52]

When the War Industries Board and the Council for National Defense were reorganized with Baruch at their head, the *New Republic*'s people were overjoyed. Not only had the president vested responsibility in a single, responsible man, but he had done so without making him into a dictator. The relevant Hard piece noted approvingly that the power to set prices was vested in a committee, not in Baruch's office, and the committee's decisions were to govern policy.[53] That committee relied for its information on Mitchell, the chief of the price section of the statistics division.

Once Wilson made Baruch's job and the War Industries Board's purpose clear, Mitchell could organize the commodity sections. In June 1918 he sent a memorandum to Gay proposing that the sections, grouped by commodity, should be set up so as to have an "intimate relation" with the price-fixing committee, providing data for each commodity whose price was to be set and giving "a vivid picture of the changes which the price system is undergoing as a whole.... This task, and the task of watching prices as an index of how the war program works, demand the same lines of systematic study. This study should be the chief concern of the price section."[54] The war gave Mitchell a chance to make a place, right in the heart of the national government, for the kind of work he was doing. He had dedicated his magnum opus to the documentation of the actions of complex economic systems, showing by careful analysis that the actions of business cycles followed patterns and could be minimized in their impact by careful and informed action. Now he could put that sort of information in the hands of actual policymakers. It took the Wilson administration more than a year to assemble the civilian side of its war machine, but once it did so, the nature of wartime bureaucracy put the economists in direct contact with the decision makers. The war presented the possibility that something might actually get done as Mitchell's analyses said it should.

Before the war, Mitchell was working on a complete survey, *Types of Economic Theory*, a work that would bring all such types into line with an evolutionary history of social thought. At the end came Veblen, who along with Dewey introduced psychology and the mind's understanding of itself to the tradition of economic analysis. By constructing this narrative of economic development, Mitchell was trying to show that society should reject dogma, a hope that matched the faith of the Beards and the Straights and other Progressives in the ability of unfettered intelligence to overcome superstition and to manage human affairs sensibly. The Columbia affair and the war interrupted this work, to which he was never able to return. Likewise, the war took him away from his family. He went home as often as he could, and sometimes Lucy came to visit.[55] His letters to Lucy dwell on her life with the children but he felt himself psychologically unable even to keep up with his storytelling duties: "When I tell a story to the children at supper I shall probably begin, 'Once there was a little mixed fertilizer. But because he had potash in his composition and British sea power checked German exports, his price rose to such unconscionable height that a chart drawn to our standard scale would be four times the length of this page. Hence the thrifty farmer planned . . . etc.'"[56] Statistics, always a fascination for him, had taken over his life. Lucy also found that the brusque demands of the war on her chosen field of endeavor made it impossible to carry on as she had. She decried the ease with which the war allowed the regimentation of education for poorer children, calling the vocational, industrial education of the war effort "the darkest of educational fields." The wartime version of education for what she had called the "here and now" took all authority away from enterprises like the Bureau of Educational Experiments.[57] Like the Straights and the Beards, the Mitchells would soon discover that they had to fend off a variety of vocal he-man authoritarians who had seized their tools for darker purposes. There was little methodological difference between educating a public for peace or for war, but war replaced the Progressive focus on moral social relations emerging from families with a morality that emphasized the needs and abilities of the state.

Mitchell pulled in Alvin Johnson from the *New Republic* to work in the price section and to help manage the commodities men. There had been little systematic effort to determine just what the armies and navies in the field would need, and how much of it would reasonably be available. Before the U.S. entry into the war, the Morgan arrangement, brokered by Davison and Straight, helped to secure decent prices for the Allies, but in their competitive bidding for items, the belligerent powers nevertheless drove up prices. As Johnson remembered, with the American entry the different representatives of the army and navy functioned much as the competing allies had; each submitted his own list of requirements, and, to be safe, often bumped up the estimated needs. Prices went up and up owing to a lack of coordination and an absence of clearly defined public interest.[58]

Mitchell and his crew had to find out what the armies really needed and what industry could really supply and at what cost. The commodities sections were therefore, as their historian writes, the "backbone" of the War Industries Board.[59] The backbone, however, was not itself certain of its steadiness. "During the war commodity statistics were developed to a higher point than ever before reached," Mitchell wrote in his official retrospective report, but, he indicated, such a compliment was due more to the sorry state of affairs before the war than to any particular accuracy his group had achieved.[60] Nobody had any reliable overall figures on how much of a given product was coming into the United States, let alone figures on where and how it was being used. Mitchell relied on consular officials, businessmen, and military officers to try to estimate the true availability of items and the true needs for them.[61]

The workings of the War Industries Board thus depended entirely on a close understanding of the wishes and needs of business. So far as Mitchell was concerned, close cooperation with business was just fine; it was what they were there to achieve. He wanted businessmen to want to provide a fair price. His only worry about the relationship was the haphazard nature of the figures he sifted from rumor, from confidential report, from estimate, and from quick counting. But it would have offended his politics to centralize or make more coercive the authority to collect these precious numbers. In a meeting of ambitious statisticians hoping for and planning a glorious postwar future, Mitchell had to fend off the enthusiasts who wanted to use the Federal Reserve Board as a "lever" to pry figures out of businessmen. Mitchell instead recommended an organization of industry leaders to persuade them of the advantage of cooperation.[62] Moreover, even though the commodities sections relied on sketchy data and interested parties to make reports to the price-fixing committee, Mitchell found they did their job rather well. As he had planned from the outset, the chief job of his group would be to assess and report on the state of the price structure built by the board and industry. When he did so for the last time, he was able to show that commodity prices had leveled off in the United States and had moved up and down less than they had in other countries, both belligerents and neutrals. He wrote, "It is difficult to explain the checking of the rise on any other ground than the substantial success of the Government's efforts to control prices."[63] Mitchell believed he had proven the he-men wrong. No authoritarian leader was necessary. Liberal efficiency and education had worked.

THE PRICE OF PROPAGANDA AND LIBERAL EFFICIENCY

Whenever the U.S. government has found it politically and constitutionally impossible to force citizens to comply with the perceived interests of the nation, then it has had to rely on persuasion, which in wartime is often called propaganda.[64] The question of how to deal with wool shortages illustrates the differences between what Gay's group could do in America and what governments could do in Europe. Armies needed wool for uniforms, so good wool had to be saved at home. Warm overcoats could be made partly of shoddy material, but dresses and skirts required, for aesthetic reasons, higher-quality sheer wool. Parisian dressmakers were (for their own inscrutable motives) contemplating lower hemlines and therefore a higher acreage of wool dedicated to skirts instead of uniforms. So Gay spoke to France's ambassador, Jules Jusserand, who said that the French government would convene and speak to the couturiers. They immediately announced that skirts would instead be shorter. The French government had acted swiftly and forcibly on the supply side of the economy, collecting the fashion industry and telling it what to do.[65] In the United States, by contrast, Gay's group believed it had to control demand, because (acting on vernacular liberal assumptions) it supposed that U.S. dressmakers had a right to sell whatever the market would absorb. Therefore the War Industries Board used its in-house speaker General Hugh Johnson, whose chief virtues were energy and a loud voice, to exhort citizens to cooperate-to choose simpler and fewer kinds of dress styles to buy.[66] They relied on informal organizations, such as Dorothy Straight's Council of Women's Organizations, an unofficial clearinghouse for charity operations, to coordinate suggestions for limited styles. Dorothy then took the matter to the Junior League, talked about the possibility of a simple, standard design, explained that there would be "an enormous amount of material and labor saved way back at the source" (and besides, "good taste could be standardized"), and the League approved it. Similar approval would have to come from other associations. Then the designs would have to be submitted to dressmaking

houses. Moreover, the whole effort had to hinge on making the wearing
of the dress a "stamp of patriotism"—otherwise how would the "rich
habitués of the Ritz" be shamed into wearing it?[67]

In the case of dressmaking, the method of cooperation might seem
more liberal than efficient (and anyway, slightly silly). But it conformed
with Progressive assumptions about how people could be made to do the
right thing: they ought not to be forced; they ought instead to be educated so they would willingly do the right thing. And in this case the project worked. But this induced voluntarism, the very model of progressive
reform-as-education though it seemed, caused great troubles down the
road. It seemed often to go too far in generating enthusiasm for cooperation, and it brought the belligerents out of the woodwork. Constant
appeals to patriotism generally had that effect. Like the Beards and the
Mitchells, the Straights found themselves fending off he-men and superpatriots of all kinds. Ralph M. Easley, of the National Civic Federation,
wrote Willard:

> This is no time for the publication of any journal that is found to
> be truckling even in the slightest degree to the German cause; and
> especially does it surprise everyone that a patriotic citizen like your-
> self would for one moment permit the use of his name as the finan-
> cial backer of such a paper. I have never agreed with the socialis-
> tic, anarchistic, syndicalistic and populistic leanings of the New
> Republic, but all that is nothing compared with its poisonous ema-
> nations since our entrance into the War.[68]

Easley's letter is clearly a product of an overactive he-man imagination:
the New Republic had, after all, favored the Allies and U.S. entrance to
the war longer than the president. Straight patiently replied that such
ideas as Easley suffered seemed to him the product of war fever and ill-
considered patriotism, which when uttered by someone in a position of
responsibility could have only a poor effect on the public. "Unfortunately
the country to be aroused must apparently be goaded. Equally unfortunately, once aroused, it will be difficult to gain any calm consideration
of what the best peace terms may be."[69] Dorothy got a similar letter from
a North Shore society man who heard a rumor that Herbert Croly had
tried to justify the sinking of the Lusitania: "Do you think he should be
interned? or at least silenced?"[70] She wrote back to say that of course
Croly had never said such a thing and diplomatically to suggest that "I

think we are all in an anxious state of mind at present in which we are prone to accuse those who disagree with us of being pro-German."[71]

The most deeply felt such bludgeonings came from the oldest ally. Theodore Roosevelt, the godfather to the Straights' (and to most Progressives') reform efforts, went off the deep end when the war came. Desperate to recapture glory, he had demanded he be sent to France to command troops; he happily sent his sons to fight. The Straights and the *New Republic* kept him at a distance, respecting him as an inspiration and as what Willard called a pacemaker, but worrying about his excesses. Roosevelt outright lied about his position on early intervention, claiming that, unlike Wilson, he wanted to fight as soon as the Germans rolled into Belgium. The *New Republic* initially believed him, but then found an old *Outlook* column in which Roosevelt had supported Wilson's policy. Dorothy thought he deserved to get the full force of the *New Republic*'s criticism "right from the shoulder," but at the same time did not want to lose him altogether, and so arranged for Lippmann and Roosevelt to have a private talk.[72] The meeting went well, but the journal had alienated the onetime president and Progressive. Willard tried to mollify him by a letter urging him to consider the nuances of the journal's liberalism. "When people are seeing 'red,' there is little love lost for the fellow who sits on the fence,"[73] he wrote. But the former president, like the superpatriots, had no time for fence-sitters. In the summer of 1918, Roosevelt, impatient with the efforts of the Straights to get him to see things their way, wrote Willard to levy his final judgment on the *New Republic*.

> You ask me to read the paper. I have read it in exactly the same way that I have read Hearst's papers. In each case I satisfied myself that probably the majority of its articles were all right, and sometimes in each case very good; but that there were a number so poisonously bad that taken as a whole the paper was like a spring where ten or fifteen percent of sewage is mixed with the pure water. . . . Hearst's papers appeal most successfully to gutter bolshevism, and the New Republic to parlor bolshevism; I do not doubt that both appeals are from their standpoints successful; and Hearst's influence is so infinitely greater that he is far more pernicious; but I feel that to cultivated people the New Republic is as mischievous as Hearst's papers are to the immense ignorant mass. . . . The New Republic in quality of paper and printing, and in its usual fastidiousness of tone appeals to cultivated people; whereas Hearst's

papers often designedly adopt a tone of screaming vulgarity, de-
bauching the taste to which they pander; but in moral quality I do
not see very much difference.[74]

The letter shows Roosevelt at his masculinist worst, sneering and stomp-
ing and insulting, and surely enjoying himself immensely. Throughout
the polemic, the voice of Roosevelt the he-man rings out, in such rhetorical ornaments as "parlor," "fastidiousness," and "pander." Willard
Straight, once the imperial golden boy of Roosevelt the bull moose, was
now shut in the parlor with the pinks, while the real men clamored to
go—not only body, but brain and soul—to the front lines.

At the front—"somewhere" in France, as the censors' colorful vague-
ness would have him write—Willard briskly polished off his War Risk
Insurance Bureau project. He worked the press to best advantage, signing himself up for the maximum insurance as an example. The papers
ate it up. After all, if Willard could, in his imperialist mode, make
accountancy exciting, he could make insurance, too, romantic, talking it
up as a "very democratic" enterprise, offering to "Private Jones" the same
coverage as to General Pershing.[75] He worked himself to exhaustion, as
he had done on every big job since China days. He shone best in such
definite projects where he could see his duty plain; when they were over,
and there seemed no use for him, he did poorly as a mere organization
man. He lost morale, and the sense of the war's futility occupied much
of his attention. His eye rested easily on the landscapes that had inspired
the great painters and he began to wonder why he was there in uniform.

> The soil is rich and brown and is just tinged with new green. It
> looks for all the world like the patina on a bit of gold bronze. The
> little mill nesting in the willows, the red tiled village in the hollow
> with the wisps of smoke rising, a man sowing, an old woman dig-
> ging up around her vines, a heavy, stalwart pair of horses with an
> old man, trudging home, in the distance the line of smoke left by
> a passing train, the long shadows stretching over all from a bluff
> along which we were riding. . . . One wanted to sing, to paint, and
> to have you share it. . . . Yet here we were getting ready for war—
> what nonsense![76]

His watercolors during this period show a decidedly pastoral, impres-
sionist influence, entirely at odds with his official military billeting. He

was shunted from communications staff to artillery school, as student and as lecturer. Nobody seemed interested in his particular talents. For his children back home, he wrote and illustrated little episodes from the history of Roman Gaul, telling about Vercingetorix and other valiant proto-poilus.[77] Letters from Dorothy came a month or six weeks after she wrote them; sometimes he did not see a newspaper or a *New Republic* for as long or longer.[78] Surrounded by muttering he-man patriots, he began to wonder if perhaps the Roosevelt line about the *New Republic* were not perhaps coming true, and in a panic cabled to find out what was all this rot about a radical free school going up on Dorothy's money.[79]

Dorothy was planning to extend her vision of a jointly useful future for their marriage by building on one of Willard's particular ambitions. She thought of this New School project from the beginning as "a sort of N.R. [*New Republic*] experiment in the educational world," in which the money backers would not have control over the intellectual side of the enterprise.[80] Willard replied, "I'm glad you contributed," though he was starting to wonder about the integrity of some of the "forward looking people. So many of them aren't honest. They don't stay put. They're not like Herbert—wise and balanced and candid."[81] Dorothy replied that of course the *New Republic* was not going all to pieces, and that the New School was hardly the half-baked venture he seemed to fear. She sent him a prospective charter for the New School's structure and mission.[82]

Willard wrote, much comforted, "I've just been reading the little pamphlet about your new university scheme. It's pretty much like the idea I'd been evolving myself for some time about a university and the way it should be handled."[83] John Dewey's and Randolph Bourne's pieces in the early numbers of the *New Republic*, describing the function of public education in creating a national community, teaching citizens to understand the structures of modern government and industry, had provoked him to write Croly about the possibility of using the *New Republic* to launch a new method of teaching American history, "proceeding as Bourne suggests from the morning paper back," trying to use the lessons of history to discuss modern social problems.[84] Bourne's fixation on the necessary function of history in explaining the newspaper and the industrial society almost certainly derived from the writings of James Harvey Robinson, who in his 1912 writings on "The New History" began with "this morning's newspaper"; he thought the historian had a duty in "explaining the immediate present."[85] Robinson, who followed Beard out of Columbia in 1917, was one of the chief movers in the New School's founding. The movement for a new school of applied social science could not have been better designed to appeal to Willard Straight. Even more telling, perhaps, of Straight's inevitable sympathy was the elevation of William Hard to importance in the *New Republic*'s New School roundtables.[86] Willard wrote Dorothy, "go to it."[87]

The New School grew out of the *New Republic*, as Dorothy planned. The Beards began showing up at the journal's dinners in the spring of 1918, along with Robinson and Dewey. They were there to consider the new educational venture, but they also ranged over topics of foreign policy and war aims. Beard became the conversation leader, offsetting, as Willard Straight had done, Croly's shy dryness.[88] Thomas Lamont, the Morgan partner, had become a regular along with his wife, and they contributed money to the New School as Dorothy did.[89] The project had begun with Robinson's, Beard's, and Dewey's quest for a university environment free of Nicholas Murray Butlers and other sources of interference like the Columbia trustees. It had crossed over, via those scholars' commitment to public activism, to the *New Republic* and its immediate social concerns, and had now inflated into a glorious vision of the perfect liberal panacea, a research and education institution that would incorporate the Bureau of Municipal Research (to which it was tied through Beard), that would educate the average citizen on the problems of government and society, that would link scholars of the nation and the world in a free environment, and bring all the knowledge of the cloisters to the service of the democratic polity. Hard's and Beard's roundtable discussion sessions built the prospective school into an enterprise for taking back American civilization from the warriors, reconfiguring the wartime administrations, like the War Industries Board, as permanent institutions, responsible to the needs of the community at peace rather than to the needs of the nation at war.[90]

Here Mitchell came in. Along with Edwin Gay he was lobbying to have their statistics division made permanent, a resource for government and business to cooperate in the control of the swings of the industrial economy. Mitchell saw the New School as an embodiment altogether of the idea that, as he told Graham Wallas, the war had swept away; he believed only careful and systematic thinking, free of interested intervention, could make civilization what it ought to be. The New School represented the "hope that the social sciences may be developed into serviceable instruments of social progress." It was his belief "that they are not yet of great value, that it is only by strenuous effort that they can be improved, and that it is important to humanity to keep a large number of people constantly at work upon these problems until the most effective methods of work have been discovered, or until the futility of trying to solve social problems by thinking has been demonstrated."[91] Mitchell had found himself caught between the Wilson administration, which thought the War Industries Board an unpleasant necessity (perhaps even unconstitutional), and the authoritarians who wanted the president to use the propitiously named Overman Act to its limits, giving them the ability to coerce businesses and unions to cooperate. In frustration, he left Washington as he had left Columbia, disgusted and searching for a place where he could ply his craft and make it useful; the New School seemed to him to represent the ideal New York he had originally envisioned.

The New School, whatever it did turn out to be, could never fulfill all the Progressives' ambitions. Its spreading, misty promise contained all of their hopes for American life, let into a single vessel whose shape itself had not yet been determined, whose many craftsmen might not agree. Willard Straight warned Dorothy that "I think there has been too great an emphasis on the 'us liberal' element and I'm afraid that one of these days there'll be a grand fight that may break things up."[92] He did well to worry. The ambition of the prewar days had nourished all kinds of experimentation in the name of liberalism and Progressivism. The war forced the Progressives to confront the troublesome problems of steering between authoritarianism and anarchy, a passage they navigated more or less together, with a common commitment to liberal efficiency. But the war had also brought them to doubt, as Mitchell gamely admitted in his brief for the New School, that social problems could be solved by teaching-a practice too easily mastered by state authority.[93]

For her own part, Dorothy Straight thought her money was better spent on the New School than on more immediate charitable needs because it worked toward the "reconstruction" of U.S. society after the war. Willard agreed; they both thought reconstruction necessary because the war had stolen the public debate away from the idea of progress in American civilization. "There is rather a discouraging wave of hate sweeping over the country now, apparently fostered by the press—and strange enough—by the churches! I hate to see us stoop to the level of the Germans," Dorothy wrote in May. Willard saw the same problem. Wartime propaganda had made him see the public discourse as hopelessly cor-

rupted: newspaper readers now seemed to him a mob of jingoes holler-
ing to have editors like Croly interned. He thought of

> the simile of the team of draft horses that went along stolidly pulling
> their load and minding their own business. It takes a lot of noise
> and beating to get them into a trot—more still to put them into a
> run. Once they're running, they look neither to the right nor left.
> You can't stop 'em or turn 'em—they're too stupid and too lack-
> ing in subtlety. They'll have to run till they're exhausted or till they
> take a fall. That is the state of mind of our public. They've come in
> late to the war. They know it and they're trying to make up for their
> former indifference by their present intolerant chauvinism. Their
> first state, like their last, is due to their lack of perception and cer-
> ebrating power.[94]

Like the Beards and the Mitchells, the Straights discovered that the war
tended to overwhelm all their hopes of teaching the U.S. democracy to
run its own affairs. The warriors had taken over the public podium and
smashed the bookshelves, and the classroom loved it.

As they all recognized, too, the war propaganda worked because it
appealed to the simplest tribal ideas about warrior men and domestic
women. War, more than any other social process, reifies discourses of gender. Through the selective-service system, the nation could separate men
from women and assign each class to its traditional role. The Straights
wrote each other to argue, both playfully and seriously, about whether
men or women sacrificed more in the war; their discussion reflected their
own experiences, but also their awareness that society had suddenly
divided drastically along those lines.[95] The minds and bodies of men were
conditioned to go to the front to fight—a process of socialization against
which the dissenters like Charles Beard, Wesley Mitchell, and Willard
Straight rebelled. Women, for their part, were organized for housekeeping and collective mother-work. True, those women who did not flinch at
opportunism were able to exploit the war to get suffrage laws passed in
New York and in the federal Congress, but Dorothy Straight's Council of
Women's Organizations had quite as much to do with supplying sweaters
and vegetables as it had to do with securing women's suffrage. Dorothy
Straight and Lucy Sprague Mitchell both served on a New York City com-
mittee to "Save 4,000 Babies This Year," at the request of "Uncle Sam"; the
German state, American women were told, showed more "solicitude" for

its children than did the American nation, which should be ashamed and should get to work.[96] If a reform-minded woman did not especially relish combining her cause with the war effort—as Mary Beard did not—she had little hope of finding allies while the war went on. In any case, war work changed the character of the cooperative public partnerships that they had been building to promote reform and instead put men and women to work for the state's most elementary needs.

The war's effectiveness in placing citizens in straitened roles thus disrupted the project of social civilization on which the Beards, Mitchells, Straights, and their allies had embarked. Most concretely, war service took husbands physically from wives, limiting the extent to which they could benefit from each other's presence. The war encouraged the he-men, whose ascendance provoked, for other men, if not a crisis, a period of deep annoyance and public incapacity. Enacting one's masculinity publicly, in a bully display, saved a man from effeminacy; hence, as Mary Ritter Beard noticed, her husband's need to make his resignation into counter-propagandistic theater. Charles's drama repudiated warrior machismo and shored up his own. Military men like Willard Straight had to suppress their dissent; habitually discreet men like Wesley Mitchell simply kept quiet. In any case, the theater of war obscured the more sensible practices of peacetime Progressivism.

More abstractly, war propaganda, which dwelt naturally on the themes of alliance and enmity, divided the world into definite categories, endangering the position of those who deliberately set out to moderate between radicals and conservatives in U.S. society. Progressives were by their nature on the fence, preferring as they did conservative means to achieve radical ends. They wanted, by processes of education, to bridge and eliminate the gap between the well-to-do and the poor, the knowledgeable and the ignorant, the native-born and the immigrant, the parents and the children. They wanted a society based on cooperation, not least of all between men and women. They believed that in this modern age the family was the principal remaining example of moral social relations and that by expanding familial relations outward they could reconstruct society. The war's propaganda dispelled that vision, and its success made them question their position as educators and social leaders. They had, at the very least, to moderate their optimism, and in most cases to modify their approaches. When they did return from the war to the enterprise of reform, they had changed in a variety of different ways; the plausibility of a distinctively democratic American civilization built on unofficial institutions seemed less evident. A remote state, concerned with its own health, had benefited from wartime enthusiasm and mastered the methods of public education.

PEACE

As Willard Straight's letters to the critics of the *New Republic* indicate, he was not only worried about the effect of propaganda on the public generally, but specifically about its effect on the peace process. After a spring and summer of bouncing from one billet to another, he had been assigned to placate Field Marshal Ferdinand Foch and reconcile him to Pershing's independent command; a government official congratulated Dorothy that her husband was "covering himself in glory" by "holding Marshal Foch's hand so successfully."[97] Once the war ended, he scrambled to get himself assigned to the treaty-negotiation teams, and with the help of Colonel Edward M. House he succeeded. Straight and Walter Lippmann were reunited in France as part of the chaotic mob that passed for the U.S. delegation.

Lippmann was assigned to the secret "Inquiry," a branch of House's informal staff supposed to discover everything they could about the European situation and so to design a workable peace arrangement. The Inquiry had reportedly helped to draft the Fourteen Points and planned negotiating strategies to limit reparations.[98] Wesley Clair Mitchell collected Inquiry data on U.S. economic dependence on other nations.[99] In his final report for the War Industries Board, he wrote:

> The outstanding fact established by the preceding tables is that the extraordinary rise of prices which started in Europe on the outbreak of war spread over the entire commercial world. Remoteness from the chief scene of the conflict did not protect Japan or Australia from a revolution in prices; difference of economic organization did not protect India; the maintenance of neutrality did not protect Argentina. No other development has ever demonstrated so forcibly the strength of the economic bonds that unite all the nations of the globe in a common fortune.[100]

Mitchell said that the price-fixing section of the War Industries Board had curbed the rise in prices. The international comparisons showed that, with proper data, the world could exercise similar control. Like Charles Beard and Willard Straight, he realized that the future of world civilization depended on the United States helping to forge cooperative coalitions among nations. Straight's work with the international banking groups established his credentials in this area, and he supported the League of Nations.[101] Beard, too, had long supported a Congress of Nations, and hoped the League would come to be one.[102] All of them worried that excesses in public opinion might endanger a useful peace.

Their suggestions, like many made by the Inquiry, went unheeded. Some of the responsibility for this inattention went to Wilson's egotism in going the negotiations alone, some to the Allies' irrepressible need for revenge; some had also to go to the he-men in the negotiating bureaucracy. Mitchell's own boss and colleague, Gay, was beginning to lean toward the authoritarian end of the spectrum. Frustrated by the confusion in Washington, he would later say, contrary to Mitchell's figure-laden analyses, that the War Industries Board had not achieved anything with its liberal efficiency. "We need not have gone through all the chaos and delay of the first year of the war," he wrote. "What should be done is to set up a dictator."[103] One of Gay's agents in Versailles worried about the "pulchritudinous youths" in the State Department crowd, and approved a comment one official made: "Someone ought to put a pink-checked dress on that boy, slap him on both cheeks, and send him home." As with most he-man pronouncements of the period, discussion of limp-wristed elements followed right on a condemnation of *"parlor socialists,"* including Walter Lippmann.[104]

Lippmann left the Inquiry after an in-house political tiff and went to France as a free agent for Colonel House, interviewing prisoners of war and army officers and studying the effects of propaganda. Someone like Gay's correspondent had got tired of Lippmann poking around, pegged him as a pink, and was about to have him sent away when Major Straight rescued him. Straight enjoyed the use of the Morgan firm's telegraph communications and its mailbag and was able to advertise himself as an affiliate of the Wall Street house when he came to pull Lippmann's chestnuts out of the fire. He also made a point of saying that the *New Republic* and Lippmann himself had supported Wilson in 1916; he probably omitted his own feelings on that election.[105] Lippmann ended up tagging along with Straight for a while.

Neither of them was enthusiastic about the evident direction of the negotiations and both wanted to get back to the United States, to the *New*

Republic, and the chance to take up once again their civilized lives. At First Army headquarters, Lippmann and Straight sat up talking all night, trying to reassure each other about the future, and not altogether succeeding, as Lippmann wrote Dorothy: "We talked far into the night, hoping, planning, sometimes doubting, but in the end renewed. In that personal loneliness which is the background of so many of us here, there was mixed also a fear that what we had meant, and what alone could justify it all, was not the meaning and the justification of those who will decide."[106]

In Washington, D.C., the day before he was to leave, Wesley Clair Mitchell walked into Edwin Gay's office to have a similar conversation. On Armistice Day, he had written Lucy that he wanted to continue advising the government's price section, but from a remove. He wanted to get back to his book on the evolution of economic theory, to teach at the New School, and most of all "to live at home again with you and the children."[107] But, he now found, there would be no more price section to advise. Wilson declined to push Congress to renew the appropriation for the Statistics Bureau; they were packing the whole office up and making final reports. Soon the temporary warren in which the war bureaucracies had lived would be knocked over to clear the Mall. On that last day in the capital, with the great effort ending, Mitchell asked Gay whether he thought economics would ever be a real science, providing useful truths. Gay was not encouraging. Maybe, he supposed, "after twenty generations of hard and painstaking work."[108] There would be no peacetime organization, no considered effort to apply economic research to social policy. The United States would go back to "muddling through," as Gay put it.[109]

Mitchell returned to New York City and to his disrupted home life. Over at the *New Republic* offices, his colleague Alvin Johnson was back from Washington, and he and some of the disaffected Columbians were meeting with Herbert Croly, talking about the New School. They were looking to the London School of Economics for aid and comfort; they were talking to Harold Laski and Graham Wallas.[110] With Dewey and Veblen in the wings, the project was a natural next step for Mitchell, who took it up, albeit with reservations. Robinson, he figured, was "a man of ideas, which is not orthodox in a historian," and so the new school had a fount of inspiration. There was money, too, so long as the Straights, the Lamonts, and their friends kept their promises, but "There is no assurance that the liberals who have supported it so far would go on with support if the faculty arrived at intellectual conclusions that shocked these liberals to their marrow. There is no assurance even that this faculty which loves liberty itself will always remain tolerant toward dissent." Like Willard Straight, he had some premonitions about the fractiousness of "us liberals." Anyway, it was an "experiment worth trying," and with that diffident comment he was back in the fold.[111]

In his presidential speech to the American Statistical Association in December 1918, which Lucy had helped him write, Mitchell tried to quell his doubts by ringing familiar optimistic progressive changes, but they now sounded hollow. "The effect of the war upon our attitude toward the use of facts for the guidance of policy links the present stage of civilization with man's savage past," he began, glumly. "The savage and the barbarian are such conservative creatures that nothing short of a catastrophe can shake them out of their settled habits, make them critical of old taboos, drive them to use their intelligence freely. . . . In matters of social organization we retain a large part of the conservatism characteristic of the savage mind." The war had done what all the progressives' sweet reason had been unable to do, showing that "under stress we make rapid progress. But when the stress is past we relapse gratefully into the thinking that has been done for us by our fathers." He dismissed the possibility of carrying on indefinitely in the Beardian manner, inciting the public by "agitation" to move forward unsteadily. Perhaps that method would work if the millennium were at hand, but if one were a student of a discipline that needed perhaps twenty generations to make its ideas clear, one had to look to the long term. "Are we not intelligent enough to devise a steadier and a more certain method of progress?" The question stood open but, as Lucy noted, when he gave the speech he still cherished hopes that the government, prodded by such institutions as the American Statistical Association, might sponsor the effort to better society intelligently. Later he could no longer so hope, and when he recycled the speech he linked the effort instead to the informal institutions and evolutionary development on which he and his kind had always to rely.[112]

"We are all living intensely, I think," Dorothy Straight wrote in 1918.[113] She had turned down countless chairmanships and presidencies, sometimes for political reasons, sometimes because Willard worried when she said she could not stop to write him until the wee hours, sometimes because she thought she ought to keep her mind more on her children. She was already chief of Mayor Mitchel's Women's Committee on National Defense, in which capacity she showed considerable administrative and diplomatic talent, coordinating the war efforts of a variety of charitable organizations, one of them her own Junior League, of which she was national president. Those activities would have been enough, but there were yet more: speeches and appearances and parades, for suffrage and food drives and charities of all kinds, heading up a Liberty Loan Drive, a Red Cross Drive, and showing up personally to can vegetables with Miriam Harriman.[114] With all that, there was yet the *New Republic* and the New School.

Like Wesley Mitchell, she, too, interpreted Armistice Day as a time for warning of the perils the war hysteria posed to civilization. "War must always remain the symbol of failure—the failure of Christian nations to live in peace and good will together. . . . Even Mars himself must laugh in sardonic glee at the spectacle of Christendom in arms. And is there no relief? Is the civilization of Western Europe marching to destruction?"[115] Even though she used the rhetoric of Christian morality to her advantage, she ultimately placed no faith in the churches, and as she could not countenance the state in arms she looked once more to an intermediate collective, an expanded family. "The group, therefore, becomes the new centre of moral and religious inspiration, its members evolving together a way of life and giving each other the mutual assistance necessary to make their code a living activating reality."[116] The war showed her, as it showed the Mitchells and the Beards, that she could not trust the state and had therefore to return her faith and her energy to the efforts to create new institutions of civilization such as those that had sustained her and her allies so far. Like Lucy Sprague Mitchell, who created her progressive school to extend the life of her family to a work-group that would fire her imagination, she expected "regeneration" to begin "with ourselves—in our personal relationships."[117]

However grimly Dorothy Straight looked on the postwar period, she preserved her faith in the essential sources of reform. As she wrote Willard, "Even T.R.'s letter to you has rolled off my back like water, and I feel able to stand up for the things I believe in, to the last gasp! There's a great challenge in the air, these days—and it's going to be an exhilarating—thrilling fight—isn't it, Best Beloved?"[118]

Willard Straight thought so. He cabled Croly that the *New Republic* must continue to support the League of Nations, admonishing him that the war had only just prevented "the destruction of liberal ideals," and that now those ideals must be once again enlivened and pushed forward. He approved of the journal's "Questions for American Conservatives," in which the "downright and virile" Roosevelt was taken to task for comparing internationalists to men who love all women as much as their own wives.[119] Straight wanted to begin reconstruction work already, to arrange to have the *New Republic* delivered to the American Expeditionary Force in France. "It is vitally important that our troops be educated prior to their return," he wrote. The war had been brutal and exciting; they all had to make ready for the "less dramatic and less specific and infinitely more difficult task" of realizing the liberal ideals for which they had nominally fought. He had only one task left in France: the peace.

Walter Lippmann was still with Willard in Paris, and the two of them constituted an informal delegation from the *New Republic* as they planned and watched the peace process. Lippmann noticed Willard was tired, saddened, and disgusted by the war, but determined to see the peace through, in the hope he could make it worthwhile by his influence. As was usual with Willard, he had been up late nights, talking and working almost to exhaustion. He had been injured, too: during the summer, when he was with Marshal Foch, he was gassed during one of the final German offensives. Someone brought him back unconscious, and, owing to the military inefficiency he had so long decried, he was not treated as a gas victim.[120] Perhaps that episode weakened his lungs; certainly his general state of overwork weakened his constitution. In any case, when the influenza epidemic swept through Paris late in November, both he and Lippmann fell sick. Lippmann got well in five days.[121] Just after midnight as December 1918 began, Willard Straight died.[122]

Five

THE NARRATIVE OF PROGRESS
VERSUS THE LOGIC OF EVENTS

The story of our life is not our life. It is our story.   —John Barth[1]

For the season of their political activism, Progressives had told themselves, each other, and anyone who would listen that they meant to urge
upon the dependent classes of society the lessons of their own experience: social categories like gender and ethnicity could not be permitted
to determine individual or social destiny, and a determined citizen could
overcome the circumstances that appeared to set his or her place at society's table. All it took was an appropriate education. And in a society dedicated to democratic ideals but evincing clear signs of inequality, the only
morally defensible position for one of the unduly privileged was that of
adoptive parent and teacher, fostering the independence of pupils who
would listen.

This sense of their mission depended on their assumption that they
could effect a transmission of culture from private to public spheres. They
did not mean to efface distinctions between one realm and the other—
and they resented it when the state-at-war began to intrude on their private lives. They staked their ambitions on the narrative logic of their own
stories: they had overcome what stood in their way; they had divested

themselves of the bourgeois gender roles that prescribed for them a confined sphere of action, and they believed now that any sufficiently enlightened citizen could do the same—and if a sufficient number of them did, then society would be able to transform itself into a democracy fulfilling the promise of American life.

If the continuation of their lives had depended on this narrative logic, they would all have died as Willard Straight did. But most people do not fall prey so easily to the dashing of their expectations, even if those expectations form the basis of their identity. Still, in the matter of Straight's death it is true (in an only marginally puckish way) that it was the discourse of masculinity propounded by the state-at-war that killed him. Straight had gone to war out of a sense of his manly duty, accepting that by virtue of his class and gender the state had a claim on his time and talents. Despite his misgivings over the use to which he and his peers were put, despite his sense that the war was creating roles for men and women that conflicted with the roles he and his wife had fought to create, he went to war out of a sense of obligation, worked at the foolish tasks he was given, and died (as so many in war do) a victim of blind, straightforward, virile obedience to incompetent instruction from above.

Indeed, the clawing tenacity of the traditional discourses of gender from which the reformers had believed themselves personally liberated affected all their endeavors. Lucy Sprague Mitchell's conversion from feminine, familial submission had meant her escape from a tubercular atmosphere in which (her doctor warned her) she would certainly turn consumptive herself if she remained. Her escape had taken her into the clear air of northern California and the heights of the Berkeley hills. But her liberation had been only partial, as the war years proved: a bout of pneumonia sent her to a doctor, and his examination revealed heavy scarring in her lungs, such as could only have come from an active case of tuberculosis. In her childhood household, everyone had been dying of consumption, so her own case went unnoticed. Now, with her lungs weakened from the pneumonia, she risked another active episode. The Mitchells built a sort of greenhouse, a glass bedroom, on the roof of their house in New York, and there she lay for months while they worried about her safety and the children's.[2]

The separate disasters that befell Lucy Sprague Mitchell and Willard Straight suggest the two greatest threats to Progressive families: a lingering, old-fashioned femininity and a new, aggressive masculinity. The two discourses pulled at the families that had thrived at the center of vigorous Progressive reformism. During wartime, masculinity had proven the greater threat, as it stigmatized reform impulses that were not somehow tied to the war effort. But submissive femininity persisted, too, and had gotten a boost from the war as it emphasized the supportive role women should play as their husbands and sons became protagonists at the front. Progressivism had thrived during a moment when traditional femininity ceased so tightly to bind women, and before aggressive masculinity had arisen to supplement the newly powerful national state.

By and large, the effects of reactionary or conservative social roles were neither as severe nor as personally devastating as in these two cases. In a sense it would have been easiest to die in the struggle for Progressivism, as the chastened survivors had to set about reconfiguring their sense of moral purpose. Because they had invested so much of themselves in their social roles, the end of the reform period was a personal crisis as much as a political one. In the end, Progressives tended rather to allow their ambitious narratives to yield to the logic of events. They had built their political castles in the air on what they believed to be the firm foundations of liberal families, constructed so as to allow husbands and wives free play with their public and private selves, and to construct an environment that would hold at bay both excessive chaos and excessive order by creating an orderly environment that fulfilled itself in its own undoing. Their children, they believed, would emerge from their period of tutelage into the world, ready as a result of their education to govern themselves. Their families would become little engines to drive social reform outward, establishing for society and for the state model relations between social equals, as well as between the powerful and the powerless, and setting a standard for the proper role of elites.

Instead they found that, with the coming of the war, the drive belts tended to run the other way: the state became a machine to drive families, and it drove them in keeping with a highly disciplined set of formulae that established limited social roles. It undid the provisional and open (even spacious) arrangements on which their ambitions had relied, and it urged them to choose, or at least to distinguish, between respectable public life and private ambition.

The reformers had sought to interpose the family as an exemplary ideal between the chaos of free markets and unfettered industry, on the one hand, and the straitening order of authoritarian structures (including state bureaucracies), on the other. But "war," as Willard Straight's favored *New Republican* culture critic Randolph Bourne wrote shortly before his own death in 1918, "is the health of the State. It automatically sets in motion throughout society those irresistible forces for uniformity." And, as Bourne and the other Progressives understood, the state in war spoiled the prospects for transformative familial relations in society, because the state became the only important parent: "And you fix your adoring gaze upon the State, with a truly filial look, as upon the Father of the flock."[3] The Progressives who tried to use the state for their own purposes were disappointed not merely because of the violence or meaninglessness of war, nor because the will to continue wartime planning faded, but because that will could not, it seemed, be used to produce to a popular sensibility of modern communion such as they had hoped to create by their own familial examples. Society seemed capable either of hierarchies of set categories or of chaos: there seemed no intermediate condition. When they returned to their own families and their own kind, they tried one last time to create a familial, informal institution that would teach a widespread public to govern itself.

THE METEORIC NEW SCHOOL

For Charles Beard, the openness that characterized the passing age ended suddenly a few weeks after the peace year of 1919 began. The Military Intelligence Service, presenting testimony to Senator Lee Overman's committee investigating the effects of German propaganda, listed Beard among sixty-two "pacifists" who propounded "dangerous and anarchic sentiments." The service cited among Beard's pacifist offenses his membership in the Intercollegiate Socialist Society and his stint as lecturer at the Rand School for Social Science.[4] Beard wrote a letter to Overman declaring, "I am not and have never been a pacifist."[5] As cases of the Red Scare go, Beard's turned out to be a mild one. But whoever made Beard a target did manage to do him damage. The accusations against him appeared on the front page of the *New York Times*; whereas his denials appeared on page eleven. Within three weeks, this planted seed bore poisonous fruit for Beard's next project.

Wesley Clair Mitchell knew trouble was in the wind for Beard and him because their allies had chosen an unpropitious name for their new project. Economics does not, as a rule, give itself to plain language, and Mitchell was always planing the rough edges off his writing in the hope of utter clarity.[6] He figured people who used too many syllables were trying to make themselves sound important, and at the same time making room for misunderstanding. So he twitted his wife for coming up with the name, "Bureau of Educational Experiments," and he never let Alvin Johnson forget another such lapse in naming their project, the New School for Social Research. The awkward name brought not only Mitchell's disapproval but also bad luck. "For this is New York," Johnson wrote, "where people are too busy to distinguish between terms that look somewhat alike." The name of the avowedly uncommitted New School for Social Research sounded too much like that of the sternly socialist Rand School of Social Science—and, Johnson said, "the delusion has persisted that they follow the same doctrine."[7] He thought the confusion came only because New Yorkers did not pay much attention, but the attack on Charles Beard, which came just before the New School's opening, helped fix the spurious link between the two in the public mind.

In a truly indecent episode, opportunistic members of the Junior League and the press took advantage of the Overman smear campaign to hound the recently widowed president of the League, Dorothy Straight, who had left town to grieve the death of her husband. "Society League Starts a Revolt," said the *Times*'s headline. Someone proposed a resolution before the Junior League objecting to the Junior League's support of "ultra-radical" professors like Charles Beard, whose cited radical adventures, familiar now to readers of the *Times*, included membership in the Intercollegiate Socialist Society and lecturing at the Rand School. "These men are not suitable teachers for the members of the League," the protesters said.[8] Once again the socialist associations made the front page, and again the reply appeared on page eleven. Dorothy's old friend Katharine Barnes noted that nobody was forcing League members to go to classes at the New School. The *Times* reporter reached Dorothy out of town. She said she believed "only a few discontented members" caused the stir, which was itself "one of the many unimportant incidents which occur in all organizations."[9]

The average Junior Leaguer in 1919 probably did not believe that William Whitney's daughter was driving the League toward a syndicalists' utopia, but by the end of the war that same average Junior Leaguer—just like the average American who would, come next fall, put Warren Harding in the White House—had tired of progress and the constant mobilization of her resources for collective needs. And Dorothy Straight seemed like a cardinal example of the reformer who asked far too much from her weary charges. "Mrs. Willard Straight's friends become more and more amused each day at her various socialistic endeavors and now that she is running the Junior League to suit herself there is great dissatisfaction in the ranks. . . . If Mrs. Straight has her way the League will be so unusual that very few of the debutantes will care to join it."[10] The more usual debutantes could use a convenient smear to excuse themselves from Dorothy's crusades.

In truth, the chief inquisitors of the Red Scare were probably much too earnest themselves for the ordinary American, bored of war and its moral equivalents, but (however paradoxically) the conservative crusade to strengthen the nation's moral fiber gave the weary an excuse to rest their consciences. As one small result of the general sentiment, the New School opened its doors under a cloud of suspicion that never dissipated. Alvin Johnson guessed the imputations of socialism cost the school "tens of thousands of students and hundreds of thousands in contributions."[11] The last great Progressive project had fallen victim to the dynamics of propaganda.

The New School started operations at 465 West Twenty-third Street, just two blocks up from the *New Republic*. The school's first days were exciting. "Every liberal I knew," Johnson wrote, "and a lot I had heard of" came to register at the price of twenty dollars apiece. For a little more than a single academic year, the New School would sparkle with the luster of the most brilliant minds in the social sciences. Not since the Harvard Philosophy Department of the 1890s had so many generally admired students of the human condition plied their study in a single place. John Dewey stood at their center as the star survivor of the fin de siècle crowd, which was also represented by the crotchety Thorstein Veblen. Robinson, Mitchell, and Beard led the remaining company, augmented in the fall by British guests Graham Wallas and Harold Laski. Because the first New School did not produce any social research, the product of that spectacular first year ended as just so much theater, an act of performance that left some imprint on the audience, but whose essence vanished altogether when the curtain descended. Dorothy Straight was the troupe's producer, promoter, and most dedicated fan. Alvin Johnson served as its chronicler.

By 1919, both Beard and Mitchell had been performing in classrooms for about twenty years. Like many good and seasoned lecturers, they preferred to do research. They thought they did more useful work in small seminars or alone in their studies than at the podium. Johnson thought this especially curious in Beard's case: as a lecturer, Beard had a great sense of theater and as a seminar leader he was hampered by his increasing deafness. Mitchell, for his part, acknowledged that his New School class on business cycles was "the best I ever had," but nevertheless thought his New School "constituency" of "the intelligent man and woman who wishes to keep abreast of the times in social matters but who for various reasons cannot or will not follow university courses" to be "numerous but less important" than the constituency he had hoped to reach through the new project. It was not enough to reach the adult interested in further education. Mitchell wanted to reach people who would make important civic, political, and business decisions.[12]

When the New School was still a dream, its creators supposed it should attract, in Willard Straight's words, "the folks who do things."[13] In his more sophisticated way, Mitchell concurred. The New School, he said, was "the product of a social process." The development of universities and the growth of the urban middle class, the advances in the social sciences, and the crisis of the war had given rise to such a school. The civilizers believed not only in such evolutionary processes—as Beard said, when they went to school there was a Darwinian "hidden in every clump of academic bushes"[14]—but also in their ability to prod and steer those processes. They gained their own independence from blind fate because they finally learned enough to have the power to do so, and they measured their maturity in terms of such independence. Consequently they must not indulge themselves in pure research, but rather serve as (in Mitchell's words) a "stimulus to social reform." As they mastered the social sciences, they could aid "the maturer man or woman who retains real intellectual interest in the midst of practical affairs"—Straight's "folks who do things"—and thus "help a very few very able people to do work of great importance which they otherwise could not accomplish."[15]

The New School, according to its founders, was therefore supposed to recapitulate their past roles as parents and teachers, only this time their audience comprised people just like themselves. Instead of adopting British labor, Chinese progressives, or anonymous masses of working women or immigrants; instead of guiding American politicians, voters, businessmen, or children (themselves, according to Lucy Sprague Mitchell, members of another culture), the reformers turned their attentions on their own kind. In their younger days, they had always assumed that their own advantages and opinions were widespread among their own people. In the explicitly imperialist days of Ruskin Hall and Willard Straight's string of China ventures, this assumption came with great and unconscious ease, and the circle of one's own kind seemed to enclose Americans indiscriminately. One could therefore ascribe failures or partial successes to problems in dealing with other, less fortunate, peoples. Over the course of the suffrage campaign and into the war years, reformers' faith that Americans instinctively recognized the self-evident need of democratic progress eroded. The circle of their own kind shrank and shrank. The war proved a special, final disaster because the very methods that Progressives had championed—education aimed at invigorating the popular will—produced not progressive democracy but rampaging intolerance. As Charles and Mary Beard wrote later about Charles's war service in the propaganda division, he and his fellows had been "assigned to 'educating' the United States," and the result stunned them. Not long before, most of the American people had wanted desperately to stay out of the European war. Now, suddenly, they were ready for a crusade. "Never before in history had such a campaign of education been organized; never before had American citizens realized how thoroughly, how irresistibly a modern government could impose its ideas on the whole nation."[16] The experience made them doubt their methods and their allies. So with the New School, the reformers quit exotic frontiers and tried instead to tend their own flock. Even if others did not yet see the light, they could at least make sure their own people did.

Charles Beard argued, perhaps plaintively and certainly without much persuasive success, that an experiment in social reform such as the New School must, by its very nature, "necessarily be conservative." After all, the nature of the classroom environment dictated that any reform it spawned or sponsored would benefit from perspective and careful judgment. Just as he had believed of Ruskin Hall's influence, he held now that "responsible thinking baffled by the world's complexities never produced half-baked radicalism."[17] Nevertheless, the people that Mitchell, Beard, and the Straights wanted never came to the school. The professors were stuck catering to Mitchell's "less important" group, those who liked lectures but were not interested in regular university courses. The folks who did things never showed up, and "the intellectual club idea," as Mitchell put it, "did not develop."[18]

Advertising, the new business based in the methods of public education and propaganda, did not help, and besides it degraded their purpose. Johnson recalled Beard's reaction to a publicity effort: "Good God! . . . They are selling us like a new brand of cheese!"[19] Mitchell spoke to sympathetic audiences and twice wrote to the *New York Evening Post* to drum up support, but nothing worked.[20] Even Dorothy Straight's money plus $20.00 apiece from every liberal Alvin Johnson knew or had heard of was not enough to keep them going without the right kind of pupils. In 1921, Beard, Dewey, Mitchell, and Robinson left the faculty of the New School. Johnson reorganized the school to focus on its de facto strength of ordinary adult education.[21]

The New School's fate demonstrated the Progressives' weakening attraction. Some people enjoyed the show they put on, but few took their ideas seriously enough to practice them. Like Theodore Roosevelt, the reformers performed brilliantly but, also as with Roosevelt, mere applause could not satisfy them. They wanted to persuade, to influence, and to shape. They wanted to enlighten, but they discovered to their chagrin that enlightenment sold poorly. In 1924, Charles Beard told a political scientist who wanted to teach at the New School that he had better spice up his topic. Unless he called it something like "the higher and dirtier psychology of super-politics" nobody would pay him any mind.[22]

PERSISTENCE

Lucy Sprague Mitchell felt the shock of the New School's demise indirectly. In 1921, when her husband left the school, she was making *The Here and Now Story Book* ready for publication, and so they came simultaneously to a lull in their activities. Lucy fell out with her onetime colleague Caroline Pratt, and their disagreement scotched her next project. Lucy had been taking notes on children's language and sense of humor in Pratt's school. Pratt's educational theories differed from Lucy's, and perhaps she envied the success of *The Here and Now Story Book*. Lucy's research notes were in the school's possession, and Pratt refused to allow her access to them.[23]

Within a year of quitting the New School, Wesley got himself reappointed to the Columbia faculty.[24] He was not isolated there: John Dewey joined him, having shrewdly scheduled his New School adventure during a sabbatical so he never officially left Columbia. Moreover, Wesley had a last extracurricular redoubt, sure to last the rest of his career. As Johnson noted, Mitchell's aptitude with numbers meant that his economic theories, no matter their implications, enjoyed a rude immunity from political assault. The numbers, people tended to believe, would not lie.[25] Even after he gave up on the more immediate prospect of reform,

Mitchell still had numbers at his beck and call. In 1920, he helped Edwin Gay to establish the National Bureau for Economic Research (NBER), with Gay as its head and Mitchell its first director of research. The bureau's Research Division would collect data on economic cycles, gradually elaborating and strengthening Mitchell's 1913 argument. Eventually, the weight of the evidence must crush all opposition, and the columns of figures and the careful graphs would finally demonstrate that reasonable and patient people could understand and tame the economy. The moral lesson of the enterprise remained implicit, and maybe only the faithful Mitchell knew it, but while he collected and analyzed data, he could proceed imperturbably as a scientist.[26]

The Bureau of Educational Experiments followed suit in the 1920s. If one wished to say how children ought to grow up, one might know first how they did grow up. One therefore needed data. As one historian writes, the field of education in the 1920s was "consumed with a passion for tabulation,"[27] and Lucy Sprague Mitchell's BEE was no exception. In the years after she came down from her glass sickroom, she and her co-workers attended to measurable phenomena, much as Wesley and his co-workers did. They measured heights and girths and bone growth. They counted teeth. They tried to observe the growth of internal organs, though it turned out they could not. They chased what Lucy called "the great white hope of education"—the IQ.[28]

Later Lucy ruefully compared this period to the entirely rationalist phase of classical economics:

> I have called this an era of discovery—the discovery of the child. Under the inspection of some early explorers, this newly discovered little human specimen looked about as realistic as "the economic man." The little people we knew and loved and wished to understand, and spoke of as "children," faded out when the ultra-scientific-minded talked of the child.[29]

Although Lucy plainly wanted to dissociate herself from the tendency of some scientists to prescribe correct behavior by referring to statistical norms, she did not want to give up the title of scientist, which she and her husband both kept. Her school was, she always insisted, a "laboratory" for performing "experiments."[30] She wanted to avoid the "ultra-scientific-minded," but not science itself. The homunculi of "the child" and "economic man" stood for the extremes of disengaged authoritarian rationalism in her discipline and her husband's—Wesley had after all done his part to demolish "economic man" by insisting on integrating psychology into economics.[31] Even while they avoided those extremes, they both clung to scientific language, principles, and method. Science was, they had both discovered, safer than politics, at least in the short term. Wesley's NBER was going to make economics into a science if it killed him—and it eventually did; he died in 1948 in the midst of editing a crowning work on business cycles. Lucy's BEE conducted scientific experiments in a laboratory environment to produce tested and approved methods of education. Both of them admitted that science had limits, but they both kept the idea and the belief of scientific progress in the foreground as they defined their endeavors.

This dalliance with scientific detachment won them several diplomatic victories. First, by becoming scientists they protected themselves against criticism on political grounds. Second, they won the right to keep the idea of progress alive in their imaginations: science progressed, from hypothesis, through experiment, to theory and law. At the same time they could also put a comfortable distance between themselves and the objects of their experiments. Reform efforts like the suffrage campaign, the New School, and adventures in government planning required them to play politics for high stakes. If they lost, they risked facing the possible falsity of their progressive principles. As scientists of social phenomena, they could eat their cake and still have it. They could believe that their work would one day change society while they kept themselves apart from the increasingly difficult business of attempting to implement social progress directly. Wesley might remark coolly that if one wished to understand current economic trends, one ought to read the latest NBER report on the subject at hand, but for himself he refused to take part in even in so conservative an effort as Herbert Hoover's experiments to "introduce intelligence into government" (as Wesley put it).[32] Lucy might "utilize all research findings to work out the best environment in which children's growth could take place," but that utilization happened only in her own school. She depended on a process of unconscious cultural absorption for those ideas to spread beyond her own little circle, and she needed to take no particular responsibility if they did not.[33]

Perhaps they stuck by their allegiance to science because they had no remaining defense against admitting that chaos underlay human affairs.

They believed rules did describe human behavior. Such rules ought not confine or define individual behavior, but if they could refine their knowledge of aggregate actions, they might reasonably request that their findings supplant instinct, ignorance, or custom as the guiding principles in human affairs. Until they did refine their knowledge of those rules, they safely hypothesized, recorded, and waited.[34]

Mary Beard, too, had ended her latest endeavors. She finished her *Short History of the American Labor Movement* in 1920.[35] The book condensed the material in longer works of labor historians like John Commons to a more easily manageable size. In keeping with her husband's contemporaneous efforts at the New School, she meant her book to help "the busy citizen" by telling such citizens the "connected story of the struggles of American workers and their rise to a position of influence in determining domestic and international relations."[36] Her efforts in this respect were more popular than his. The book went through several printings and she brought out new editions in 1924 and 1931. In it she dealt delicately with the elements of social politics that had so troubled her recently. She defined what she believed was a "definite feminist movement"—one that occurred when women "declared their inherent right to choose their own occupations." Labor unions were not always sympathetic to such feminism, as Beard noted, though in the face of the Supreme Court's hostility to protective legislation for women workers, unions had appeared to her to respond, however tepidly, to the pleas of women labor leaders. Still, the most important effort of the labor movement was its "deep social and spiritual significance. It draws men and women together in a great coöperative undertaking which grows in strength day and night and develops ideals of peace and well-being in society." It fostered a community larger than the family, pulling men and women together in a sense of common purpose that transcended demands for wages, hours, or legal protections. In this cultural sense, the movement was by her lights truly revolutionary, though in a chastened progressive sense of which (as she wrote) even Edmund Burke could have approved.[37]

She continued her long and painful dissociation from the ranks of organized feminism. Having quit the National Woman's Party in 1917, she had in 1919 to ask them to stop using her name on their letterhead.[38] Still, through 1921 she stayed in touch with some of her "erstwhile pals," as she called them, even when they began to push the Equal Rights Amendment, which she opposed.[39] Like Dorothy Straight, Florence Kelley, Alice Hamilton, and other proponents of women's rights, Beard believed the ERA might "overthrow all protective industrial legislation for women." She especially worried that women might be conscripted for battle.[40] She did not relish the idea of equality if it meant equality in service of the industrial order and the state.

In the years after Willard's death, Dorothy Straight did not slow her activities or decrease the number of her responsibilities. If anything, she undertook more and greater good deeds. She continued running the Junior League tenement project. She sponsored meetings for the Women's Trade Union League, for a committee to oppose the ERA, and for Senator William Borah's lobby to free political prisoners, including members of the Industrial Workers of the World arrested in the United States during the war.[41] At the request of Herbert Hoover, she organized women's charities to meet the relief needs of the starving and displaced Europeans.[42] She sponsored a charity luncheon at which the donors ate only rice, in sympathy with the hungry millions in China.[43] She headed the Pueblo Defense Committee, which tried to persuade the government to keep the Lincoln administration's long-ago promise that the Pueblos might stay on their lands.[44] She led the delegation of women's organizations that attended President Warren Harding's 1921 disarmament conference.[45] Through all this, she continued to keep Herbert Croly and the *New Republic* in business. As she later wrote, "After Willard's death I immersed myself in work of many kinds."[46]

A curious phrase in Willard's will launched Dorothy on her last project of American reform. He asked in his last testament that some of his money be used to make Cornell University "a more human place."[47] Dorothy did not begin to think about realizing the bequest until the fall of 1920, when Leonard Elmhirst, an Englishman and a student of the Cornell agricultural school, visited her at the Colony Club in New York. Elmhirst, like many of her visitors, wanted to get money from her for a worthy cause—in his case, a university club for international students. He singled himself out by a making a Straightean remark about "the business short-comings of professors,"[48] and persuaded her thereby to go to Ithaca.

She hired William Delano, who had built her house on Fifth Avenue, to consider the design for a student union. Delano wrote, "Mrs. Straight emphasised the need for a place where 'ideas can get loose and be discussed,' 'where faculty can meet students informally or over a meal,' and 'where friendships can emerge and blossom.' "[49] His building would try to create this space within a structure that recalled the imperial spires and buttresses of Oxford, borrowing traditional authority for modern innovation.

The project immediately ran into trouble. Dorothy's increased public visibility in a time of political conservatism did her reputation no good. She knew about the "cruel intolerance" that pervaded U.S. political discourse in the early 1920s,[50] but she expected better from the universities. But Cornell, like the vast majority of the nation, now lay outside the charmed circle of progressive reform. As Herbert Croly said, it was truly American, "a middle western coeducational college,"[51] and it was therefore little interested in Dorothy Straight's interference. Cornell history professor Wallace Notestein told Leonard Elmhirst, "Our whole country . . . is today in danger of being run by women," and he found the Cornell project to be no exception. Women in education, Notestein complained, were trouble. "They don't know how to handle the boys." Willard Straight Hall did finally get built, but it segregated students by sex and had a separate entrance for women. It was the last of Dorothy's reform projects. She had so fallen out of love with her own country that she agreed to marry Elmhirst in 1925 and move with him and her children to England.[52]

CHILDREN

When Lucy Sprague Mitchell looked back on the Chicago businessmen of her father's generation, she wrote,

> They wished to found families, to have their sons carry on their work. . . . But their children often ended in sanitariums. Many drank themselves into illness or death, many were just ineffective or commonplace. There are more among the third generation, I believe, who show a fighting quality, or at least an ability to adapt to what life brings them. It is a puzzling rhythm in our American culture which I wish I understood.[53]

That rhythm marked time as American progress staggered from one generation to the next. Lucy saw that children rarely shared the ambitions of their parents, and she herself (though she made herself a success) began by rejecting her father's apparent principles. At the same time, she put all of her hopes and dreams into understanding her own children and the children of her generation. Even if one reduced the scope of progress to the accumulation of merely scientific knowledge, one still relied on the next generation to pick up where one left off, to share one's opinions as to which parts of life had importance.

Her puzzlement in this matter affected her deeply and painfully. After all, the passage of will and principle from one generation to the next underlay her own struggle to obtain her freedom, and also her own decision to surrender her hard-won freedom to some degree by entering a marriage. She barely escaped from traditional familial duties that were literally killing her. She had to exert her will to gain her independence, and this exertion of her will was perhaps more important than any of her allies and all the chances that presented themselves to her. When she met Robin Mitchell, she found a man whose will matched her own. The two of them built a moral universe based on their own strongly willed belief in human potential, and they made their marriage and their house into the center of that universe. But all their efforts served no purpose if that little world were static and sterile. It had to grow and to last if it were to succeed. They had to pass on their beliefs and their knowledge to their own children, the nearest and most suggestible of pupils. On the other hand, the children represented also (as Progressives could not so readily see) the question of the relative strengths of enlightenment and emotion. In their family relations, there was as much frustration as education, and will and willfulness were closely linked.

The Mitchells' house was a Progressive school. The family shared space with theorists and teachers and the children of other households. Moreover, Lucy made her children the subjects and objects of her experiments in forging the links between a child's experience and a parent's teachings. The older children, Jack and Sprague, began at the BEE's experimental school when they were three, and Marni and Arnold entered the BEE's nursery even earlier, at two and a half and one and a half.[54] Lucy later wrote of her marriage,

> I think the fact that we were both workers *did* prove to be such a bond in the life we built together—a life that included more than the two of us. It included children. Did my work hurt them? The wonderful thing about my life—and I have had a wonderful life— was the way my work helped me with my children. Trying to learn what children are like helps any mother with her own children. I

know I made mistakes with my children. But I believe I would have
made even more without my work.[55]

The Mitchell children, when they looked back on it later, thought less
highly of the connection between their mother's work and their upbringing. They were always the target of their mother's professional scrutiny
as much as they were the object of her maternal sympathy. They appear
by name throughout *The Here and Now Story Book*, so the private scenes
of their childhoods are a matter of public record. Another child-object
of such a literary transformation wrote later that he believed his father
had, in some way, "filched from me my good name and had left me with
nothing but the empty fame of being his son."[56] The junior Mitchells felt
likewise, believing their mother was too much the scientist and writer,
using them as material rather than appreciating them as children. As historian Joyce Antler found when interviewing the Mitchell children, they
believed that the progressive ideal of encouraging their independence and
getting them to make their own decisions had left them freer than they
would have liked. They wanted more advice and direction.[57] As their
mother had when considering marriage, they yearned for freedom from
their liberty.

Charles and Mary Beard supplemented Miriam's and William's home
schooling with their political education, which included their appearances in suffrage parades and their later travel around the United States
and overseas to Europe and Asia. In Europe they saw the results of the
war. Women mourned husbands and children and struggled to feed
themselves. There was little enough food even for prosperous American
travelers. In Japan they met municipal planners, feminists, and politicians of all stripes. The adults' dinner conversations made impressions
on the children, as Miriam later recalled.[58] The world they saw was vastly
more varied and troublesome than the world their parents had known
when they were young, infinitely more resistant to the impress of even
the hardiest goodwill.

By the time the Beard children went off to college, they had a thorough background in the same matters their parents were busily teaching
themselves and their fellow citizens, but they had it much sooner than
ever their parents could. Their schooling appeared unorthodox to the
outside observer, and Charles's expressed theories (about the child's
learning from its immediate environment) echoed those of progressive
educators like Dewey and Lucy Sprague Mitchell. But from the children's

point of view, the familiarity of their parental teachers eclipsed the strangeness of the theories that underlay the process. That strangeness would have been evident only to an outsider. Unlike the Mitchell children, whose house became a laboratory school where they and other subjects toiled in the interest of producing scientific principles, the Beard children had their lessons from their parents in an unsystematic order tailored to their particular needs.

Eventually both Miriam and William must have learned their arithmetic, as well as their politics. She became a historian of business, he a political scientist. Neither ever expressed the sort of resentment common among the Mitchell children, and indeed William later collaborated with Charles on a study of industrial America.[59] Both took part willingly in interviews commemorating their parents' achievements and they worked together to assemble the remains of their parents' papers for DePauw University. The only indication that they might have had some difficulty escaping their parents' shadow is that neither spoke at Charles's centennial, leaving that job to Miriam's son, who began by remarking that so far as he knew there was no such psychological phenomenon as a grandfather complex.[60] Still, both the younger Beards became scholars of complexity. They had become more scientific, more descriptive, and more detached than their politically purposeful parents.

Like the Mitchell and Beard children, the children of Dorothy Whitney's first marriage had an unusual education. The youngest, Michael Straight, later speculated that if Willard had lived, the children's lives might have been less unusual. They felt Willard's death not only in his absence but also in the effect of his end on their mother. Dorothy, according to her own testimony, threw herself into her work after Willard died. In his memoir, Michael Straight asks, "Why, I wonder, did she find solace in work rather than in her children?"[61]

When Dorothy Straight decided to marry Leonard Elmhirst and move to England, she did so on the condition that the two of them would build a progressive school suitable for educating her American children, who otherwise would find themselves at sea in English culture. She put Leonard in charge of finding a suitable place. He picked Dartington Hall, in Devonshire, originally the home of John Holand, duke of Exeter and half-brother to Richard II.[62] The resulting school at Dartington Hall became the heart of a utopian community with the Elmhirsts at its head. One of Dartington's devotees called it "feudalism without feudalism" because the school's formal structure was strictly democratic while its spiritual and actual leaders were indisputably the lord and lady of Dartington manor. Another lifelong student of the Dartington experiment called it an effort in which "Rousseau *was* cross-bred with Baden-Powell."[63] In short, the Dartington school recapitulated the same dichotomy that invariably characterized the experiments of the reformers who believed in civilization, and it tended rather to confuse its subjects, including the Straight children.

Dartington tried to reconcile imperialism with democracy, to use the means of the former to produce the latter: it was, for American Progressives, a familiar ambition. Children of the school determined their own curriculum and developed their interests by roaming the countryside, much as the Beard children did. On the other hand, they were part of a self-governing community rather larger than their own family, and so had political problems outside the usual realm of domestic crises. When Dorothy wanted to spend a large sum, she put the question as to how it might best be used. When the democracy spoke and said it wanted a bowling alley, it got a dance company—and a lesson—instead. Dorothy believed in democracy, but like a good parent she believed in a guided democracy, and Dartington and her children alike tried to find where she meant to guide them.[64]

Not every marriage that lasts is happy, and not every happy marriage makes for a happy family. If the Mitchells, Beards, and Straights had been ordinary professional couples with children, then the various opinions of their children might have reflected only those particular ways in which happy families are alike and unhappy families are each unique. But the Mitchells, Beards, and Straights all mixed up their public lives with their marriages and their families and tried to reach out from their families to society while trying to bring social concerns into their families. Each of them knew he or she had been caught in a web of familial strictures from the moment of his or her birth. Each knew also that in choosing a mate he or she stepped across a threshold into mature independence. For the educated person of some means, family was the first bond they learned to accept and marriage the first bond they chose. If they had ever accepted the petty tyranny of familial circumstance, they also qualified their sense of subjection. Their dependence would be limited to their youth and their freedom would commence with their maturity. In the meantime, they would enjoy the benefits of an upbringing that should teach them to behave responsibly when they were free. And the Progressives' parents tended to collude in their plans, giving them money and schooling and supporting them as they went out into the world. And out there they sought not liberty, but duty.

Nothing and nobody made Dorothy Whitney or Lucy Sprague choose marriage; about Mary Ritter one cannot be sure, though one certainly suspects she had her own head even when she was young. But they did choose it, not out of need, but from desire. They knew full well they could have careers of their own outside marriage, away from men altogether, if they wanted. For each of them, marriage and family entailed a set of responsibilities that they made essential to their lives. Each of them took material from her husband's life and used it to suit him to a cooperative role—for in another life each such man could have been a career man, a middle-class man all but separate from his family. Instead, Dorothy Whitney, by her constant political curiosity and interest, determinedly made Willard Straight over into a Progressive activist. Mary Ritter took Charles Beard's imperialist populism and began to mold it into a vision of an inclusive civilization. Lucy Sprague forced Wesley Mitchell to demonstrate that his dry academicism really concealed a spirited social experimenter and not merely a dry academic. Of course, too, each man brought such changes on himself by his choice of a wife. Each chose a mate who had ideas and a life of her own. The nature of intimate partnerships remains finally secret, but the public manifestations of such hidden workings are plain.

These couples were reformers before they were parents. Each took on dependent charges before they had children of their own. As they tried to imagine the imperial relation or the class relation, their own experiences of subjection or association crept in at the gaps in their understanding. They could understand the subject position of students or children. They could not understand irreducible human difference, and when offered the chance, generally would not take it: that way lay hate and contempt. Therefore the friendly metaphor of the parental relation interposed itself between elites and subjects, between imperialism and democracy. Families provided immediate and particular data about social relations, data far more persuasive than theory could be. Reformers who had appreciated these relationships could identify the process of education with the process of evolution and civilization. Only thus could they understand present injustices and inequities: in the end all manner of things would be well.

The idea that children might be innately, permanently troublesome was therefore ridiculous. Children needed only the proper environment and they would educate themselves to the limits of their ability. Paradoxically (for reformers who believed in the value of social mixing and the erosion of social distinction), the Beard children may have fared best in their nearly sealed environment. At the New Milford house, which Charles had specifically designed so that the trees hid even the small town below, one could imagine oneself alone with nature and a library—two marvelous experiential textbooks—without having to envy other objects of parental attentions. The Mitchell and Straight children, on the other hand, had always to contend with others within a world built by their parents specifically (it must have seemed at times) to test them, ruled over by detached scientific principles and a promiscuous parental affection. The tyrannical bonds of the blood seemed to matter more when they were tried in a social environment. For example, Joyce Antler found that the Mitchells' adopted children resented their Progressive upbringing more than the others. The Mitchells told Jack and Marni they were adopted (presumably because knowledge is always better than ignorance), and so, Antler speculates, these two children might have felt inadequate or insecure. By contrast, the Mitchells' natural children, Sprague and Arnold, felt the weight of their inheritance as a demand to succeed in terms they did not understand in a world they never made.[65] Maybe the relation of parent to child did not work so well as a metaphor for soluble relations between haves and have-nots. Parents were always with their children, even after children grew up and went away, and even a parental death did not give a puzzled child dominion over its own fate. The staggered rhythm of capability passing unevenly from generation to generation confused Lucy Sprague Mitchell because it looked very little like the steady flow of imagined progress.

THE WORLD WELL LOST ONCE MORE

Progressive optimism had been born in a world with permeable boundaries.[66] Wesley Mitchell's advocacy of a U.S. central bank depended on his perception that the United States lagged European nations in this regard. Dorothy Straight's sense of the potential for civilization in America derived from her contact with civilization in Europe. The Beards had both reached political maturity during their stint in Britain, and their first set of reforms depended on an American-Anglo-Saxon ideal culture that transcended nations. Lucy Sprague insisted her Chicago education had been "just as much European" as anything else.[67] Willard Straight's informal imperialism required the formal framework and precedent examples of other nations' imperialism to give it shape, and the Open Door stayed open only through U.S. coordination (however unwilling or ungainly) with European and Asian powers to maintain a balance. Furthermore, Progressive reforms weakened other boundaries. The family promoted the transmission of culture across the boundary between private and public life. Progressives' cooperative reforms blurred the distinction between women's and men's spaces, both physically and culturally.

World War I destroyed the old balance of power and with it the sense that the world would safely submit to their compass. When Charles Beard lamented the loss of those "spacious" days, he suggested the significant shift in capability that the war wrought. The Progressive world shrank, and efforts to reach beyond its immediate boundaries met with quick rebuffs. The fate of the New School certainly suggested as much. When, after that, Dorothy Straight left for England and made it her home, she escaped into a castle where she could pursue her reform efforts in a snug isolation. The Mitchells also invested less of their time in cosmopolitan New York and began to think of their summer place in Vermont as their true home. The Beards did begin one new international effort, but found it ending almost immediately: Charles's municipal reform work had made him popular among Japanese officials, and when the Beards traveled to Japan as a family, Mary's work on issues of women in history and the labor movement brought her into contact with Japanese reform circles. But Japan soon began to change. One friend warned, "Young men . . . do not think that America is making new experiments in the way of government," and another that "the democratization of Japan became almost like a fading dream."[68] Isolation crept over them all, and by degrees they welcomed it. They had too much to do on their own doorstep to look further any longer.

Their families had in short acquired that insulation that was supposed to characterize American middle-class families, but which was deadly to their intended species of reform. Where before they believed their own households would extend into the world and the world into their households, they now effected a separation between the two, and their reform projects, though not so brutally ended as they might have been, persisted only in attenuated relations to the world at large, emphasizing the kinds of reform that only slightly exposed reformers to the consequences of their actions. The *New Republic*, once an extension of the Straights' ambition and the launching pad for the New School, became merely a magazine, in the 1920s more interested in psychological and cultural matters than political or social ones. The BEE and the National Bureau for Economic Research published reports that plummeted into the murk of public opinion, where they achieved effects only by Brownian motion, if at all. The Beards, in their home atop their Connecticut hill, continued mightily to publish, but their books and articles no longer represented the core of a set of social commitments. They were singular political actions in their own right: noble, well-intentioned, and even influential, but not so risky as had been the extension of their personal relations into public.

WHAT IS WORTH WHILE TO STRIVE FOR

Over the course of the preceding chapters, I have sought to demonstrate that the Progressives treated their personal relationships as models for social relationships. I have also tried to demonstrate that in the course of describing desirable social relations, they tended rather to reject the prescriptive power of gender discourse, in large measure because they recognized deep parallels between men's and women's desire for social usefulness. They preferred instead to emphasize the power of empathy to dissolve invidious distinctions between classes of persons. They made this empathy, this conviction of fundamental connection between human persons, the basis of their hopeful faith that education could transform a troubled society into a public of self-governing citizens. And they offered themselves and their families as examples and driving engines of reform—an offer that might result in great forfeit if they proved wrong.

As they tempered their social optimism to account for intractable circumstances, they began to place a greater burden on others to meet the obligations they had, in their youth, incurred. The original narrative of Progressive success would have reached a climax within a single generation, as a concentrated series of grand gestures devolved knowledge and power to the benighted, who in turn would obligingly emerge into the light as mature, responsible, independent-minded citizens. Once this blessed day had failed, repeatedly, to dawn, Progressives faced a choice: they could stick stubbornly to their stories, insisting on their eventual fulfillment, or they could change their expectations in the light of contrary facts. Perhaps the second choice required greater courage, as it meant surrendering long-held ideas—ideas that were the basis of their very identities. But it also meant investing subsequent generations with the obligation of social reform, imposing the desires of the past on the dreams of the future.

For such a talkative generation of reformers, the Progressives often foundered when it came to explaining what, really, they wanted: or else they protested much too much, citing fourteen desiderata when only one would have done. But they knew at bottom "what was worth while," as both Wesley Mitchell and Dorothy Straight said: anything that tended to humanize the relations between people who had been shuffled about and classified by the complex interactions between their own wishes and the needs of industrial economies.[69]

To us today, it may seem naive that Progressives should have looked to the family for the appropriate description of such relations, and it moreover seems painfully naive that they hoped their families should have become the agencies of dramatic social change. But we nowadays benefit from (or labor under) the immense effects of a century during which the augmentation of government institutions has been essential to the pursuit of civil rights, of economic welfare, and of international influence, and we can therefore only remotely feel the possibilities that other, informal, neighborly institutions seemed to present in the early years of the twentieth century. Not only was the state a newly grown creature, but the great institutions that preserve and transmit culture—the universities, the museums, the civic associations—had barely been born, and held an uncertain authority. But the habits of families, of teachers and students, were (or so Progressives believed) well-understood, powerful, and easily exploited. Moreover, in a world transformed by industry—by what Mitchell called "the money economy," which made all values into cash values, and made all relations into business transactions—the human affections were vanishing from public life, supplanted by rational valuation and arbitrary allegiance. But if the affections had fled from society, the family remained their refuge, and could become the starting point from which they reached outward once more.

Nor, with our present sense that the political valence of "family" is hierarchical and reactionary, can we intuitively grasp the association between family and freedom that was so essential to Progressivism. The Progressive family was supposed to create repeatedly, through the education of generations of children, the conditions for freedom. The process of education combined with the parental affections should (Progressives believed) have been sufficient to generate an American citizenry capable of managing its own affairs, and that also knew the value of relations that the money economy could not describe. These relations—these values— should have been sufficient to create an American politics that could democratically, and morally, manage the modernization of a continental economy.

The Progressives' faith in the transformative power of these simple relations could not survive the war, which exalted an efficient orderliness in social relations over any sense of moral obligation or justice. This tendency was probably generic to old-fashioned wars, which necessarily made the mere preservation of a polity a priority. Order and efficiency become ends in themselves. Had Progressives themselves desired an orderly or efficient society, World War I would have proved an unvarnished blessing to them. But, as Mitchell wrote, "sounder organization" and "better training" could not by themselves be worthy social goals. They were not "what is worth while to strive for." And the only worthwhile things Mitchell could imagine were familial relations. If the war could demonstrate that families were inadequate to the reform of society, it could not destroy the intrinsic moral value of the relations within them. Those aspects—if those alone—of the Progressive vision survived the history of their times, and persisted in the morals of the stories they told about themselves.[70]

EPILOGUE: THE RISE AND FALL OF
THE RISE OF AMERICAN CIVILIZATION;
OR, A FURTHER PARABLE ON THE NARRATIVE
OF PROGRESS AND THE LOGIC OF EVENTS

Even though nothing in life ends so dramatically as narrative logic suggests it should, the wave of deaths at the end of the war did seem to signal the passage of an era, especially as one of the deaths was Theodore Roosevelt's. Roosevelt had the decency to eulogize Willard Straight— "both he and his wife had in their souls that touch of heroism"—and within weeks of sounding this grace note, he died, passing "with the tide" and taking with him his inspiration for "all men who loved right more than ease," as Edith Wharton wrote.[1]

Still, if vigorous Progressivism had ended, progress of a kind continued through the 1920s. In 1927, in New York, Americans saw Charles Lindbergh off on his trans-Atlantic flight and greeted the heroic age of aviation. The automobile came into its own as the Triborough Bridge was proposed (initially with its terminal diphthong intact) and the Holland Tunnel opened. The fruits of this progress sometimes tasted funny: "No victory was ever more hollow than the success of the new Holland Tunnel. You approach with eagerness, you drive through it with speed and éclat, you emerge at the other end with joy and thanksgiving. And where are you? In Jersey City," as E. B. White wrote.[2] With Prohibition in the Constitution and Calvin Coolidge in the White House, it was "difficult to be solemn."[3]

This was the year Charles and Mary Beard earned their fame with the publication of *The Rise of American Civilization*. After their trip to Japan, they spent most of their time out of New York, up at their Connecticut farm. Despite their immersion in historical sources over these years, they, too, had not been solemn. Now that their children had gone to college, they could freely enjoy "a jolly party" on an occasional trip into town, as Charles wrote H. L. Mencken. And if the book that emerged could be judged by its black and gold cover, it was a product of that time and place. A small gold medallion relieves the black background, containing within it a jagged design that might either be ancient and tribal or modern and electric, but in either case is powerful. Within the bindings was an equally powerful, sweeping synthesis of American history—we might even say *the* powerful, sweeping synthesis of American history, as its interpretive ambition has never been matched. The book is proper literature: erudite and written always with a sense of humor. And its narrative coherence belongs unmistakably to the Progressive period. The Beards' "civilization" refers to all the top-down reform efforts that spark bottom-up activity. The book documents this process of civilization and was itself an intentional installment in that process: as the Beards wrote in the introduction to the first reissue of the book, "The history of a civilization, if intelligently conceived, may be an instrument of civilization."[4] As the Beards had long maintained, the narrative of progress, if propounded upon the hustings, could enliven the populace to take control of its own destiny. The notion that written history would now serve the purpose that once politics, new schools, impassioned speeches, and emotional energy had served reflected the chastening experiences of the decade since the war had begun. But the intent remained: to use education to encourage independence and thus fulfill the promise of American life.

Traditionally, historians have treated *The Rise of American Civilization* as a better or worse elaboration of Charles's *An Economic Interpretation of the Constitution*.[5] But recently, historians have suggested that the contribution of Mary Beard to the *Rise* consisted not only in adding women to the social history of the work but in propounding the idea of civilization itself. This idea made the work what it was: "an organic book," as the Beards themselves wrote, a coherent whole in which the progressively ramified American culture gave meaning to the advance of American civilization.[6] The principal method of advancing such a culture from parents to children (as the book says) was "nurture—the climate of books and learning, the occupations and conversations of parents and adult friends."[7]

The Beards suggested the importance of culture in the principal precedent they attacked: Henry Adams, who appears at the beginning and end of the book. Adams had long been and would indeed continue to be a haunt in Charles's intellectual attic, but here the Beards conjured him specifically to exorcise him.[8] Adams, the descendant of presidents and the dour dean of the previous generation of historians, had framed his own *History of the United States* by asking whether the American democracy could produce a civilization of its own: "Of all possible triumphs, none could equal that which might be won in the regions of thought if the intellectual influence of the United States should equal their social and economical importance," he wrote.[9] His *History* did not altogether dash these hopes, but he plainly did not make much of the cultural product of democracy in the new world. The Beards' work skewers this pessimism as often as possible. If (for example) Adams reluctantly conceded some originality to Washington Irving, the Beards offered up Irving, Cooper, Emerson, Hawthorne, and Fuller, among many others: there were, too, Catharine Beecher and Frances Wright, Mercy Otis Warren and the famous army of scribbling women who so offended Hawthorne; James, Howells, Twain, and Godey's *Lady's Book*.[10] Adams was wrong: culture vindicated democracy, and the Beards looked hopefully forward to a coming age when the money imperative on culture would recede, allowing (à la Mitchell) the craft impulse once more to flourish, so "fine arts and industry, put asunder by the machine, must be somehow reunited," principally of course by new kinds of schools.[11]

The book concluded with a conditional statement tinged with triumph: "If the generality of opinion, as distinguished from that of poignant specialists [i.e., Adams], was taken into account, there was no doubt about the nature of the future in America. . . . If so, it is the dawn, not the dusk, of the gods."[12] They were, of course, plural gods, the deities of democrats.

The Rise of American Civilization was a tremendous success. It became a Book of the Month Club selection and generated sufficient demand for multiple revisions and sequels. As historian Richard Hofstadter later wrote, "*The Rise of American Civilization* was received with all but universal enthusiasm, enjoyed splendid sales, and did more than any other book of the twentieth century to define American history for the reading public."[13] It succeeded grandly both high and low and seemed to become precisely the effective, motivating synthesis the Beards had hoped it would, reaching readers rich and poor.

Then the obstinate procession of history produced, once more, a dramatic irony that irresistibly affected the narrative of progress toward the dawn of the gods. In 1930, after the Great Crash but before the Great Depression, the Beards reissued the book with a new, admonitory and ambiguous introduction that reflected the uncertainty of the moment.

> Business enterprise has been built upon a heritage of civilization, and its directors are likely to be civilized in proportion as they understand the history of their inheritance without which they would be economic infants. More than that. They are in turn the makers of civilization as well as patrons of the arts. In some mysterious way thought and the materials of life evolve together.[14]

With this new beginning, their old ending seemed even more cautious. And by 1933, the old ending had to go altogether, as the logic of events once more shredded the narrative of Progressive optimism. They concluded no longer with trumpets for democratic civilization triumphing over Adamsian skepticism, but with "Thought, weary Titan," climbing painfully upward, to an unknown goal at an unknown distance from his present perch.[15]

The Beards began this decade as friends and allies of the new Roosevelt, the Democratic one. Charles's books of 1934, co-written with George H. E. Smith, plainly tried to steer Franklin Roosevelt in a Beardian direction.[16] Charles also wrote a pamphlet endorsing the Good Neighbor policy toward Latin America and got a warm presidential thank-you for it: "I need not tell you how delighted we all are and how very much I appreciate your doing this, hope I shall see you soon again," FDR wrote.[17] In 1938, Charles praised Roosevelt's second inaugural address as a "great state paper" and privately wished the president had pushed harder for the World Court: "He should have fought."[18] Mary meanwhile became a friendly correspondent with Eleanor Roosevelt, and in 1936 enlisted her help in trying to establish a World Center for Women's Archives.[19]

Throughout the 1930s, the Beards continued to expound the idea of civilization. Mary lectured at Stanford on "Women's Share in the Civilizing Process."[20] Charles plotted with Abraham Flexner to establish a new school dedicated to a cross-disciplinary study of "the application of the arts and sciences to civilization."[21] Mary told an audience in 1936 that civilization was women's "primordial urge," and challenged her listeners to discover "what share have women actually had in elevating ambition, individualism, greed, slavery, power, pomp, ferocity, parasitism, war and general depravity to major manifestations of the human spirit? What share have women had in the humanistic enterprise which has held societies together?"[22] She gestured here in the direction her prejudices led her: away from the association of women with specific, gendered virtue, and toward a comprehensive view of their involvement in all of the organic civilization that humankind had created. The effort would culminate in her 1946 *Woman as Force in History*, which thumpingly (if not conclusively) rejected the doctrine of woman's subordination to men and placed women squarely in the common life of society.[23] Charles worked on the call-and-response volumes *Whither Mankind?* and *Toward Civilization* to mount "sweeping criticism of modern life and institutions" without "a scrapping of the scientific knowledge and equipment which men have won," thus identifying the civilization project closely with Enlightenment thought.[24] Later, when Charles wrote a blurb for a book by David Lilienthal, director of the Tennessee Valley Authority, he described Lilienthal's vision of "grass-roots democracy" as the core of "civilization," adding, "the word civilization used above is carefully chosen as expressing all the human values represented in human achievements described in the book."[25]

By the late 1930s, though, the Beards increasingly feared their old Rooseveltian enemies—war and Caesarism. In 1935 Charles predicted the Pacific War in *Scribner's*—"There will be an 'incident,' a 'provocation,'" he ominously wrote—and so when the war came, he saw what he had feared he would see.[26] Even though during the war he once again worked for the government as a propagandist, writing "Dialogues on Democracy!" for the Office of War Information, he found himself branded an isolationist and even a traitor for his attacks on FDR, which were, to be sure, vitriolic: he accused the president of plotting "a real holy war" and of making himself the American "*Fuehrer*," the nation's "indispensable man."[27] These efforts earned Charles a comparison to Adolf Hitler from historian Samuel Eliot Morison, who called into question the whole course of the Beards' career and their very notion of history for a purpose.[28]

Near the end of her life, Mary Beard wrote a long answer to a request to elucidate the Beards' thinking. The letter was uncharacteristic; she generally refused to write about herself, her husband, or her writings. But this time she tried to put down on paper what, as she wrote, "I think we thought":

> The failure of the "Founding Fathers" to come to grips with slavery postponed but did not avoid the slavery issue; may indeed have heightened it. If the great plantations could have been run without slaves at the time, the issue of slavery, presumably, would not have been so tempestuous. If slavery had been tackled in the constitutional convention, perhaps the Union of States could not have been effected. But . . . evidently the will to unite was deterministic. . . .
>
> My own Quaker stock, when Lincoln called for Volunteers, answered that call when [my father] was a junior in college and the junior class of young men went to war together. He was only mustered out at the end of the war. Then he turned for occupation to become a lawyer—in Indianapolis. When I was of high school age, I asked my father why he volunteered to fight and he always said: "To save the Union." I believe that was true. . . . If we [Charles and Mary] had made it [the interpretation] wholly economic, there might or might not have been critics. I think that every war is a failure of statesmanship but statecraft is a recent idea and a phenomenon not yet achieved.[29]

Mary Beard here strove to explain the Beards' thinking on two episodes for which they were often attacked. In both cases, critics said, *The Rise of American Civilization* had—like *An Economic Interpretation of the Constitution* before it—sullied the memory of a preceding generation by imputing to economic causes the dramatic effects (a powerful union and re-union of states) on which the progress of American civilization depended. In these two paragraphs, Mary tied herself to the Civil War generation, whose desire to save the Union she credited and who themselves were merely set to solve the problem the Founding Fathers had left them. The Progressives' generation, in turn, set about solving the problems left them by their parents. It was for this reason that "The Gilded Age," covering the decades after the Civil War—the Beards' own youth—is the pivotal chapter in the Beards' *Rise*. At ninety-six pages, it is the longest chapter in the second volume.[30] In this section, they developed the notion that the United States, emerging from the Civil War newly unified and industrialized, stood on the brink of recapitulating the rise of older empires, who advanced on the shoulders of their own oppressed, in a distinctly American manner.

> History seemed to be repeating itself. Ancient Rome had its proletarian quarters; London, Paris, and Berlin their slums. Nero's House of Gold rose near the waste of dark tenements. . . . Queen Victoria drew revenues from rack-renting in London misery. . . . As Calhoun remarked, somebody had to pay for culture. . . . And yet, though there was poverty in American cities, stark and galling enough to blast human nature, there was no proletariat in the Roman sense of the word. Among the American working classes, all save the most wretched had aspirations; there was a baton in every tool-kit. The public schools which flung wide for all the portals to the mysterious world of science, letters, and art opened the way for the talented to rise in to the professions—at least that of politics.[31]

Here was the problem and here also was the hope for its solution. In this America there arose "a wide and active middle class" whose "cultural operations beyond question set the central pattern for the future in America."[32] This class—"this respectable middle class," the Beards wrote, almost without irony—"carried the burden of American civilization," and it was not alone: "Except in some of the mountain regions of the South, the aspirations of the middle class were on the whole joyously emulated by the agricultural masses and by the merchants of tiny villages."[33] In these middle classes especially, but also in working classes where women had jobs and in the leisure class where they had the freedom to educate themselves, the world of women changed, too: "The gravity of women's interests steadily moved from the center of the family outward toward the periphery of that circle where it merged into the larger humanities."[34]

This rising middle class, emulated far and wide, which gave rise to educated and ambitious women, and men ambitious for their children, undertook to destroy a cozy bourgeois insularity. Women and men alike saw at first hand the world of poverty juxtaposed with their own comforts, and were sensible not only of its injustice but also of the potential for relieving it. This immediate experience of wrong and the belief that it could and should be readily addressed gave rise to the reform movement that followed for women and men alike: "It was no accident that Jane Addams, head of Hull House, stood with Theodore Roosevelt at Armageddon in 1912 when the plutocracy was challenged in the name of 'decent government and fair play.' " Both had come of that class and had enjoyed its comforts. Both had seen poverty with their own eyes and were ready to change it by education and by exalting social obligations that challenged the "cash nexus."[35]

The Beards' new history was neither parricidal nor filiopietistic, but rather moved toward an acceptance of a principle of precession rather than progress to explain the transmission of knowledge from one generation to the next. Their synthesis had to comprehend incidental retrograde motion amid general forward movement. Increasingly, as they wrote themselves into the past and began contemplating the prospect before (and after) their generation, they began to make places for error as well as success. Their hard reckoning with the judgment of the 1940s on their own past led them first to burn, then to reorder and preserve part of their own historical record. Charles's death in 1948 (of a fatal allergy to sulfa) left Mary to reckon with their legacy. To Alfred A. Knopf's suggestion that a biography of Charles might help, she wrote, "No one is to have access to CAB's papers unless such a person is truly competent to use them and . . . no such person is yet visible to me." Knopf consoled her that a "promising youngster" would turn up someday. She wrote, "I'll be dead by that time." Even while she brusquely refused to consider the scholarly examination of the Beard papers in her own time, she labored to prepare them for such scrutiny. Not only did she keep and organize the papers, but she inserted notes to offer interpretive insight— or spin, as the case may be: "As many of these letters show, CAB was invited or about to be invited to teach in other institutions after he resigned from Columbia. . . . He accepted no such invitation. [signed] Mary"; "Beard did not engage in party politics of any kind. Was not a member of the Socialist Party"; "When Henry M. could not get a resolution passed at Barnard . . . expressing at least appreciation of CAB as teacher there, he resigned—but quietly. [signed] Mary," and so on. She plainly meant the archive as a defense against their attackers. In the same cause, she labored over explanations of their life and work, explications of their "purposes and performances," continuing to insist that there was no secret, private life apart from their public texts: "You ask me for some personal items with which to brighten your paper about me. I am now 76 years of age and my *hobby* for twenty years—even longer—has been studying history and writing about it[, b]oth as co-author with my husband and as my separate writing and study for it."[36]

Once, before the Civil War, farms and small towns and college encompassed the existence of the ordinary American family. Then fathers became soldiers and the families moved to cities, where chances abounded. The newly educated children of the victorious armies advanced on the apparently malleable metropolis of the emerging empire, determined to make themselves mothers and fathers to a new world of their own. They built a society of independent institutions meant to teach the American democracy to govern itself. New York, whose most important power was the power to back, stood with its resources at the ready. Then a new war changed the evident course of events.

The Beards should have forgiven themselves for succumbing once again to their optimism in 1927. Like most Americans, they had not felt the devastation of World War I as their European counterparts had. The sort of America they had imagined before the war seemed once again possible. Even if the war's imperatives had separated men from women and had overtaken public discussion of social issues, by the middle 1920s the excesses of the war exercise had faded. Women seemed, according to Mary, to gain steadily in their assertion of their rights.[37] If labor unions and African Americans and immigrants still struggled, the rude health of the U.S. economy seemed likely to support indefinite experimentation and adjustment. Civilization seemed once more attainable.

But by the end of the 1930s, New York backed Washington, its only hope. The recently Progressive middle class seemed ready now to stampede at the behest of any new despot with dramatic talents. Now empire and progress parted company. Just as with World War I (which now was plainly but the first world war) the impending World War II began to part men from women in the service of the state, thereby setting back hopes for civilization again. Now Germany, once the mythic begetter of democracy, became instead a mythically masculine Fatherland under the imaginative influence of a vigorous, even hysterical, performer. Now Mary Beard hopefully suggested Americans might think of their nation by contrast as a peaceful Motherland, even going so far as to nominate Eleanor Roosevelt as a "great white Mother," hoping to preserve peace by taking advantage of the publicly separated parental principles. (Roosevelt's response—"I am amused"—suggested how artificial this solution sounded even then.)[38] But empires would be empires, built as engines of the state, which had already proven its ability to manipulate the democratic will. Women would now encourage and willingly submit to the war-lust of men. Now mothers and fathers would have to set aside their united peaceful ambitions.

In 1927, "the last days of normalcy," all had looked well, as the Beards wrote in the 1933 edition of the *Rise*. "Never had the world seemed brighter to those who enjoyed the brightness."[39] But they concluded by noting that all that had changed. They noted that John Chamberlain, in a book titled *Farewell to Reform: The Rise, Life and Decay of the Progressive Mind in America*, had "laid Theodore Roosevelt, Robert M. La Follette, and Woodrow Wilson away in their tombs with Charles I, Louis XVI, and Nicholas II."[40] The Beards rarely performed without a certain self-aware irony, and this curtain call was no exception. Chamberlain had bustled the Beards offstage along with those other reformers: "The works of . . . Beard and company are like magnificent machines with no dynamos attached: there is nothing to start the conveyor belts moving," he wrote.[41] So in turn the Beards lumped him in with those other recent writers who "surged up on the left" to do away with their generation.[42] The cycles of history precessed, and the Beards prepared to make themselves content with their contribution to the wheel's progress. As Charles observed to Carl Bridenbaugh in 1938, surely with mixed feelings, "It is clear the youngsters will write the history of civilization in America."[43] In 1943, the then-youngster Richard Hofstadter wrote of the Beards' project that their calling on the great minds of the past and saying that they "invoked 'civilization' seems little more revealing than that they all accepted monogamy; perhaps less so, for the meaning of monogamy is generally understood."[44] The general understanding of marriage—of family, of children, of all consequent social relations—on which the Beards and their allies in fact depended had, it turned out, escaped the youngsters who followed them.

NOTES

INTRODUCTION

1. Honoré de Balzac, *Le contrat de mariage* (Paris: Michel Lévy Frères, 1892), 25.

2. Tamara Hareven, "Family History at the Crossroads," *Journal of Family History* 12, nos. 1–3 (1987): ix–xxiii; quotation on x.

3. This definition of Progressivism within a global context draws on James T. Kloppenberg, *Uncertain Victory: Social Democracy and Progressivism in European and American Thought, 1870–1920* (New York: Oxford Univ. Press, 1986), 298–394, and Daniel T. Rodgers, *Atlantic Crossings: Social Politics in a Progressive Age* (Cambridge: Harvard Univ. Press, 1998), 52–75. For the various elements of Progressivism, see also Kloppenberg, "Political Ideas in Twentieth-Century America," in *The Virtues of Liberalism* (New York: Oxford Univ. Press, 1998), esp. 126–32; Rodgers, "In Search of Progressivism," *Reviews in American History* 10, no. 4 (1982): 113–32; David M. Kennedy, "Overview: The Progressive Era," *Historian* 37, no. 3 (1975): 20–34; and Peter G. Filene, "An Obituary for 'The Progressive Movement,'" *American Quarterly* 22, no. 1 (1970): 453–68.

4. Kloppenberg, "Political Ideas," 129; Casey Nelson Blake, *Beloved Community: The Cultural Criticism of Randolph Bourne, Van Wyck Brooks, Waldo Frank,*

and Lewis Mumford (Chapel Hill: Univ. of North Carolina Press, 1990), 24; Robert H. Wiebe, *The Search for Order, 1877–1920* (New York: Hill & Wang, 1967). For a critique of the orderly thesis for foreign policy, see Walter LaFeber, *The American Search for Opportunity, 1865–1913*, vol. 2 of *The Cambridge History of American Foreign Relations,* ed. Warren I. Cohen (Cambridge: Cambridge Univ. Press, 1993).

5. Christopher Lasch, *Women and the Common Life: Love, Marriage, and Feminism,* ed. Elisabeth Lasch-Quinn (New York: Norton, 1997), 168.

6. This account of immigration draws on Timothy J. Hatton and Jeffrey G. Williamson, *The Age of Mass Migration: Causes and Economic Impact* (New York: Oxford Univ. Press, 1998); John Bodnar, *The Transplanted: A History of Immigrants in Urban America* (Bloomington: Indiana Univ. Press, 1985), esp. 45–71; see also Steven J. Diner, *A Very Different Age: Americans of the Progressive Era* (New York: Hill & Wang, 1998), 76–101.

7. On the English movement, see Lawrence Goldman, *Dons and Workers: Oxford and Adult Education Since 1850* (Oxford: Clarendon, 1995), 45–50. On the distinctly female character of the American movement, see also Rodgers, *Atlantic Crossings,* 64.

8. Jane Addams, *Democracy and Social Ethics,* ed. Anne Firor Scott (1902; Cambridge: Harvard Univ. Press, 1964), 72–73. See also Estelle B. Freedman, "Separatism as Strategy: Female Institution Building and American Feminism, 1870–1930," *Feminist Studies* 5, no. 3 (1979): 512–29; Blanche Wiesen Cook, "Female Support Networks and Political Activism: Lillian Wald, Crystal Eastman, Emma Goldman," *Chrysalis* 3 (fall 1977): 43–61; and Kathryn Kish Sklar, "Hull House in the 1890s: A Community of Women Reformers," *Signs* 10, no. 4 (1985): 658–77. On Christian sacrifice and chaste reform, see Mina J. Carson, *Settlement Folk: Social Thought and the American Settlement Movement, 1885–1930* (Chicago: Univ. of Chicago Press, 1990).

9. Elaine Tyler May, *Great Expectations: Marriage and Divorce in Post-Victorian America* (Chicago: Univ. of Chicago Press, 1980), esp. 50–53; also William O'Neill, *Divorce in the Progressive Era* (New Haven: Yale Univ. Press, 1967). On shifts in family structure, see Steven Mintz and Susan Kellogg, *Domestic Revolutions: A Social History of Family Life* (New York: Free Press, 1988), 107–31; also Linda J. Nicholson, *Gender and History: The Limits of Social Theory in the Age of the Family* (New York: Columbia Univ. Press, 1986), 106–14. Michael Grossberg sees divorce law as upholding a double standard for women, rather than recognizing their liberation: see Grossberg, *Governing the Hearth: Law and the Family in Nineteenth-Century America* (Chapel Hill: Univ. of North Carolina Press, 1985), 250–53.

10. William H. Chafe, *The Paradox of Change: American Women in the Twentieth Century* (New York: Oxford Univ. Press, 1991), 16; emphasis in the original.

11. See Robyn Muncy, *Creating a Female Dominion in American Reform, 1890–1935* (New York: Oxford Univ. Press, 1991), 38–65, esp. 43ff. and Molly Ladd-Taylor, *Raising a Baby the Government Way: Mothers' Letters to the Children's Bureau, 1915–1932* (New Brunswick: Rutgers Univ. Press, 1986).

12. Seth Koven and Sonya Michel, *Mothers of a New World: Maternalist Politics and the Origins of Welfare States* (London: Routledge, 1993), 2.

13. Freedman, *Maternal Justice: Miriam Van Waters and the Female Reform Tradition* (Chicago: Univ. of Chicago Press, 1996), 78. For a commentary on the term *maternalist* as a noun, see Koven, "The Ambivalence of Agency: Women, Families, and Social Policy in France, Britain, and the United States," *Journal of Women's History* 9, no. 1 (1997): 68.

14. Gail Bederman, " 'The Women Have Had Charge of the Church Work Long Enough': The Men and Religion Forward Movement of 1911–1912 and the Masculinization of Middle-Class Protestantism," *American Quarterly* 41, no. 3 (1989): 451; Arnaldo Testi, "The Gender of Reform Politics: Theodore Roosevelt and the Culture of Masculinity," *Journal of American History* 81, no. 4 (1995): 1521.

15. Seth Koven and Sonya Michel, "Womanly Duties: Maternalist Politics and the Origins of Welfare States in France, Germany, Great Britain and the United States, 1880–1920," *American Historical Review* 95, no. 4 (1990): 1092.

16. Seth Koven and Sonya Michel, "Conference Report: Gender and the Origins of the Welfare State," *Radical History Review* 43 (January 1989): 117. See also Molly Ladd-Taylor, *Mother-work: Women, Child Welfare, and the State, 1890–1930* (Urbana: Univ. of Illinois, 1994) for a thorough taxonomic elaboration of varieties of maternalism and their limits.

17. Theda Skocpol, *Protecting Soldiers and Mothers: The Political Origins of Social Policy in the United States* (Cambridge: Harvard Univ. Press, 1992), 2. For discussion of Skocpol's argument, see Paula Baker's review of Skocpol's *Protecting Soldiers and Mothers* in *American Historical Review* 98, no. 2 (1993): 458–60, and Alice Kessler-Harris's review of the same work in *Journal of American History* 80, no. 3 (1993): 1035–37; note also Skocpol, *Protecting*, table 9, 446–47 and appendix 2, 543–55.

18. For a small example of other metaphors, see the discussion of "the child crop," in Muncy, *Creating a Female Dominion*, 39.

19. Skocpol, *Protecting*, 529.

20. Koven and Michel, *Mothers of a New World*, 1–2.

21. MRB, "The Twentieth Century Woman Looking Around and Backward," *Young Oxford* 2 (December 1900): 101; MRB, "The Legislative Influence of Unenfranchised Women," *Annals of the American Academy of Political and Social Science* 56 (November 1914): 61; Charles A. Beard and Mary R. Beard, *The Rise of American Civilization*, 2 vols. (New York: Macmillan, 1927), 2:405; MRB to a Mr. Oberholzer, 19 November 1952, Beard Papers.

22. Joyce Antler, "Feminism as Life-Process: The Life and Career of Lucy Sprague Mitchell," *Feminist Studies* 7, no. 1 (1981): 153. Antler has expanded this article into a remarkable biography, *Lucy Sprague Mitchell: The Making of a Modern Woman* (New Haven: Yale Univ. Press, 1987).

23. Rosalind Rosenberg, *Beyond Separate Spheres: The Intellectual Roots of Modern Feminism* (New Haven: Yale Univ. Press, 1982), and Rosenberg, "In Search of Woman's Nature, 1850–1920," *Feminist Studies* 3, nos. 1–2 (1975): 141–54. See also

the congruent analysis of Lillian Wald and Jane Addams in Jill K. Conway, *The First Generation of American Women Graduates* (New York: Garland, 1987).

24. Joseph Bucklin Bishop, *Theodore Roosevelt and His Times, Shown in His Own Letters* (London: Hodder, 1920), 10, 25, 50. On TR and masculine Progressivism, see Bederman, *Manliness and Civilization: A Cultural History of Gender and Race in the United States, 1880–1917* (Chicago: Univ. of Chicago Press, 1995) and Testi, "Gender." For Bederman particularly, masculinity is much more tied up with race than with class.

25. Margaret Marsh, "Suburban Men and Masculine Domesticity, 1870–1915," *American Quarterly* 40, no. 2 (1988): 165–86, 176, and 181 n. 4. Regarding Marsh's argument about the tendency toward masculine domesticity, cf. Testi, who believes this process amounted to "a male recapture of the domestic space," ("Gender," 1521), but it is amply clear that Roosevelt's behavior here was not "strict father" but "nurturant parent," to borrow the terms of analysis of George Lakoff, *Moral Politics: What Conservatives Know that Liberals Don't* (Chicago: Univ. of Chicago Press, 1996). On Roosevelt and his children, see also *A Bully Father: Theodore Roosevelt's Letters to His Children*, ed. Joan Patterson Kerr (New York: Random House, 1995).

26. Some biographers have dealt creatively with this issue, though looking at individual cases often makes them look more exceptional than this list suggests. See, for example, Desley Deacon, *Elsie Clews Parsons: Inventing Modern Life* (Chicago: Univ. of Chicago Press, 1997); Bernard A. Weisberger, *The LaFollettes of Wisconsin: Love and Politics in Progressive America* (Madison: Univ. of Wisconsin Press, 1994); Elizabeth Ann Payne, *Reform, Labor, and Feminism: Margaret Dreier Robins and the Woman's Trade Union League* (Urbana: Univ. of Illinois Press, 1988); see also A. M. McBriar, *An Edwardian Mixed Doubles: The Bosanquets versus the Webbs: A Study in British Social Policy, 1890–1929* (Oxford: Clarendon, 1987); Beatrice Webb, *Our Partnership* (London: Longmans, Green, 1948).

27. Gore Vidal, "Love on the Hudson," review of *Closest Companion*, by Geoffrey Ward, *New York Review of Books* 42, no. 8 (1995): 4.

28. Cook, *Eleanor Roosevelt*, vol. 1, *1884–1933* (New York: Viking, 1992), 245.

29. Joseph P. Lash, *Eleanor and Franklin* (New York: Norton, 1971), 498.

30. Addams, *Democracy and Social Ethics*, 77–78.

31. Ibid., 14, 63, 79.

32. On Addams, the settlement-house movement, and the Progressive Party, see Allen F. Davis, "Social Workers and the Progressive Party, 1912–1916," *American Historical Review* 69, no. 3, (1964): 671–88.

33. Theodore Roosevelt, "Social Justice," essay of 1917, in *The Foes of Our Own Household*, vol. 19 of *The Works of Theodore Roosevelt*, national edition, ed. Hermann Hagedorn (New York: Scribner's, 1926), 92, 93.

34. Roosevelt, "The Meaning of Free Government," speech at Saint Louis, 28 March 1912, in *Social Justice and Popular Rule: Essays, Addresses, and Public Statements Relating to the Progressive Movement, 1910–1916*, vol. 17 of *Works*, 173.

35. Roosevelt, "Social Justice," 88; "Americanism," speech of 1915 in *America and the World War, Fear God and Take Your Own Part, Letters to His Chil-*

dren, vol. 18 of *Works*, 395; "Social Justice," 84; also, for example, introduction to *Foes*, 25ff; "The Terms of Peace," speech of 1918 in *Foes*, 372; see also "Questions for American Conservatives," *New Republic*, 21 September 1918, 213.

36. See Rebecca Edwards, *Angels in the Machinery: Gender and American Party Politics from the Civil War to the Progressive Era* (New York: Oxford Univ. Press, 1997), for example, 165.

37. On the family as an organizing principle for politics, see Lakoff, *Moral Politics*; Lasch, 1980 review essay reprinted as "Life in the Therapeutic State," in *Women and the Common Life*; Lasch, *Haven in a Heartless World: The Family Besieged* (New York: Basic, 1977); Jacques Donzelot, *The Policing of Families*, trans. Robert Hurley (1977; Baltimore: Johns Hopkins Univ. Press, 1997); Jay Fliegelman, *Prodigals and Pilgrims: The American Revolution against Patriarchal Authority* (Cambridge: Cambridge Univ. Press, 1982); Chris Dixon, *Perfecting the Family: Anti-Slavery Marriages in Nineteenth-Century America* (Amherst: Univ. of Massachusetts Press, 1997). On Progressivism and social order generally, see Wiebe, *Search*; Samuel P. Hays, *The Response to Industrialism, 1885–1914* (1957; 2d ed., Chicago: Univ. of Chicago Press, 1995); and Hays, "The Politics of Reform in Municipal Government in the Progressive Era," *Pacific Northwest Quarterly* 55 (1964): 157–69. The notion current in the late 1960s and 1970s that Progressives wanted to impose a repressive social order is effectively debunked in, for example, Kloppenberg, *Uncertain Victory*, esp. 377–94; also Kloppenberg, "Political Ideas," 126–37; cf. the historiography in Glenn C. Altschuler, *Race, Ethnicity, and Class in American Social Thought, 1865–1919* (Wheeling, Ill.: Harlan Davidson, 1982), 76–113.

38. Randolph S. Bourne, "The State," in *War and the Intellectuals: Essays by Randolph S. Bourne, 1915–1919*, ed. Carl Resek (New York: Harper, 1964), 97. On the legacy of "the educational style" in politics for both men and women, and more generally as a means of combating unthinking allegiance (in this case to party), see Michael E. McGerr, "Political Style and Women's Power, 1830–1930," *Journal of American History* 77, no. 3 (1990): 864–85, esp. 870–71; also McGerr, *The Decline of Popular Politics: The American North, 1865–1928* (New York: Oxford Univ. Press, 1986), 66ff.

39. See Ladd-Taylor, *Raising a Baby*.

40. This account of the shifting role of marriage and family draws on Morton Keller, *Affairs of State: Public Life in Late Nineteenth Century America* (Cambridge: Harvard Univ. Press, 1977), 461–72; Nancy F. Cott, "Giving Character to Our Whole Civil Polity: Marriage and the Public Order in the Late Nineteenth Century," in *U.S. History as Women's History: New Feminist Essays*, ed. Linda K. Kerber, Alice Kessler-Harris, and Kathryn Kish Sklar (Chapel Hill: Univ. of North Carolina Press, 1995); and Grossberg, 289–307.

41. On the primacy of experience in shaping Progressive morality, see Kloppenberg, "Democracy and Disenchantment" in *Virtues of Liberalism*; cf. Lasch on the "religion of experience" in *The New Radicalism in America, 1889–1963: The Intellectual as a Social Type* (New York: Knopf, 1965), for example, 62–65 and 99–103.

42. S.G.T. (pseud. for WDS), "Philanthropy or Social Leadership?" *New Republic*, 27 March 1915, 208–9.

43. Cited in Genevieve P. Herrick, "Women in the News," *Country Gentlemen*, May 1936, Beard microfilm in Beard Papers.

44. See discussion of Addams, above. For the growing proportion of married educated women, see Helen Lefkowitz Horowitz, *Campus Life: Undergraduate Cultures from the End of the Eighteenth Century to the Present* (New York: Knopf, 1987), 197–99; also Cott, *The Grounding of Modern Feminism* (New Haven: Yale Univ. Press, 1987), 147–48 and 180ff.

45. WCM, "The Backward Art of Spending Money," *American Economic Review* 2 (June 1912): 270–71.

46. Isaiah Berlin, "Joseph de Maistre and the Origins of Fascism," *The Crooked Timber of Humanity: Chapters in the History of Ideas*, ed. Henry Hardy (New York: Vintage, 1992), 162.

47. WCM, "Backward Art," 280.

48. Richard Wightman Fox, "The Culture of Liberal Protestant Progressivism, 1900–1925," *Journal of Interdisciplinary History* 23, no. 3 (1993): 639–60, quotation on 658. Fox's essay belongs to a discussion of the Protestant dimension of Progressivism, elements of which are argued also in Robert M. Crunden, *Ministers of Reform: The Progressives' Achievement in American Civilization, 1889–1920* (New York: Basic, 1982); and Carson, *Settlement Folk*.

49. DWSE (see note in the list of abbreviations) autobiographical notes, DWSE Papers.

50. Cited in Antler, *Lucy Sprague Mitchell*, 222.

51. MRB to Elizabeth Rogers, 17 November 1917, in Cott, *A Woman Making History: Mary Ritter Beard through Her Letters* (New Haven: Yale Univ. Press, 1991) (hereafter cited as *WMH*), 97–98.

52. Michael P. McCarthy, "Urban Optimism and Reform Thought in the Progressive Era," *Historian* 51, no. 2 (1989): 239–62, quotation on 262.

53. Each of the six reformers has left some manuscript collections; the Straights' papers are held in the Carl A. Kroch Library of Cornell University, the Beards' in the Roy O. West Library of DePauw University, and the Mitchells' in the Nicholas Murray Butler Library of Columbia University. DePauw has worked hard to make up for the Beards' destruction of some of their papers by accumulating new materials from relatives and correspondents, including recent accessions to do with the Beards' early years. Because I am interested more in the organizing principle of the family rather than in the thing itself, I have not suffered too greatly from the absence of letters between the two Beards: I want to know what they expected the idea of personal relationships to imply, and they have written about this elsewhere.

54. For the effects of World War I generally, see David M. Kennedy, *Over Here: The First World War and American Society* (New York: Oxford Univ. Press, 1980); cf. Neil A. Wynn, *From Progressivism to Prosperity: World War I and American Society* (New York: Holmes & Meier, 1986).

55. MRB, "Twentieth Century Woman," 103–4.

56. WCM, "Backward Art."

57. HC, *Willard Straight* (New York: Macmillan, 1924), 458–59.

58. For this critique of liberalism, see Peter Steinfels, *The Neo-conservatives: The Men Who are Changing America's Politics* (New York: Simon & Schuster, 1979).

59. Glenn C. Altschuler and Stuart F. Blumin, introduction to *Rude Republic: Americans and Their Politics in the Nineteenth Century* (Princeton, N.J.: Princeton Univ. Press, 2000), 9–10.

60. See for example Dixon, *Perfecting the Family*; also Blumin, *The Emergence of the Middle Class: Social Experience in the American City, 1760–1900* (New York: Cambridge Univ. Press, 1989); Mary P. Ryan, *Cradle of the Middle Class: The Family in Oneida County, New York, 1760–1865* (New York: Cambridge Univ. Press, 1981).

61. See, for example, Newt Gingrich, *To Renew America* (New York: Harper-Collins, 1995); for evidence of Gingrich's opposition to the Progressives' view of civilization, note his discussion of the "so-called business cycle," 67; CAB to David Lilienthal, 6 and 7 January 1944, Beard Papers—he was praising Lilienthal's work at the Tennessee Valley Authority. This argument about the liberal view of civilization runs counter to that in Bederman, *Manliness and Civilization*.

62. Freedman makes a similar point about the way separatist institutions change the perspective of all women: "The history of separatism also helps explain why the politics of lesbian feminism have been so important in the revival of the women's movement. Lesbian feminism, by affirming the primacy of women's relationships with each other and by providing an alternative feminist culture, forced many nonlesbians to reevaluate their relationships with men, male institutions, and male values." Freedman, "Separatism as Strategy," 524.

63. For similarly problematized analyses reaching somewhat different conclusions, see Lakoff, *Moral Politics*, and Donzelot, *Policing*.

64. See, for example, William Hard, "Efficiency and the 'He-Man,'" *New Republic*, 9 March 1918, 165–67.

65. On the relation of elites to the public in the Progressive era, see Leon Fink, *Progressive Intellectuals and the Dilemmas of Democratic Commitment* (Cambridge: Harvard Univ. Press, 1997). Fink discusses the sometimes disastrous effects of Progressive ambitions on experimental marriages—in this case an explicitly socialist experiment, rather than the liberal ones considered here—in his chapter on Anna Strunsky Walling, 147–83.

66. See E. J. Dionne, *They Only Look Dead: Why Progressives Will Dominate the Next Political Era* (New York: Simon & Schuster, 1996); Jacob Weisberg, *In Defense of Government: The Fall and Rise of Public Trust* (New York: Scribner's, 1996); Michael Tomasky, *Left for Dead: The Life, Death, and Possible Resurrection of Progressive Politics in America* (New York: Free Press, 1996); Michael Lind, *The Next American Nation: The New Nationalism and the Fourth American Revolution* (New York: Free Press, 1995); Ben J. Wattenberg, *Values Matter Most: How*

Republicans or Democrats or a Third Party Can Win and Renew the American Way of Life (New York: Free Press, 1995); see also President Bill Clinton's remarks on an effort to "mend our social fabric" that "began with the Progressive Era," "Remarks by the President, Pennsylvania State University Graduate School Commencement," White House press release, 10 May 1996.

1. DOROTHY WHITNEY AND WILLARD STRAIGHT

1. Leslie Kaufman-Rosen, "Newt's One-Woman Focus Group," *Newsweek,* 13 February 1995, 31.

2. Undated stationery, late 1913 or early 1914, bears the "liberal democracy" motto. DWSE Papers.

3. Cited in W. A. Swanberg, *Whitney Father, Whitney Heiress* (New York: Scribner's, 1980), 89. On Whitney, see Allan Nevins, *Grover Cleveland: A Study in Courage* (New York: Dodd, Mead, 1933), 507; see also Mark D. Hirsch, *William C. Whitney: Modern Warwick* (New York: Dodd, Mead, 1948).

4. DWSE autobiographical notes, DWSE Papers.

5. *Junior League National Bulletin* 1, June 1915, 6.

6. Ibid. 2 (December 1915): 1.

7. "Society Girls Band Together for Ministering to the Poor," *New York Herald,* 3 January 1909, clipping in DWSE Papers. The article was a review of the organization's history.

8. Anne Firor Scott, "Women's Voluntary Associations: From Charity to Reform," in *Lady Bountiful Revisited: Women, Philanthropy, and Power,* ed. Kathleen D. McCarthy (New Brunswick: Rutgers Univ. Press, 1990), 48. On the history of home visits, see Christine Stansell, *City of Women: Sex and Class in New York City, 1789–1860* (New York: Knopf, 1986), 64ff; see also Addams, *Democracy and Social Ethics,* 13ff.

9. "H. P. Whitney Gets Half," *New York Tribune,* 25 February 1904, clipping in DWSE Papers; DWSE autobiographical notes, DWSE Papers.

10. DWSE diary, 21 December 1904 and 30 January 1905, DWSE Papers.

11. DWSE diary, 16 September, 10 December 1905; BB to DWSE in letters of May and June 1912; "prejudice" in BB to DWSE, 24 May 1912, DWSE Papers.

12. DWSE autobiographical notes, DWSE Papers; DWSE diary, 5 February 1908.

13. DWSE to Katharine Barney Barnes, 29 January 1910, DWSE Papers.

14. DWSE diary for April and May 1911; *Junior League Bulletin* 1 (December 1914): 5; "Clubhouse for Girls," *New York Times,* 16 May 1911, 8:3.

15. "Working Girls Now Live Like the 400," *New York Daily News,* 24 June 1922; clipping in DWSE Papers.

16. "Society Leader Pleading for Women's Suffrage at Hotel Astor Luncheon," *New York World,* 16 January 1909; see also for example DWSE diary, 6 May 1911; "Wealthy Women Who are Attempting to Solve Problems of To-Day," *New York*

Herald, 26 January 1913, clippings in DWSE Papers; *Bulletin* 1, April 1915, 5. On avoiding suffrage in favor of less divisive issues, see Karen Blair, *The Clubwoman as Feminist: True Womanhood Redefined, 1868–1914* (New York: Holmes & Meier, 1980), 44. On the ostensibly masculine activities of women's organizations, see Lori D. Ginzberg, *Women and the Work of Benevolence: Morality, Politics, and Class in the Nineteenth-Century United States* (New Haven: Yale Univ. Press, 1990), 37 and 59. On the characteristically feminine, hands-on approach to reform, see, for example, Linda Gordon, *Pitied but Not Entitled: Single Mothers and the History of Welfare* (New York: Free Press, 1994) and Gordon's discussion of "the female relational, nurturant ego" in "Putting Children First: Women, Maternalism and Welfare in the Early Twentieth Century," *U.S. History as Women's History*, 73.

17. DWSE autobiographical notes, DWSE Papers.

18. DWSE diary, 2 February 1905, 22 May 1907 and 4 May 1911, 28 April 1908, 13 February 1907, 19 January 1905.

19. DWSE diary, 30 April 1909.

20. DWSE diary, 5 February, 17 March, 12 May, 18 May 1911.

21. DWSE diary, 3 February 1906.

22. Quoted in Emma Straight's diary, as cited in HC, *Straight*, 16.

23. HC, *Straight*, 32; for "Foster Father," see, for example, 15 December 1908, HMS Papers.

24. WDS to DWSE, March 1915, DWSE Papers; WDS to HC, 29 December 1914, WDS Papers; cited in Helen Dodson Kahn, *The Great Game of Empire: Willard D. Straight and American Far Eastern Policy*, Ph.D. diss., Cornell, 1968, 154; see also Eric Rauchway, "Willard Straight and the Paradox of Liberal Imperialism," *Pacific Historical Review* 66, no. 3 (1997): 363–97.

25. HMS, *Syllabus of Lectures on the History of the British Empire* (Ithaca: Ithaca Journal, 1901), 17 and 40; HMS, "Four Phases of Kipling's Work," *University Chronicle* (Berkeley) 3 (1900): 249.

26. WDS inscribed a copy of his privately printed 1912 speech, *China's Loan Negotiations*, to HMS as "from one whom he sent to China." HMS's copy of the speech is in the general circulating collection at the University of California, Berkeley.

27. See, for example, Robert Hart to James Duncan Campbell, 24 May 1903, *The I.G. in Peking: Letters of Robert Hart, Chinese Maritime Customs, 1868–1907*, ed. John King Fairbank, Katherine Frost Bruner, and Elizabeth MacLeod Matheson (Cambridge: Harvard Univ. Press, 1975), 2:1360.

28. WDS diary, 28 September 1903, WDS Papers.

29. WDS to HMS, 11 August 1909, HMS Papers.

30. WDS diary, 22 June 1905.

31. Kahn, 18; WDS "As a Tramp Would See It: The Story of a Little Journey through Northern New York," in *The Era* 33 (1900–1): 33; for WDS portraiture, see, for example, HC, *Straight*, 201. WDS, *China's Loan Negotiations*, 32. On the relation of empathy to liberal moral behavior, see Lakoff, 114ff.

32. Bederman, *Manliness and Civilization*, 26.

33. HMS, "Four Phases," 249; WDS diary, 4 October 1902.

34. *Cornellian and Class Book*, 1901; WDS to Whitney Willard Straight, 10 December 1917, WDS Papers; WDS to HMS, undated 1903, and WDS to HMS, 3 July 1906, HMS Papers.

35. Sao-ke Alfred Sze, *Reminiscences of His Early Years*, trans. Amy C. Wu (Washington, D.C.: 1962), 19; Alfred Sze to HMS, 2 December 1899, HMS Papers.

36. HMS, "Four Phases," 248–49.

37. WDS diary, 4 October 1902.

38. Ibid., 268; WDS to HMS, 25 November 1901, HMS Papers.

39. Emily S. Rosenberg, "Revisiting Dollar Diplomacy: Narratives of Money and Manliness," *Diplomatic History* 22, no. 2 (1998): 174.

40. WDS to HC, 1 August 1917, WDS Papers.

41. George Marvin, cited in HC, *Straight*, 255. On Straight's role in the State Department, see HC, *Straight*, and also Walter LaFeber, *The Clash: U.S.-Japanese Relations throughout History* (New York: Norton, 1997), 65–127 passim.

42. On Roosevelt, realpolitik, and Japan, see LaFeber, *The Clash*, 91ff; cf. Frank Ninkovich, "Theodore Roosevelt: Civilization as Ideology," *Diplomatic History* 10, no. 3 (1986): 221–45.

43. WDS to DWSE, 5 April 1910, DWSE Papers (he was writing about earlier events); see also Michael H. Hunt, *Frontier Defense and the Open Door: Manchuria in Chinese-American Relations, 1895–1911* (New Haven: Yale Univ. Press, 1973), 154ff; WDS to George Marvin, 5 April 1908 and 14 April 1908, WDS Papers; see also HC, *Straight*, 258–60.

44. DWSE note to herself, undated (1907?), Grand Hotel stationery, DWSE Papers.

45. WDS to DWSE, 20 January 1909, DWSE Papers.

46. Idem, 4 September 1909.

47. DWSE diary, 1910, DWSE Papers.

48. DWSE to Katharine Barney Barnes, 18 November 1909, DWSE Papers.

49. Idem, 11 February 1910.

50. DWSE Grand Hotel note.

51. Maurice Hewlett, *Open Country: A Comedy with a Sting* (New York: Scribner's, 1909), 67.

52. WDS to DWSE, 6 January 1910, DWSE Papers. Such peculiar use of dashes characterizes the letters of both Straights.

53. WDS to DWSE, 9 January 1910, DWSE Papers.

54. Hewlett, *Open Country*, 125.

55. Quoted in WDS to DWSE, 14 August 1910, DWSE Papers.

56. WDS to DWSE, 7 August 1910, DWSE Papers.

57. Idem, 12 August 1910.

58. "Willard Straight, Who Is to Marry Dorothy Whitney," *New York Times*, 30 July 1911, clipping in DWSE Papers.

59. B. H. Friedman, *Gertrude Vanderbilt Whitney: A Biography.* (Garden City: Doubleday, 1978), 296.

60. DWSE to WDS, 7 February 1911, DWSE Papers.

61. WDS to DWSE, 13 September 1910, DWSE Papers.

62. DWSE, Grand Hotel note, and diary, 8 January 1912, DWSE Papers.

63. DWSE diary, 19 October 1911.

64. DWSE diary, 10, 18, 27 November 1911.

65. DWSE diary, 12 February, March, passim, and 4 April 1912.

66. Marainne Bend to DWSE, 8 September 1911, DWSE Papers.

67. WDS to Marainne Bend, 23 June 1911; WDS to BB, 1 December 1911 and 13 May 1912, DWSE Papers.

68. BB to DWSE, 12 May 1912, DWSE Papers.

69. BB to DWSE, 24 May 1912, DWSE Papers.

70. BB to DWSE, 23 June 1912, DWSE Papers.

71. DWSE diary, 10 August 1912, DWSE papers.

72. H. G. Wells, *Marriage* (1912; reprint, New York: Duffield, 1913), 416, 504.

73. "Mrs. Straight Refuses to Talk,' *New York Press*, 26 October 1912, DWSE Papers.

74. DWSE diary, 21 October 1912, DWSE Papers.

75. DWSE diary, 6 November and the rest of the month, 1912.

76. WDS to DWSE, 4 September 1910, DWSE Papers.

77. DWSE to WDS, undated 1912, DWSE Papers.

78. Idem, 11 July 1913.

79. WDS to DWSE, 13 September 1910, DWSE Papers.

80. DWSE to WDS, 31 March 1918, DWSE Papers; she was recalling her earlier feelings.

81. Wells, *Marriage,* 496.

82. DWSE diary, 8 June 1913.

83. DWSE to WDS, 31 March 1918, DWSE Papers; in this letter, as before, she was recalling her earlier feelings.

84. Herbert Croly, *The Promise of American Life* (1909; Boston: Northwestern Univ. Press, 1989).

85. WDS to HC, 29 December 1914, WDS Papers.

86. DWSE diary, 8 November 1913.

87. HC to DWSE, undated 1914, DWSE Papers; David W. Levy, *Herbert Croly of The New Republic: The Life and Thought of an American Progressive* (Princeton: Princeton Univ. Press, 1985), 199.

88. Bruce Bliven, "The First Forty Years," *New Republic*, 22 November 1954, 6.

89. Felix Frankfurter, *Felix Frankfurter Reminisces* (New York: Reynal, 1960), 92.

90. HC to WDS, 19 November 1914, WDS Papers. See also DWSE to WDS, 22 March 1916 and 19 October 1918 for descriptions of Straight at *New Republic* dinners.

91. Croly on the radicals: HC to WDS, 29 November 1914, WDS Papers; Hackett on HC and Lippmann: Francis Hackett, *American Rainbow: Early Rem-*

iniscences (New York: Liveright, 1971), 287–89; on the subject of Walter Lippmann, see also Charles A. Beard (who unofficially served in Willard's role at the *New Republic* for some time after his death) to Maury Maverick, 8 September (no year stated, but 193–), Beard Papers; Littell on Willard, Philip Littell to DWSE, 10 December 1918, DWSE Papers; Levy, 205; Philip Littell to DWSE, 10 December 1918, DWSE Papers; WDS to Henry Prather Fletcher, 15 September 1915, WDS Papers; "Willard Straight Retires," *New York Times,* 18 September 1915, 13:4; Walter Lippmann to WDS and DWSE, 23 May 1917, DWSE Papers.

92. Gerald Gunther, *Learned Hand: The Man and the Judge* (New York: Knopf, 1994), 200.

93. Herbert Croly, *Progressive Democracy* (New York: Macmillan, 1914).

94. *Progressive Democracy,* 211ff, recapitulates Croly's speech on the founding of the *New Republic,* which is in the WDS Papers. On the report, see HC, *Straight,* 472.

95. Ibid.

96. DWSE to WDS, 22 March 1916, DWSE Papers.

97. Michael Young, *The Elmhirsts of Dartington: The Creation of an Utopian Community* (London: Routledge, 1982), 72.

98. HC to DWSE, 20 April 1914, DWSE Papers.

99. Idem, 4 November 1914.

100. DWSE to WDS, 23 December 1914, DWSE Papers; see *New Republic,* 5 December 1914, 19–20 and 20–22.

101. DWSE to WDS, 17 March 1916, DWSE Papers.

102. Francis Hackett, "The Sacred Cow," *New Republic,* 3 June 1916, 116, and "Father Blakely States the Issue," *New Republic,* 29 July 1916, 319–20.

103. WDS to HC, 5 March 1915, WDS Papers; S. G. T., "Philanthropy or Social Leadership?" *New Republic,* 27 March 1915, 208–9.; DWSE to WDS, 29 December 1914, DWSE Papers; DWSE to WDS, 25 December 1914, DWSE Papers.

104. DWSE to WDS, 21 February 1918, DWSE Papers.

105. HC, *Straight,* 474.

106. "A Letter from Mr. Straight," *New Republic,* 28 October 1916, 313–14.

107. Berkeley Toeby (circulation chief of the *New Republic*) to WDS, 23 November 1916, DWSE Papers.

108. Charles Forcey, *The Crossroads of Liberalism: Croly, Weyl, Lippmann, and the Progressive Era, 1900–1925* (New York: Oxford Univ. Press, 1961), 334n.

2. MARY RITTER AND CHARLES BEARD

1. Leon Edel, "The Man in the Woman," review of *Willa: The Life of Willa Cather,* by Phyllis C. Robinson, *New Republic* 189, no. 20 (14 November 1983): 34–36; quotation on 34.

2. Cited in Cott, *WMH,* ix. Ever since Ellen Nore's excellent biography of CAB in 1983, it has been commonplace to note the joint character of the Beards'

joint works. Nancy Cott especially has drawn out the extent to which MRB's concerns gave *The Rise of American Civilization* its scope beyond political history. I have gratefully drawn on these works but am focusing here on a different problem: the extent to which the Beards, both separately and together, used a parental and familial model to justify their reform efforts. The nature of the collaboration (which was, the Beards frequently insisted, private) is not as important here as the fact of the collaboration and the conclusions it led them to—specifically, the usefulness of marriage and the family as a source of Progressive reform—and I argue here that this familial ideal gave an ideological unity to their various efforts. See Ellen Nore, *Charles A. Beard: An Intellectual Biography* (Carbondale: Southern Illinois Univ. Press, 1983), 112–13; Thomas Bender, "The New History: Then and Now," *Reviews in American History* 12, no. 4 (December 1984): 612–22; Cott, *WMH*; and Cott, "Two Beards."

3. These letters, along with others the archivists have collected from various Beard children and grandchildren, are in the Beard Papers at DePauw University. The collection also includes many of MRB's later letters, in which she often described the early years of her marriage and work with CAB. These letters, which frequently retell the same or similar episodes, are clearly an effort to replace what had been destroyed—which is to say, MRB's sense of the Beards' story—and to supply some, albeit later, documentation of it.

4. Cited in Cott, *WMH*, 339 n. 2.

5. Ibid., 11.

6. CAB to Eric Goldman, 13 February (1948?); CAB to Carl Becker, 4 February (year not stated; 1930s?); re Vachel Lindsay and the Beards, see CAB to Ernest Hopkins, 25 July 1922; Beard Papers. On "spacious days," see Vachel Lindsay, "Litany of the Heroes," *Collected Poems* (New York: Macmillan, 1925), 193.

7. On the Beards' general relationship to the public record, see Bender, "New History," 615.

8. On the Beards, see MRB, *The Making of Charles A. Beard: An Interpretation* (New York: Exposition, 1955), 9–12; on the Ritters, see MRB to Thomas E. Bonner, undated, but 1954, Beard Papers and also Cott, *WMH*, 4–5. Ann J. Lane attributes MRB's politics to her mother—a theory Nore doubts; see *Mary Ritter Beard: A Sourcebook*, ed. Ann J. Lane (New York: Schocken, 1977), 13ff, and Nore, *Charles Beard*, 21.

9. *DePauw Mirage*, 1899, DePauw University Archives. It was common for coeducational universities to permit men to visit women's dormitories and be allowed some privacy provided they kept sufficient illumination going.

10. *DePauw Mirage*, 1897, DePauw University Archives.

11. *Mirage*, 1899.

12. William Warren Sweet, *Indiana Asbury-DePauw University, 1837–1937* (New York: Abingdon, 1937), 149.

13. Claude G. Bowers, *Beveridge and the Progressive Era* (New York: Literary Guild, 1932), 18.

14. Registrar's record of Charles Beard, DePauw University Archives; MRB, *Making of Charles Beard*, 15.

15. Lawrence Goodwyn, *The Populist Moment: A Short History of the Agrarian Revolt in America* (New York: Oxford Univ. Press, 1978), 178–79.

16. Bowers, 16.

17. *DePauw Mirage*, 1899.

18. *Fifty-eighth Yearbook of DePauw University* (1895–1896): 41–42; Beard's affinity for Dr. Stephenson's courses is mentioned in the *DePauw Mirage*, 1899.

19. CAB's biographer Ellen Nore discusses this topic at some length; see Nore, *Charles Beard,* 10ff.

20. Registrar's Records of Charles Beard and Mary Ritter, DePauw University Archives.

21. Lane, 16.

22. MRB, "Memory and Human Relations," *Kappa Kappa Gamma Key*, December 1936, Beard Papers.

23. Frederick York Powell to CAB, 3 March 1899, Beard Papers. For "nicest American" see Burleigh Taylor Wilkins, "Frederick York Powell and Charles A. Beard: A Study in Anglo-American Historiography and Thought," *American Quarterly* 11 (spring 1959): 21–39; quotation on 23.

24. Wilbur K. Kurtz to Eleanor Commack, undated, Beard Papers.

25. Barbara K. Turoff, *Mary Beard as Force in History*, Monograph Series, Number 3 (Dayton: Wright State Univ. Press, 1979), 15.

26. "Beard–Ritter: DePauw Graduates Unite in Marriage," *DePauw Palladium,* 12 March 1900.

27. CAB, "An Interesting Letter," *DePauw Palladium*, 17 October 1898.

28. E. P. Thompson, *The Making of the English Working Class* (New York: Random House, 1964); see for example 807.

29. "Oxford Movement: The Success of Charles Beard '98 and Walter Vrooman" *DePauw Palladium*, 10 April 1899. On the Vroomans, see Ross E. Paulson, *Radicalism and Reform: The Vrooman Family and American Social Thought, 1837–1937* (Lexington: Univ. of Kentucky Press, 1968).

30. CAB had "heroic" but unspecified help from Mary Payne Giles. See CAB to Lionel Elvin, 18 December 1945, cited in "Documents: Charles A. Beard on the Founding of Ruskin Hall," ed. Burleigh Taylor Wilkins, *Indiana Magazine of History* 52 (September 1956): 277–84; esp. 283.

31. "The Ruskin Hall Movement in Wigan: The Wonderful Century," *Wigan Observer and District Advertiser* 21 December 1900; clipping in Beard Papers. There are also newspaper accounts of speeches at Chorley and Macclesfield.

32. Ibid.

33. Ibid. See also CAB, *The Industrial Revolution,* 2d ed. (London: Allen & Unwin, 1902 (1st ed. 1901)), 37–38.

34. See also Nore, *Charles Beard,* 24–25.

35. Cited in Genevieve P. Herrick, "Women in the News," *Country Gentlemen,* May 1936, clipping in Beard Papers.

36. On the original statement of the subjective and objective needs for Pro-

gressive reform, see Addams, *Twenty Years at Hull House* (1910; reprint, New York: Penguin, 1961), 94ff.

37. On the "common autobiographical ploy" of the conversion experience in Progressives' own stories, see David M. Kennedy, *Birth Control in America: The Career of Margaret Sanger* (New Haven: Yale Univ. Press, 1970), 17. Turoff, *Mary Beard*, 16–17, doubts the force of this particular instance and also discusses the importance of conversion experiences.

38. MRB, "The Twentieth Century Woman Looking Around and Backward" and "The Nineteenth Century Woman Looking Forward," *Young Oxford* 2, no. 16 (1901): 119–22. Cott remarks on these essays in *WMH* and mentions their debt to Charlotte Perkins Gilman but does not note their focus on marriage as problem and solution. See *WMH*, 19–20; for example, "following Gilman, she envisioned collective solutions, such as communal cooking and laundry, to end 'household slavery.'" Cott does, however, mention MRB's interest in marriage in "Two Beards," at 282.

39. MRB, *Making of Charles Beard*, 20.

40. MRB, "Twentieth Century Woman," 101.

41. Ibid., 102–4.

42. MRB, "Nineteenth Century Woman," 119–22.

43. Ibid., 120. Cott makes a specific link between the idea of race progress and Gilman's critique of women's place in society, which MRB does seem to echo in her assertions of women's "oversexed" estate. But her cited authorities in critiquing modern marriage were Edward Carpenter, Havelock Ellis, Mrs. Frank Leslie (by way of a joke more than anything else), and, with highest approval, Elizabeth Cady Stanton. See Cott, *WMH*, 19–20; MRB, "Nineteenth Century Woman," 119ff.

44. On Pankhurst, see Emmeline Pankhurst, *My Own Story* (London: Eveleigh Nash, 1914). On visits to the Pankhursts, see William Beard and Miriam Beard Vagts, introduction to Beard microfilm, Beard Papers. It is possible that Miriam remembered some visits but she could have been only one year old or so at the time. The "spurred me" quotation is cited in *WMH*, 7.

45. MRB, *Making of Charles Beard*, 21.

46. CAB to Lionel Elvin, 18 December 1945, in Wilkins, "Founding of Ruskin," 284.

47. Cited in Cott, *WMH*, 10–11.

48. MRB to Leonora O'Reilly, 1 January 1912, ibid., 64.

49. Interview with William Beard, Eleanor Commack, Beard Papers.

50. Ernest Hopkins to CAB, 14 November 1922, Beard Papers. CAB's farmerly pronouncements are legendary. For example: "There are three kinds of farmers: tired farmers, retired farmers, and rubber-tired farmers"—CAB was the first kind (James A. Farrell, "America's Eminent Historian," *DePauw Alumnus*, January 1940; clipping in Beard Papers); "As long as there's corn in Indiana and hogs to eat the corn, Charlie Beard will bow to no man" (cited in MRB, *Making of Charles Beard*, 22).

51. For the description of the Beards' homestead, see MRB to Eula Gotcher, 23 October 1952, Beard Papers. On the Beards' suite in the Hotel des Artistes, see Nore, *Charles Beard,* 127; on parties, see, for example, CAB to H. L. Mencken, 12 April 1924, Beard Papers.

52. "New Ideas for the Training of Children," *New York Times,* 10 October 1909, 5:4. See also the discussion in Nore, *Charles Beard,* 236 n. 2.

53. MRB to Eula Gotcher, 23 October 1952, Beard Papers.

54. CAB to Lewis Mayers, 15 September 1911 ("bully") and 6 August 1912 ("Holy Ghost"), Beard Papers; MRB, "The Legislative Influence of Unenfranchised Women," *Annals of the American Academy of Political and Social Science* 56 (November 1914): 54–61; for their reluctance to be identified with TR's Progressivism, see, for example, CAB's description of TR as a "shifty gentleman," CAB to Robert La Follette, 14 May 1913, Beard Papers; MRB's scolding of John Chamberlain for depicting CAB as "a party Progressive follower of Theodore Roosevelt," MRB to John Chamberlain, 29 September 1951, Beard Papers; MRB note: "Beard did not engage in party politics of any kind," Beard Papers.

55. A remark of 1914 cited in *Charles A. Beard: An Observance of the Centennial of His Birth,* ed. Marvin C. Swanson (Greencastle, Ind.: DePauw University Press, 1974), 56.

56. CAB to William E. Dodd, 12 December 1921; CAB to Albert J. Beveridge, undated (1920?); Beard Papers.

57. MRB to Robert E. Thomas, 1 March 1952, Beard Papers.

58. Cott, "Two Beards," 279.

59. Cited in Howard Kennedy Beale, ed., *Charles A. Beard: An Appraisal* (Lexington: Univ. of Kentucky Press, 1954), 6.

60. CAB, "The Constitution of Oklahoma," *Political Science Quarterly* 24 (March 1909): 95–114, quotation on 114; CAB, "The Ballot's Burden," *Political Science Quarterly* 24 (December 1909): 598.

61. CAB to Robert La Follette, 14 May 1913, Beard Papers.

62. CAB, *The Supreme Court and the Constitution* (1912; revised 1938; reprint, Englewood Cliffs, N.J.: Prentice-Hall, 1962), 94 and 85.

63. CAB to John Fairlie, 10 July 1911, Beard Papers.

64. CAB, *American City Government: A Survey of Newer Tendencies* (New York: Century, 1912), 80, 94–109, 150. There are other examples of the theater of municipal education; see, for example, CAB's evident delight with the breathing dolls that show the benefits of good ventilation (281).

65. Ibid., ix, 12, 24–25, 311, 30. On this last point, cf. Thomas Bender, "The Historian and Public Life: Charles A. Beard and the City," *Intellect and Public Life: Essays on the Social History of Academic Intellectuals in the United States* (Baltimore: Johns Hopkins Univ. Press, 1993), 95.

66. MRB to Alice Paul (early 1913), Cott, *WMH,* 68; see Turoff, 22; Harriot Stanton Blatch and Alma Lutz, *Challenging Years: The Memoirs of Harriot Stanton Blatch* (New York: Putnam, 1940), 92–93; *The History of Woman Suffrage,* ed. Ida Husted Harper et al. (National American Woman Suffrage Association, 1922),

5: 378. Cott records MRB's early and sometimes vigorous efforts to persuade her husband to campaign for the suffrage in *WMH*, 342 n. 16.

67. William Beard and Miriam Beard Vagts, introduction to Beard microfilm, Beard Papers. For Paul's objections, see Cott, *WMH*, 351 n. 5.

68. Interview with William Beard, Eleanor Commack, Beard Papers.

69. MRB congressional testimony, Beard microfilm, Beard Papers.

70. Harper, *History*, 5:397.

71. See "Points to Wilson's Silence on Women," *New York Times*, 20 November 1914, 6:2; *New Republic*, 5 December 1914, 6; MRB to Alice Paul, 30 November 1914, Cott, *WMH*, 82.

72. CAB, "Woman Suffrage and Strategy," *New Republic*, 12 December 1914, 22–23.

73. Cited in Nore, *Charles Beard*, 63.

74. CAB to Max Farrand, 5 May 1913, Beard Papers.

75. Cited in Richard Ratcliffe, *Along the Banks of Brook Bezor: A History of the Spiceland Community* (n.p.. 1963), 31.

76. CAB, *An Economic Interpretation of the Constitution of the United States* (1913; reprint, New York: Free Press, 1986), 1, 24; CAB to Robert La Follette, 10 May 1913, Beard Papers.

77. Richard Hofstadter, *The Progressive Historians: Turner, Beard, Parrington* (Chicago: Univ. of Chicago Press, 1968), 211 and 207. On the impact of the book, see also John P. Diggins, "Power and Authority in American History: The Case of Charles A. Beard and His Critics," *American Historical Review* 86, no. 4 (October 1981): 701–30, esp. 702.

78. MRB to a Miss Dunn, 12 March 1914, Beard Papers.

79. MRB, "Legislative Influence." The article was part of a volume dedicated to the suffrage question and began with Jane Addams's assertion that women's suffrage was "a part of that evolutionary conception of self-government" (1).

80. Ibid., 54, 56, 60–61.

81. Ibid., 56, 61.

82. "Women Threaten Wilson," *New York Times*, 12 November 1917, 1:5; "Suffragists Call the President Weak," *New York Times*, 12 November 1916, 6:4.

83. Cited in Harper, *History*, 5:432; MRB and Florence Kelley, "Votes for Women; Amending State Constitutions: A Study of Constitutions which Lack Suffrage Amendments," June 1916, Beard Papers.

84. CAB, "Jefferson and the New Freedom," *New Republic*, 14 November 1914, 18–19.

85. CAB, *Economic Interpretation*, 22 n.

86. CAB to Lewis Mayers, 2 May 1912, Beard Papers.

87. Idem, 24 November 1911 and 31 January 1913, Beard Papers; CAB, *Contemporary American History, 1877–1913* (New York: Macmillan, 1914), v, 271ff, 379. CAB was here clearly developing an argument along lines similar to those of his friend James Harvey Robinson. See Robinson, *The New History* (New York: Macmillan, 1912). Cf. Cott, "Two Beards."

88. CAB, *American City Government*, 84–85.

89. MRB, *Women's Work in Municipalities*, National Municipal League Series (1915; reprint, New York: Arno, 1972).

90. Ibid., 170, vi, and 322.

91. Introduction to Beard microfilm, Beard Papers.

92. Cott, *WMH*, 15 and 342 n. 17, writes that MRB was the instigator of the coauthorship. Nore, *Charles Beard*, 47, mentions the Beards' interest in families in this work.

93. CAB and MRB, *American Citizenship* (1914; new and revised edition, New York: Macmillan, 1921), vi–vii.

94. Ibid., 7, 22–23, 25.

95. Ibid., 31–32.

96. Ibid., 74, 293.

97. MRB, "Legislative Influence," 61.

98. CAB, "The Biological Woman," *New York Times*, 18 July 1915, 6.10:1–3.

3. LUCY SPRAGUE AND WESLEY CLAIR MITCHELL

1. William James, *The Principles of Psychology* (1890; reprint, 2 vols. in 1, New York: Dover, 1950), 1:294; emphasis in the original.

2. Mark C. Smith, "Wesley Mitchell and the Quantitative Approach," in *Social Science in the Crucible: The American Debate over Objectivity and Purpose, 1918–1941* (Durham: Duke Univ. Press, 1994), 49–83, writes, "Beginning in the late 1800s with his research on business cycles and becoming more pronounced with his government service during World War I, Mitchell downgraded his concern for normative goals" (51). Cf. Jeff Biddle, "A Citation Analysis of the Sources and Extent of Wesley Mitchell's Reputation," *History of Political Economy* 28, no. 2 (1996): 137–69, where the significant shift comes after the war.

3. WCM to LSM, 5 December 1911, LSM Papers.

4. LSM, *Two Lives: The Story of Wesley Clair Mitchell and Myself* (New York: Simon & Schuster, 1953), 15–21.

5. WCM, ed., *What Veblen Taught: Selected Writings of Thorstein Veblen* (New York: Viking, 1936), xvi–xvii.

6. WCM to LSM, 18 October 1911, LSM Papers.

7. Cited in Arthur Frank Burns, ed., *Wesley Clair Mitchell, the Economic Scientist* (New York: National Bureau of Economic Research, 1952), 94.

8. Cited in LSM, *Two Lives*, 23.

9. See Thomas Wakefield Goodspeed, *The Story of the University of Chicago, 1890–1925* (Chicago: Univ. of Chicago Press, 1925), 33–72 passim.

10. See *Cap and Gown*, the university yearbook, for WCM's class of '96.

11. WCM to LSM, 18 October 1911, LSM Papers.

12. Horowitz, *Campus Life*, 14.

13. WCM to LSM, 18 October 1911, LSM Papers.

14. LSM, notes for a speech of 21 October 1949, LSM Papers; emphasis in the original.

15. Robert Westbrook, *John Dewey and American Democracy* (Ithaca: Cornell Univ. Press, 1991), 92.

16. Cited in LSM, *Two Lives*, 86.

17. WCM, *What Veblen Taught*, xxxvi.

18. Cited in Alfred Bornemann, *J. Laurence Laughlin: Chapters in the Career of an Economist* (Washington, D.C.: American Council on Public Affairs, 1940), 89.

19. J. Laurence Laughlin, "Some Recollections of Henry Adams," *Scribner's* May 1921, 578.

20. J. Laurence Laughlin, *The Study of Political Economy: Hints to Students and Teachers* (New York: Appleton, 1885), 139.

21. J. Laurence Laughlin, *Facts about Money, Including the Debate with W. H. Harvey* (Chicago: Weeks, 1895).

22. Cited in LSM, *Two Lives*, 85–86.

23. Laughlin, *Study of Political Economy*, 105.

24. WCM to LSM, 18 October 1911, LSM Papers.

25. WCM, *A History of the Greenbacks, with Special Reference to the Economic Consequences of Their Issue, 1862–1865* (Chicago: Univ. of Chicago Press, 1903), 419, 350.

26. Ibid., 419, 404.

27. "Steel Strikers Use Violence," *Chicago Tribune*, 3 September 1901; "Tinplate Men May End Strike," *Chicago Tribune*, 4 September 1901; "End of the Steel Strike," *Chicago Tribune*, 16 September 1901; on the Amalgamated, see Jesse S. Robinson, *The Amalgamated Association of Iron, Steel, and Tin Workers*, Johns Hopkins University Studies in Historical and Political Science 38, no. 2 (Baltimore: Johns Hopkins Univ. Press, 1920).

28. LSM, *Two Lives*, 13; LSM Oral History, 24.

29. LSM Oral History, 35.

30. LSM, *Two Lives*, 58.

31. LSM Oral History, 31.

32. Antler, *Lucy Sprague Mitchell*, 119.

33. LSM Oral History, 34.

34. LSM, *Two Lives*, 69.

35. LSM Oral History, 25–26.

36. LSM, *Two Lives*, 102–5.

37. Ibid., 115.

38. See record of Lucy Sprague, Radcliffe College Archives. On the exceptional Harvard Department of Philosophy, see Bruce Kuklick, *The Rise of American Philosophy: Cambridge, Massachusetts, 1860–1930* (New Haven: Yale Univ. Press, 1977).

39. Gertrude Stein, *The Autobiography of Alice B. Toklas* (New York: Vintage, 1933), 78.

40. LSM, *Two Lives*, 120.

41. Cited in Donald Fleming, "Harvard's Golden Age?" in Bernard Bailyn et al., *Glimpses of the Harvard Past* (Cambridge: Harvard Univ. Press, 1986), 87.

42. LSM, *Two Lives*, 121 and 51.

43. Ibid., 129, 133; LSM Oral History, 37–38.

44. LSM Oral History, 40–42; LSM, *Two Lives*, 194.

45. BIW to LSM, 1 October 1907, Presidents' Papers.

46. LSM to BIW, 6 June 1908; BIW to LSM, 9 June 1908; LSM to BIW, 18 September 1908; LSM to BIW, 16 November 1908, Presidents' Papers.

47. Cited in Lynn D. Gordon, *Gender and Higher Education in the Progressive Era* (New Haven: Yale Univ. Press, 1990), 59.

48. BIW to LS, 25 August 1908, Presidents' Papers; LSM Oral History, 44.

49. LSM, *Two Lives*, 139.

50. LSM Oral History, 49.

51. LSM, *Two Lives*, 207, 198.

52. Ibid., 51.

53. Cited in Gordon, 71.

54. LSM to BIW, 11 March 1911.

55. LSM to BIW, 6 January 1911, 27 December 1911, Presidents' Papers.

56. Otho Sprague to BIW, 31 January 1907, Presidents' Papers.

57. LSM to Women's Undergraduate Student Affairs Committee, 4 April 1911, Presidents' Papers.

58. LSM to BIW, 11 April 1911, Presidents' Papers.

59. BIW to LSM, 10 April 1911, 11 April 1911, 19 April 1911, Presidents' Papers. See also Antler, *Lucy Sprague Mitchell,* 102 and 381 nn. 17–21.

60. In her chapter "A Passionate Woman" (159–78), Antler provides a thorough analysis of the Mitchells' courtship correspondence, emphasizing the "contradiction . . . between her rational and her emotional self" that LSM felt tearing at her (174), and the dual passions LSM felt—for a reform career and for love. In this section, I offer a shorter account focusing on the Mitchells' logical argument about the use of marriage for ambitious men and women who wanted to separate themselves from the social claim of gender in the interest of pursuing a reform career. I am therefore more impressed with WCM's efforts to extricate himself from the demands of masculinity (cf. Antler, 174), though essentially in agreement on the ways in which LSM reconciled her traditional needs with her modern ones. Antler writes that this rational debate came to no conclusion; that only time spent together could reconcile the two hearts. Because in this study I am concerned with how the Mitchells' "experimental dual-career marriage" affected their "progressive reform in education and in economics" (Antler, *Lucy Sprague Mitchell,* xv), I have emphasized the extent to which the thoroughly rational WCM made a central place for irrational attractions in his intellectual work. Thus, rather than making a decision between the relative effi-

cacy of hearts and of minds in this negotiation, I have tried to make a case for the ideas of their hearts they carried in their minds, and therefore for their common interest in the social import of marriage and family.

61. LSM, *Two Lives*, 150.

62. WCM Diary, 5 February and the rest of 1905; see also 24 January 1907 and 10 February 1908, WCM Papers.

63. LSM, *Two Lives*, 175; WCM diary, 4 May 1909 and the rest of 1908–9, WCM Papers.

64. Cited in LSM, *Two Lives*, 175. For Mitchell as an economist of institution, see Biddle.

65. WCM, "The Rationality of Economic Activity," part 1, *Journal of Political Economy* 18, no. 2 (1910): 97–113; part 2 appeared in the following issue: 197–216; quotation at 208.

66. Ibid., part 1 at 98 and part 2 at 214.

67. WCM, "Money Economy and Modern Civilization," ed. Malcolm Rutherford, *History of Political Economy* 28, no. 3 (1996): 329–57; quotations at 329–30, 338–39, and 348.

68. Ibid., 356–57.

69. WCM, "Backward Art," 270.

70. Ibid., 272, 270, 273.

71. Ibid., 280.

72. LSM to WCM, 29 October 1911, LSM Papers.

73. WCM to LSM, 6 November 1911, LSM Papers.

74. Idem, 15 November 1911.

75. Idem, 5 December 1911.

76. Idem, 9 December 1911.

77. LSM to WCM, 19 December 1911, LSM Papers.

78. WCM to LSM, 24 December 1911, LSM Papers.

79. LSM to WCM, 26 December 1911, LSM Papers.

80. Antler, *Lucy Sprague Mitchell*, 190.

81. LSM, *Two Lives*, 210.

82. LSM to WCM, December 1911 (more exact date not stated), LSM Papers.

83. WCM to LSM, 15 December 1911, LSM Papers.

84. LSM, *Two Lives*, 232.

85. Ibid., 319.

86. "Rich Adopt Foundling," *New York Times*, 1 April 1914, 1:1; see Antler, *Lucy Sprague Mitchell*, 231.

87. WCM to Graham Wallas, 3 February 1915, WCM Papers.

88. WCM to LSM, 13 March 1914, LSM Papers.

89. Cited in LSM, speech of 21 October 1949, LSM Papers.

90. LSM, *Two Lives*, 273–74; see also Antler, *Lucy Sprague Mitchell*, 220ff.

91. Helen Boardman, *Psychological Tests: A Bibliography* (New York: Bureau of Educational Experiments, 1917).

92. LSM, *Here and Now Story Book: Two- to Seven- Year Olds; Experimental

Stories Written for the Children of the City and Country School (formerly the Play School) and the Nursery School of the Bureau of Educational Experiments, illus. Hendrik Willem Van Loon (New York: Dutton, 1921), 50.

93. Ibid., 8–20.

94. Ibid.; see, for example, "The Children's New Dresses."

95. Cited in Barbara Biber, "Lucy Sprague Mitchell, 1878–1967," 19, LSM Papers.

96. LSM, *Two Lives*, 150.

97. WCM, "Pecuniary Logic," notes, for the "The Money Economy" MS, WCM Papers.

98. WCM, *Business Cycles*, Memoirs of the University of California 3 (Berkeley: Univ. of California Press, 1913), 570–77.

99. Ibid., 599.

100. Ibid., vii.

101. Milton Friedman, "Wesley C. Mitchell as an Economic Theorist," *Journal of Political Economy* 58, no. 6 (1950): 470. See Biddle on Mitchell's influence.

4. WAR AND THE PROGRESSIVE FAMILY

1. Randolph S. Bourne, "A War Diary," in *Essays*, 40–41.

2. On reading TNR, see Antler, *Lucy Sprague Mitchell*, 204; WCM to Graham Wallas, 1 February 1915, WCM Papers.

3. WCM, notes for a talk at the Women's Political Union, 11 February 1915, WCM Papers.

4. See LSM, *Two Lives*, 296–97 and Herbert Heaton, *A Scholar in Action: Edwin F. Gay* (Cambridge: Harvard Univ. Press, 1952), 110.

5. Cited in Jean Ferriss Leich, *Architectural Visions: The Drawings of Hugh Ferriss* (New York: Whitney Library of Design, 1980), 52–53.

6. The Beards make this point in the last chapter of *Rise of American Civilization*, 2:786ff.

7. Cited in Pamela Scott and Antoinette J. Lee, *Buildings of the District of Columbia* (New York: Oxford Univ. Press, 1993), 49.

8. WDS diary, December-January 1914–15.

9. HC, *Straight*, 478; Swanberg, *Whitney*, 355.

10. See for example WDS, *The European War and Our Opportunity in Foreign Trade*, address before the Illinois Manufacturers' Association, 27 October 1914 (New York: n.p., 1914); WDS, *Foreign Relations and Oversea Trade*, address before the Southern Commercial Congress, 30 April 1915 (New York: n.p., 1915).

11. WDS, deceased alumnus file, Cornell Univ.

12. WDS diary, January 1915.

13. Allen F. Davis, "Welfare, Reform, and World War I," *American Quarterly* 19, no. 3 (1967): 516–33, quotations on 523.

14. WDS to DWSE, 23 December 1917, DWS E Papers.

15. WDS to Henry P. Fletcher, 16 September 1915, WDS Papers; WDS to DWSE, 21 December 1917, DWSE Papers; idem, 30 January 1918.

16. WDS to DWSE, 19, 21, 23 December 1917, DWSE Papers.

17. *Military Records of Cornell University in the World War* (Ithaca: Cornell, 1930), 118.

18. DWSE to WDS, 4 May 1918, DWSE Papers.

19. WDS to HC, 1 March 1915, WDS Papers.

20. Beard cited in Carol S. Gruber, *Mars and Minerva: World War I and the Uses of Higher Learning in America* (Baton Rouge: Louisiana State Univ. Press, 1975), 88.

21. Ibid., 151.

22. Frederic L. Paxson, ed., *War Cyclopedia* (Washington, D.C.: Government Printing Office, 1918).

23. Gruber, *Mars,* 148 n. 62.

24. Ibid., 198, 22, 35.

25. Ibid., 64, 39.

26. "Insults to the Flag," *New York Times,* 27 April 1917, 12:2.

27. CAB, "A Statement by Charles A. Beard," *New Republic,* 29 December 1917, 249.

28. MRB to Alice Paul, 14 December 1914, Cott, *WMH,* 82.

29. MRB to Carrie Chapman Catt, 8 June 1915, ibid., 88.

30. MRB to Alice Paul, 26 July 1916, ibid., 94.

31. Nore, *Charles Beard,* 73.

32. "Women's Fund for Hughes," *New York Times,* 3 July 1916, 5:5.

33. "Invitation to Woman Suffrage Party Patriotic Suffrage Meeting" for 20 October 1917, DWSE Papers.

34. "Suffrage Women Threaten Wilson," *New York Times,* 12 November 1917, 1:5.

35. "Suffragist Pickets Get Arrested Again," *New York Times,* 13 November 1917, 4:1.

36. MRB to Elizabeth Rogers, 17 November 1917, Cott, *WMH,* 97–98.

37. Unidentified clipping, 18 December 1917, DWSE Papers.

38. Cited in Gruber, *Mars,* 204.

39. Ibid., 188.

40. CAB to Abraham Flexner, 15 August 1931, Beard Papers.

41. CAB, "A Statement by Charles A. Beard," *New Republic,* 29 December 1917, 249.

42. Thomas R. Powell to CAB, Alfred Z. Reed to CAB, both dated 1917 (month mot stated); Frederick Breithut to CAB, 15 October 1917, Beard Papers.

43. Harriot Stanton Blatch to CAB, 19 October 1917, Beard Papers.

44. MRB note, n.d., Beard Papers.

45. MRB to Elizabeth Kalb, 9 April 1919, Cott, *WMH,* 98.

46. Alvin Johnson, *Pioneer's Progress: An Autobiography* (New York: Viking, 1952), 252; Bernard M. Baruch, *Baruch: The Public Years* (New York: Holt, 1960), 25ff.

47. Bernard M. Baruch, *American Industry in the War: A Report of the War Industries Board (1921)* (New York: Prentice-Hall, 1941), 115.

48. William Hard, "Retarding the Allies," *New Republic*, 29 December 1917, 238.

49. William Hard, "Efficiency and the 'He-Man,'" *New Republic*, 9 March 1918.

50. DWSE to WDS, 15 December 1917, DWSE Papers.

51. Idem, 24 March 1918.

52. Idem, 24 April 1918.

53. William Hard, "Wilson Defines Baruch," *New Republic*, 23 March 1918.

54. WCM to Edwin F. Gay, 3 June 1918, Gay Papers.

55. See, for example, Gay diary, 24 March 1919, Gay Papers.

56. Cited in LSM, *Two Lives*, 301.

57. See Antler, *Lucy Sprague Mitchell*, 222–23.

58. Johnson, *Pioneer's Progress*, 252.

59. Robert D. Cuff, *The War Industries Board: Business-Government Relations during World War I* (Baltimore: Johns Hopkins Univ. Press, 1973), 150.

60. WCM, *International Price Comparisons*, History of Prices during the War (Washington, D.C.: Government Printing Office, 1919), 3.

61. Ibid.

62. Minutes of a meeting of the statistical group, 28 January 1919, Gay Papers.

63. WCM, *International Price Comparisons*, 53 and 11.

64. For a discussion of propaganda as the price of liberal efficiency with reference to democratic conditions, see Kennedy, *Over Here*, 136–43.

65. Johnson, *Pioneer's Progress*, 256.

66. Heaton, *Scholar*, 125.

67. DWSE to WDS, 8 January 1918, DWSE Papers.

68. Ralph M. Easley to WDS, 25 September 1917, WDS Papers.

69. WDS to Ralph Easley, September 1917, WDS Papers.

70. William Jay Schiefflin to DWSE, 27 August 1918, DWSE Papers.

71. DWSE to William Jay Schiefflin, 30 August 1918, DWSE Papers.

72. DWSE to WDS, 7 April 1916, DWSE Papers.

73. WDS to Theodore Roosevelt, 25 March 1916, WDS Papers.

74. Theodore Roosevelt to WDS, 14 July 1918, DWSE Papers.

75. Unidentified clipping, 8 January 1918, DWSE Papers.

76. WDS to DWSE, 18 March 1918, WDS Papers.

77. WDS to Whitney Willard Straight, 17 April 1918, WDS Papers.

78. See, for example, WDS to DWS, 31 March 1918, WDS Papers.

79. DWSE mentions the cable in a letter to WDS, 30 May 1918, DWSE Papers.

80. DWSE to WDS, 21 April 1918, DWSE Papers.

81. WDS to DWSE, 21 April 1918, WDS Papers.

82. DWSE to WDS, 24 April 1918 and 30 May 1918, DWSE Papers.

83. WDS to DWSE, 30 July 1918, WDS Papers.

84. WDS to HC, 1 January 1915, WDS Papers.

85. Robinson, *The New History*, 1 and 69.

86. See, for example, DWSE to WDS, 19 October 1918, DWSE Papers.

87. WDS to DWSE, 30 July 1918, WDS Papers.

88. DWSE to WDS, 4 May 1918, DWSE Papers.

89. DWSE to WDS, 19 October 1918, DWSE Papers.

90. DWSE to WDS, 19 October 1918, DWSE Papers.

91. WCM, notes for a talk at Greensboro, Vermont, 14 August 1920, WCM Papers.

92. WDS to DWSE, 30 July 1918, WDS Papers.

93. For another angle on the war's effect in breaking up onetime allies, see James J. Connolly, *The Triumph of Ethnic Progressivism: Urban Political Culture in Boston, 1900–1925* (Cambridge: Harvard Univ. Press, 1998).

94. Cited in HC, *Straight*, 527.

95. See, for example, WDS to DWSE, 21 April 1918, WDS Papers.

96. *New York Evening Telegram*, 17 March 1918, DWSE Papers.

97. DWSE to WDS, 15 November 1918, DWSE Papers.

98. Ronald Steel, *Walter Lippmann and the American Century* (London: Bodley Head, 1980), 128–43; see C. K. Leith to Edwin F. Gay, 24 March 1919, Gay Papers: "The fourteen points were written by the Inquiry and transmitted through Colonel House." According to this memorandum, the House of Morgan was another unofficial negotiating entity; apparently Thomas Lamont was supposed to try to persuade the British and the French to reduce their reparations demands.

99. Undated memorandum, Gay Papers.

100. WCM, International Price Comparisons, 53.

101. See WDS to HC, 7 November 1918, WDS Papers.

102. "For Congress of Nations," *New York Times*, 21 January 1916, 9:4; see also CAB to Huntington Gilchrist, 24 February 1920, Beard Papers.

103. See E. F. Gay, notes on a conversation with Herbert Hoover, 18 November 1926, Gay Papers.

104. C. K. Leith to E. F. Gay, 24 March 1919, Gay Papers; emphasis in the original.

105. Steel, *Lippman*, 149.

106. Walter Lippmann to DWSE, 1 December 1918, WDS Papers.

107. WCM to LSM, 11 November 1918, cited in LSM, *Two Lives*, 300.

108. Heaton, *Scholar*, 196.

109. E. F. Gay, "Outline of the Problem," 1926, E. F. Gay Papers.

110. Johnson, *Pioneer's Progress*, 272.

111. WCM, talk at Greensboro, Vermont, 14 August 1920, WCM Papers.

112. LSM, *Two Lives*, 303–5.

113. DWSE to WDS, 6 February 1918, DWSE Papers.

114. See DWSE to WDS, 4 May 1918; "Start $100,000,000 Red Cross Drive," *Evening Mail*, 26 May 1917, DWSE Papers; unidentified clipping, DWSE Papers.

115. DWSE, essay on 11 November 1918, DWSE Papers.

116. DWSE, notes, n.d., DWSE Papers.

117. DWSE, essay on 11 November 1918, DWSE Papers.

118. DWSE to WDS, 3 November 1918, DWSE Papers.

119. "Questions for American Conservatives," *New Republic*, 21 September 1918, 213.

120. *Military Records of Cornell University in the World War*, 118.

121. Steel, *Lippmann*, 151.

122. "Willard D. Straight," *New Republic*, 7 December 1918, 163.

5. THE NARRATIVE OF PROGRESS VERSUS THE LOGIC OF EVENTS

1. John Barth, *The Tidewater Tales: A Novel* (New York: Fawcett Columbine, 1987), 142.

2. LSM, *Two Lives*, 408.

3. Bourne, "The State," in *Essays*, 71 and 75.

4. "Lists Americans as Pacifists," *New York Times*, 25 January 1919, 1:4.

5. "On Pacifist List, but Serve Nation," *New York Times*, 26 January 1919, 8:1.

6. LSM, *Two Lives*, 245.

7. Johnson, *Pioneer's Progress*, 275.

8. "Society League Starts a Revolt," *New York Times*, 17 February 1919, 1:2; also *New York Palladium*, 18 February 1919, clipping in DWSE Papers.

9. "Explains Lecture Plan," *New York Times*, 18 February 1919, 11:4.

10. *Town Topics*, 25 October 1919, clipping in DWSE Papers.

11. Johnson, *Pioneer's Progress*, 275.

12. WCM, notes on a talk at Greensboro, WCM Papers. Hereafter cited as Greensboro talk.

13. WDS to DWSE, 30 July 1918, DWSE Papers.

14. CAB to Carl Becker, 4 February (1930s), Beard Papers.

15. Greensboro talk.

16. *Rise of American Civilization* 2:639–40.

17. Cited in Nore, *Charles Beard*, 91.

18. Greensboro talk.

19. Johnson, *Pioneer's Progress*, 279.

20. Greensboro talk and letters to the *Evening Post*, 5 February and 31 March 1920, WCM Papers.

21. See Johnson, *Pioneer's Progress*, 281ff; Peter Rutkoff and William B. Scott, *New School: A History of the New School for Social Research* (New York: Free Press, 1986), 29ff; Nore, *Charles Beard*, 90; and LSM, *Two Lives*, 342.

22. CAB to Lewis Mayer, 11 October 1924, Beard Papers.

23. LSM, *Two Lives,* 408.

24. Nicholas Murray Butler to WCM, 7 March 1922, WCM Papers; *New York Times,* 19 March 1922, 2.8:3.

25. Johnson, *Pioneer's Progress,* 273.

26. LSM, *Two Lives,* 349–62.

27. Lawrence A. Cremin, *The Transformation of the School: Progressivism in American Education, 1876–1957* (New York: Knopf, 1961), 181.

28. LSM, *Two Lives,* 459.

29. Ibid.

30. See, for example, LSM 1935 speech on the BEE or LSM speech on John Dewey, 21 October 1949, LSM Papers.

31. See, for example, WCM, "The Rationality of Economic Activity," 97.

32. See, for example, WCM, draft essay for the *New York Herald Tribune* on public works, 5 June 1931, WCM Papers; WCM to Herbert Hoover, 3 August 1921, WCM Papers.

33. LSM, 1935 speech on the BEE or LSM speech, October 1949, on Dewey.

34. For another interpretation of social science in Mitchell's cosmology, see Smith, *Social Science.*

35. MRB, *A Short History of the American Labor Movement* (1920; reprint, New York: Greenwood, 1968), v.

36. MRB, notes on the back of a letter of 1922, Beard Papers.

37. MRB, *Short History,* 154, 192, 9, 113.

38. MRB to Elizabeth Kalb, 9 April 1919, Cott, *WMH.*

39. MRB to Elsie Hill, 10 July 1921, ibid.

40. Ibid. On DWSE, Kelley, and Hamilton, see "Open Fund to Fight Women's Equality," *New York Times,* 16 May 1922, 19:1, and "Equal Rights," ibid., 17 May 1922, 18:4.

41. "Borah Makes Plea for War Prisoners," 12 March 1923, unidentified clipping, DWSE Papers.

42. Report of the Women's Emergency Committee of the European Relief Council, 1 March 1921, DWSE Papers.

43. "Society to Eat Luncheon Made Entirely from Rice," 24 January 1921, unidentified clipping in DWSE Papers.

44. DWSE to Friends of the Pueblo, 29 January 1923, DWSE Papers.

45. Young, *Elmhirsts,* 72.

46. Cited in Michael Straight, *After Long Silence* (New York: Norton, 1983), 24.

47. Cited in Young, *Elmhirsts,* 62.

48. Leonard K. Elmhirst, *The Straight and Its Origin* (Ithaca: Willard Straight Hall, 1975), 21.

49. Cited in Elmhirst, *The Straight,* 113.

50. DWSE, autobiographical notes, DWSE Papers.

51. HC to DWSE, 17 June 1924, DWSE Papers.

52. Elmhirst, *The Straight,* 96–97.

53. LSM, *Two Lives,* 62.

54. Ibid., 259.

55. Ibid., 540; emphasis in the original.

56. Christopher Milne, *The Enchanted Places* (London: Eyre Methuen, 1974), 165.

57. Antler, *Lucy Sprague Mitchell,* 361.

58. Nore, *Charles Beard,* 96, 103, 105. See also the narrative for the film of the Beards' visit to Japan, Beard Papers.

59. Charles A. Beard and William Beard, *The American Leviathan: The Republic in the Machine Age* (New York: Macmillan, 1930).

60. Detlev Vagts, "A Grandson Remembers His Grandfather," in Swanson, 18.

61. Straight, *After Long Silence,* 24.

62. Young, *Elmhirsts,* 105.

63. Ibid., 160; emphasis in the original.

64. Michael Straight to the author, 12 August 1994.

65. Antler, *Lucy Sprague Mitchell,* 360–61.

66. For the most elegant recent development of this theme, see Rodgers, *Atlantic Crossings.*

67. LSM Oral History, 22.

68. Yusuke Tsurumi to CAB, 20 April 1922, Beard Papers; Shidzue Kato to MRB, 21 October (no year stated; 1920s), Beard Papers.

69. On "what is worth while," see pages 21 and 44 above.

70. Ibid.

EPILOGUE

1. Theodore Roosevelt, "The Men Whose Lot Has Been Hardest," *Kansas City Star,* 11 December 1918, clipping in DWSE Papers; Edith Wharton, "With the Tide," *New York Times,* 6 April 1919, 7.9:2.

2. "Talk of the Town," *New Yorker,* 26 November 1927, 19.

3. Ibid., 19 February 1927, 17.

4. *Rise,* 1-vol. edition (New York: Macmillan, 1930), vii.

5. For example, Richard Hofstadter thought the book "overpresses the economic interpretation"; Ellen Nore thinks the Beards "pull back" as they near a "class analysis." Hofstadter, *Progressive Historians,* 299; Nore, *Charles Beard,* 115.

6. Cott, "Two Beards," 282ff.

7. *Rise,* 2:435.

8. Adams appears in *Rise,* at 1:4 and 2:799–800. On CAB and Adams, see CAB, "Henry Adams," *New Republic,* 31 March 1920, 162–63; also CAB, introduction to *The Law of Civilization and Decay,* by Brooks Adams (1896; New York: Vintage,

1943); CAB somewhat improbably wrote Carl Becker that Adams had "added to our literature of joyful noise." CAB to Carl Becker, 14 May (1933?), Beard Papers.

9. Henry Adams, *History of the United States of America during the Administrations of Thomas Jefferson and James Madison* (1889–91; New York: Library of America, 1986), 54.

10. *Rise*, 1:643; 2:441ff.

11. Ibid., 2:453.

12. Ibid., 2:800.

13. Hofstadter, *Progressive Historians*, 299.

14. *Rise* (1930), xi.

15. *Rise* (1933), 2:837.

16. CAB and George H. E. Smith, *The Open Door at Home: A Trial Philosophy of National Interest* (New York: Macmillan, 1934) and *The Idea of National Interest: An Analytical Study of American Foreign Policy* (New York: Macmillan, 1934).

17. Franklin D. Roosevelt to CAB, 19 March 1936, Beard Papers. The Beards' keeping of this letter when they burned others reveals something about the record they hoped to preserve.

18. CAB to Daniel Carter Beard, 18 November 1938, and CAB to William E. Dodd, 12 April 1938, Beard Papers.

19. MRB kept a note from Eleanor Roosevelt of 14 November 1933 thanking her for a kind book review; see also MRB to Rosika Schwimmer, 14 February 1936, Cott, *WMH*.

20. Edgar E. Robinson to MRB, 27 March 1932, Beard Papers.

21. CAB to Abraham Flexner, 22 April 1931, Beard Papers.

22. MRB, "Memory and Human Relations," in *Kappa Kappa Gamma Key*, December 1936, Beard Papers.

23. MRB, *Woman as Force in History: A Study in Traditions and Realities* (New York: Macmillan, 1946); see Cott, *WMH*, 52ff.

24. CAB to S. Flexner, 18 October 1927, Beard Papers; CAB, *Whither Mankind? A Panorama of Modern Civilization* (New York: Longmans, Green, 1928); CAB, *Toward Civilization* (New York: Longmans, Green, 1930).

25. See David Lilienthal to CAB, 6 January 1944, and CAB to David Lilienthal, 7 January 1944, Beard Papers.

26. Cited in Nore, *Charles Beard*, 172.

27. CAB, "Giddy Minds and Foreign Quarrels: An Estimate of American Foreign Policy," *Harper's*, September 1939, 345; Hofstadter, *Progressive Historians*, 344; CAB, *President Roosevelt and the Coming of the War, 1941: A Study in Appearances and Realities* (New Haven: Yale Univ. Press, 1948), 579.

28. Samuel Eliot Morison, "History through a Beard," *By Land and by Sea: Essays and Addresses* (New York: Knopf, 1953).

29. MRB to Thomas E. Bonner, dated only 1954, Beard Papers.

30. "The Gilded Age" runs from page 383 to 479 in vol. 2 of the original *Rise*.

The longest chapter in the whole work is "Democracy, Romantic and Realistic" (99 pages), which concludes the first volume and sets the stage for the further development of democracy in the modern era.

31. *Rise*, 2:394–95.

32. Ibid., 2:399.

33. Ibid., 2:401–2.

34. Ibid., 2:404.

35. Ibid., 2:423.

36. MRB notes dispersed throughout Beard Papers; MRB to Robert E. Thomas, 1 March 1952, Beard Papers; MRB to Eula Gotcher, 23 October 1952, Beard Papers; emphasis in the original. Thomas had just written "A Reappraisal of Charles A. Beard's *An Economic Interpretation of the Constitution of the United States,*"*American Historical Review* 57, no. 2 (1952): 370–75. Thomas opened by putting Prufrock's words in the maligned CAB's mouth: "That is not it at all / That is not what I meant, at all," 370.

37. MRB, "A Test for the Modern Woman," undated 1932, Beard Papers. She remarks here that the Great Depression halted women's progress, which postwar prosperity abetted.

38. MRB, "America through Mother's Eyes," undated, but 1930s, and Eleanor Roosevelt to MRB, 14 November 1933, Beard Papers. Koven and Michel make the point that the paternalist rhetoric of National Socialism displaced the rhetoric of maternalism in the Soziale Frauenschulen. "Womanly Duties," 1106–7.

39. *Rise* (1933), 2:719 and 721.

40. Ibid., 2:837.

41. John Chamberlain, *Farewell to Reform: The Rise, Life, and Decay of the Progressive Mind in America*, 2d ed. (New York: Day, 1933), 216.

42. *Rise* (1933), 2:832.

43. CAB to Carl Bridenbaugh, 17 December 1938, Beard Papers.

44. Richard Hofstadter, "The Beards, Part IV," *New Republic* 4 January 1943, 28.

WORKS CITED

SELECTED PRIMARY AND CONTEMPORARY SOURCES

Addams, Jane. *Democracy and Social Ethics.* Ed. Anne Firor Scott. 1902. Reprint, Cambridge: Harvard University Press, 1964.

——. *Twenty Years at Hull House.* 1910. Reprint, New York: Penguin, 1961.

Baruch, Bernard M. *American Industry in the War: A Report of the War Industries Board (1921).* New York: Prentice-Hall, 1941.

——. *Baruch: The Public Years.* New York: Holt, 1960.

Beard, Charles A. *American City Government: A Survey of Newer Tendencies.* New York: Century, 1912.

——. "The Ballot's Burden." *Political Science Quarterly* 24 (December 1909): 589–614.

——. "The Constitution of Oklahoma." *Political Science Quarterly* 24 (March 1909): 95–114.

——. *Contemporary American History, 1877–1913.* New York: Macmillan, 1914.

——. *An Economic Interpretation of the Constitution of the United States.* 1913. Reprint, New York: Free Press, 1986.

——. "Giddy Minds and Foreign Quarrels: An Estimate of American Foreign Policy." *Harper's,* September 1939.

———. "Henry Adams." *New Republic*, 31 March 1920, 162–63.

———. *The Industrial Revolution*. 1st ed. 1901; 2d ed., London: Allen & Unwin, 1902.

———. Introduction to *The Law of Civilization and Decay*, by Brooks Adams. 1896. Reprint, New York: Vintage, 1943.

———. *President Roosevelt and the Coming of the War, 1941: A Study in Appearances and Realities*. New Haven: Yale University Press, 1948.

———. *The Supreme Court and the Constitution*. 1912. Rev. 1938. Reprint, Englewood Cliffs, N.J.: Prentice-Hall, 1962.

———. *Toward Civilization*. New York: Longmans, Green, 1930.

———. *Whither Mankind? A Panorama of Modern Civilization*. New York: Longmans, Green, 1928.

Beard, Charles A., and Mary R. Beard. *American Citizenship*. 1914. New and rev. ed., New York: Macmillan, 1921.

———. *The Rise of American Civilization*. 2 vols. New York: Macmillan, 1927.

Beard, Charles A., and William Beard. *The American Leviathan: The Republic in the Machine Age*. New York: Macmillan, 1930.

Beard, Charles A., and George H. E. Smith. *The Idea of National Interest: An Analytical Study of American Foreign Policy*. New York: Macmillan, 1934.

———. *The Open Door at Home: A Trial Philosophy of National Interest*. New York: Macmillan, 1934.

Beard, Mary R. "The Twentieth Century Woman Looking Around and Backward." *Young Oxford* 2, no. 15 (1900): 100–104. The byline appears as Mrs. Charles Beard.

———. "The Legislative Influence of Unenfranchised Women." *Annals of the American Academy of Political and Social Science* 56 (November 1914): 54–61.

———. "The Nineteenth Century Woman Looking Forward." *Young Oxford* 2, no. 16 (1901): 119–22. The byline appears as Mrs. Charles Beard.

———. *The Making of Charles A. Beard: An Interpretation*. New York: Exposition, 1955.

———. *A Short History of the American Labor Movement*. 1920. Reprint, New York: Greenwood, 1968.

———. *Woman as Force in History: A Study in Traditions and Realities*. New York: Macmillan, 1946.

———. *Women's Work in Municipalities*. National Municipal League Series. 1915. Reprint, New York: Arno, 1972.

Blatch, Harriot Stanton and Alma Lutz. *Challenging Years: The Memoirs of Harriot Stanton Blatch*. New York: Putnam, 1940.

Boardman, Helen. *Psychological Tests: A Bibliography*. New York: Bureau of Educational Experiments, 1917.

Bourne, Randolph S. *War and the Intellectuals: Essays by Randolph S. Bourne, 1915–1919*. Ed. Carl Resek. New York: Harper, 1964.

Croly, Herbert. *The Promise of American Life*. 1909. Reprint, Boston: Northeastern University Press, 1989.

———. *Progressive Democracy*. New York: Macmillan, 1914.

Elmhirst, Leonard K. *The Straight and Its Origins*. Ithaca: Willard Straight Hall, 1975.

Frankfurter, Felix. *Felix Frankfurter Reminisces*. New York: Reynal, 1960.

Hackett, Francis. *American Rainbow: Early Reminiscences*. New York: Liveright, 1971.

Hewlett, Maurice. *Open Country: A Comedy with a Sting*. New York: Scribner's, 1909.

Johnson, Alvin. *Pioneer's Progress: An Autobiography*. New York: Viking, 1952.

Laughlin, J. Laurence. *Facts about Money, Including the Debate with W. H. Harvey*. Chicago: E. A. Weeks, 1895.

——. *The Study of Political Economy: Hints to Students and Teachers*. New York: Appleton, 1885.

Lindsay, Vachel. *Collected Poems*. New York: Macmillan, 1925.

Mitchell, Lucy Sprague. *Here and Now Story Book: Two- to Seven-Year Olds: Experimental Stories Written for the Children of the City and Country School (formerly the Play School) and the Nursery School of the Bureau of Educational Experiments*. Illus. Hendrik Willem Van Loon. New York: Dutton, 1921.

——. *Two Lives: The Story of Wesley Clair Mitchell and Myself*. New York: Simon & Schuster, 1953.

Mitchell, Wesley Clair. "The Backward Art of Spending Money," *American Economic Review* 2 (June 1912): 219–81.

——. *Business Cycles*. Memoirs of the University of California 3. Berkeley: University of California, 1913.

——. *A History of the Greenbacks, with Special Reference to the Economic Consequences of Their Issue, 1862–1865*. Chicago: University of Chicago Press, 1903.

——. "Money Economy and Modern Civilization." Ed. Malcolm Rutherford. *History of Political Economy* 28, no. 3 (1996): 329–57.

——. *International Price Comparisons*. History of Prices during the War. Washington, D.C.: Government Printing Office, 1919.

——. "The Rationality of Economic Activity." *Journal of Political Economy* 18 (1910). Part 1 in issue no. 2: 97–113; part 2 in issue no. 3: 197–216.

Mitchell, Wesley Clair, ed. *What Veblen Taught: Selected Writings of Thorstein Veblen*. New York: Viking, 1936.

Pankhurst, Emmeline. *My Own Story*. London: Eveleigh Nash, 1914.

Paxson, Frederic L., ed. *War Cyclopedia*. Washington, D.C.: Government Printing Office, 1918.

Robinson, James Harvey. *The New History*. New York: Macmillan, 1912.

Roosevelt, Theodore. *The Works of Theodore Roosevelt*. 20 vols. Ed. Hermann Hagedorn. National ed., New York: Scribner's, 1926.

Stein, Gertrude. *The Autobiography of Alice B. Toklas*. New York: Vintage, 1933.

Stephens, Henry Morse. "Four Phases of Kipling's Work." *University Chronicle* (Berkeley) 3 (1900).

——. *Syllabus of Lectures on the History of the British Empire*. Ithaca: Ithaca Journal, 1901.

Straight, Michael. *After Long Silence*. New York: Norton, 1983.

Straight, Willard. *China's Loan Negotiations*. New York: n.p., 1912.

——. *The European War and Our Opportunity in Foreign Trade*. Address before the Illinois Manufacturers' Association, 27 October 1914. New York: n.p., 1914.

——. *Foreign Relations and Oversea Trade*. Address before the Southern Commercial Congress, 30 April 1915. New York: n.p., 1915.

Sze, Sao-ke Alfred. *Reminiscences of His Early Years*. Trans. Amy C. Wu. Washington, D.C.: n.p., 1962.

Wells, H. G. *Marriage*. 1912. Reprint, New York: Duffield, 1913.

Wilkins, Burleigh Taylor, ed. "Documents: Charles A. Beard on the Founding of Ruskin Hall." *Indiana Magazine of History* 52 (September 1956): 277–84.

HISTORICAL AND CRITICAL SOURCES

Altschuler, Glenn C. *Race, Ethnicity, and Class in American Social Thought, 1865–1919*. Wheeling, Ill.: Harlan Davidson, 1982.

Altschuler, Glenn C., and Stuart F. Blumin. *Rude Republic: Americans and their Politics in the Nineteenth Century*. Princeton, N.J.: Princeton University Press, 2000.

Antler, Joyce. "Feminism as Life-Process: The Life and Career of Lucy Sprague Mitchell." *Feminist Studies* 7, no. 1 (1981): 134–57.

——. *Lucy Sprague Mitchell: The Making of a Modern Woman*. New Haven: Yale University Press, 1987.

Bailyn, Bernard, et al. *Glimpses of the Harvard Past*. Cambridge: Harvard University Press, 1986.

Beale, Howard Kennedy, ed. *Charles A. Beard: An Appraisal*. Lexington: University of Kentucky Press, 1954.

Bederman, Gail. *Manliness and Civilization: A Cultural History of Gender and Race in the United States, 1880–1917*. Chicago: University of Chicago Press, 1995.

——. " 'The Women Have Had Charge of the Church Work Long Enough': The Men and Religion Forward Movement of 1911–1912 and the Masculinization of Middle-Class Protestantism." *American Quarterly* 41, no. 3 (1989): 432–65.

Bender, Thomas. *Intellect and Public Life: Essays on the Social History of Academic Intellectuals in the United States*. Baltimore: Johns Hopkins University Press, 1993.

——. "The New History: Then and Now." *Reviews in American History* 12, no. 4 (1984): 612–22.

Berlin, Isaiah. *The Crooked Timber of Humanity: Chapters in the History of Ideas*. Ed. Henry Hardy. New York: Vintage, 1992.

Biddle, Jeff. "A Citation Analysis of the Sources and Extent of Wesley Mitchell's Reputation." *History of Political Economy* 28, no. 2 (1996): 137–69.

Bishop, Joseph Bucklin. *Theodore Roosevelt and His Times Shown in His Own Letters*. London: Hodder, 1920.

Blair, Karen J. *The Clubwoman as Feminist: True Womanhood Redefined, 1868–1914.* New York: Holmes & Meier, 1980.

Blake, Casey Nelson. *Beloved Community: The Cultural Criticism of Randolph Bourne, Van Wyck Brooks, Waldo Frank, and Lewis Mumford.* Chapel Hill: University of North Carolina Press, 1990.

Blumin, Stuart F. *The Emergence of the Middle Class: Social Experience in the American City, 1760–1900.* New York: Cambridge University Press, 1989.

Bodnar, John. *The Transplanted: A History of Immigrants in Urban America.* Bloomington: Indiana University Press, 1985.

Bornemann, Alfred. *J. Laurence Laughlin: Chapters in the Career of an Economist.* Washington, D.C.: American Council on Public Affairs, 1940.

Bourne, Randolph S. *War and the Intellectuals: Essays by Randolph S. Bourne, 1915–1919.* Ed. Carl Resek. New York: Harper, 1964.

Bowers, Claude G. *Beveridge and the Progressive Era.* New York: Literary Guild, 1932.

Burns, Arthur Frank, ed. *Wesley Clair Mitchell, the Economic Scientist.* New York: National Bureau of Economic Research, 1952.

Carson, Mina J. *Settlement Folk: Social Thought and the American Settlement Movement, 1885–1930.* Chicago: University of Chicago Press, 1990.

Chafe, William H. *The Paradox of Change: American Women in the Twentieth Century.* New York: Oxford University Press, 1991.

Chamberlain, John. *Farewell to Reform: The Rise, Life and Decay of the Progressive Mind in America.* 1932; 2d ed., New York: John Day, 1933.

Clinton, William J. "Remarks by the President, Pennsylvania State University Graduate School Commencement," White House press release, 10 May 1996.

Connolly, James J. *The Triumph of Ethnic Progressivism: Urban Political Culture in Boston, 1900–1925.* Cambridge: Harvard University Press, 1998.

Conway, Jill K. *The First Generation of American Women Graduates.* New York: Garland, 1987.

Cook, Blanche Wiesen. *Eleanor Roosevelt.* Vol. 1, *1884–1933.* New York: Viking, 1992.

——. "Female Support Networks and Political Activism: Lillian Wald, Crystal Eastman, Emma Goldman." *Chrysalis* 3 (fall 1977): 43–61.

Cott, Nancy F. *The Grounding of Modern Feminism.* New Haven: Yale University Press, 1987.

——. "Two Beards: Coauthorship and the Concept of Civilization." *American Quarterly* 42, no. 2 (1990): 274–300.

——. *A Woman Making History: Mary Ritter Beard through Her Letters.* New Haven: Yale University Press, 1991.

Cremin, Lawrence A. *The Transformation of the School: Progressivism in American Education, 1876–1957.* New York: Knopf, 1961.

Croly, Herbert. *Willard Straight.* New York: Macmillan 1924.

Crunden, Robert M. *Ministers of Reform: The Progressives' Achievement in American Civilization, 1889–1920.* New York: Basic, 1982.

Cuff, Robert D. *The War Industries Board: Business-Government Relations during World War I.* Baltimore: Johns Hopkins University Press, 1973.

Davis, Allen F. "Social Workers and the Progressive Party, 1912–1916." *American Historical Review* 69, no. 3 (1964): 671–88.

———. "Welfare, Reform, and World War I." *American Quarterly* 19, no. 3 (1967): 516–33.

Deacon, Desley. *Elsie Clews Parsons: Inventing Modern Life.* Chicago: University of Chicago Press, 1997.

Diggins, John P. "Power and Authority in American History: The Case of Charles A. Beard and His Critics," *American Historical Review* 86, no. 4 (1981): 701–30.

Diner, Steven J. *A Very Different Age: Americans of the Progressive Era.* New York: Hill & Wang, 1998.

Dionne, E. J. *They Only Look Dead: Why Progressives Will Dominate the Next Political Era.* New York: Simon & Schuster, 1996.

Dixon, Chris. *Perfecting the Family: Anti-Slavery Marriages in Nineteenth-Century America.* Amherst: University of Massachusetts Press, 1997.

Donzelot, Jacques. *The Policing of Families.* Trans. Robert Hurley. 1977. Reprint, Baltimore: Johns Hopkins University Press, 1997.

Edwards, Rebecca. *Angels in the Machinery: Gender and American Party Politics from the Civil War to the Progressive Era.* New York: Oxford University Press, 1997.

Fairbank, John King, Katherine Frost Bruner, and Elizabeth MacLeod Matheson, eds. *The I.G. in Peking: Letters of Robert Hart, Chinese Maritime Custons, 1868–1907.* Cambridge: Harvard University Press, 1975.

Filene, Peter G. "An Obituary for 'The Progressive Movement.'" *American Quarterly* 22, no. 1 (1970): 453–68.

Fink, Leon. *Progressive Intellectuals and the Dilemmas of Democratic Commitment.* Cambridge: Harvard University Press, 1997.

Fliegelman, Jay. *Prodigals and Pilgrims: The American Revolution against Patriarchal Authority.* Cambridge: Cambridge University Press, 1982.

Forcey, Charles. *The Crossroads of Liberalism: Croly, Weyl, Lippmann, and the Progressive Era, 1900–1925.* New York: Oxford University Press, 1961.

Fox, Richard Wightman. "The Culture of Liberal Protestant Progressivism, 1900–1925." *Journal of Interdisciplinary History* 23, no. 3 (1993): 639–60.

Freedman, Estelle B. *Maternal Justice: Miriam Van Waters and the Female Reform Tradition.* Chicago: University of Chicago Press, 1996.

———. "Separatism as Strategy: Female Institution Building and American Feminism, 1870–1930." *Feminist Studies* 5, no. 3 (1979): 512–29.

Friedman, B. H. *Gertrude Vanderbilt Whitney: A Biography.* Garden City: Doubleday, 1978.

Friedman, Milton. "Wesley C. Mitchell as an Economic Theorist." *Journal of Political Economy* 58, no. 6 (1950).

Gingrich, Newt. *To Renew America.* New York: HarperCollins, 1995.

Ginzberg, Lori D. *Women and the Work of Benevolence: Morality, Politics, and Class in the Nineteenth-Century United States.* New Haven: Yale University Press, 1990.

Goldman, Lawrence. *Dons and Workers: Oxford and Adult Education since 1850.* Oxford: Clarendon Press, 1995.

Goodspeed, Thomas Wakefield. *The Story of the University of Chicago, 1890–1925.* Chicago: University of Chicago Press, 1925.

Goodwyn, Lawrence. *The Populist Moment: A Short History of the Agrarian Revolt in America.* New York: Oxford University Press, 1978.

Gordon, Linda. *Pitied but Not Entitled: Single Mothers and the History of Welfare.* New York: Free Press, 1994.

Gordon, Lynn D. *Gender and Higher Education in the Progressive Era.* New Haven: Yale University Press, 1990.

Grossberg, Michael. *Governing the Hearth: Law and the Family in Nineteenth-Century America.* Chapel Hill: University of North Carolina Press, 1985.

Gruber, Carol S. *Mars and Minerva: World War I and the Uses of Higher Learning in America.* Baton Rouge: Louisiana State University Press, 1975.

Gunther, Gerald. *Learned Hand: The Man and the Judge.* New York: Knopf, 1994.

Hareven, Tamara. "Family History at the Crossroads." *Journal of Family History* 12, nos. 1–3 (1987): ix–xxiii.

Harper, Ida Husted, Elizabeth Cady Stanton, Susan B. Anthony, and Matilda Joselyn Gage, eds. *The History of Woman Suffrage.* 6 vols. National American Woman Suffrage Association, 1922.

Hatton, Timothy J., and Jeffrey G. Williamson. *The Age of Mass Migration: Causes and Economic Impact.* New York: Oxford University Press, 1998.

Hays, Samuel P. "The Politics of Reform in Municipal Government in the Progressive Era." *Pacific Northwest Quarterly* 55 (1964): 157–69.

———. *The Response to Industrialism, 1885–1914.* 1957. 2nd ed., Chicago: University of Chicago Press, 1995.

Heaton, Herbert. *A Scholar in Action: Edwin F. Gay.* Cambridge: Harvard University Press, 1952.

Hirsch, Mark D. *William C. Whitney: Modern Warwick.* New York: Dodd, Mead, 1948.

Hofstadter, Richard. "The Beards, Part IV." *New Republic,* 4 January 1943, 28.

Hofstadter, Richard. *The Age of Reform: From Bryan to FDR.* New York: Knopf, 1955.

Hofstadter, Richard. *The Progressive Historians: Turner, Beard, Parrington.* Chicago: University of Chicago Press, 1968.

Horowitz, Helen Lefkowitz. *Campus Life: Undergraduate Cultures from the End of the Eighteenth Century to the Present.* New York: Knopf, 1987.

Hunt, Michael H. *Frontier Defense and the Open Door: Manchuria in Chinese-American Relations, 1895–1911.* New Haven: Yale University Press, 1973.

Kahn, Helen Dodson. *The Great Game of Empire: Willard D. Straight and American Far Eastern Policy.* Ph.D. diss., Cornell University, 1968.

Keller, Morton. *Affairs of State: Public Life in Late Nineteenth-Century America.* Cambridge: Harvard University Press, 1977.

Kennedy, David M. *Birth Control in America: The Career of Margaret Sanger.* New Haven: Yale University Press, 1970.

———. *Over Here: The First World War and American Society.* New York: Oxford University Press, 1980.

———. "Overview: The Progressive Era." *Historian* 37, no. 3 (1975): 20–34.

Kerber, Linda K., Alice Kessler-Harris, and Kathryn Kish Sklar, eds. *U. S. History as Women's History: New Feminist Essays.* Chapel Hill: University of North Carolina Press, 1995.

Kerr, Joan Patterson, ed. *A Bully Father: Theodore Roosevelt's Letters to His Children.* New York: Random House, 1995.

Kloppenberg, James T. *Uncertain Victory: Social Democracy and Progressivism in European and American Thought, 1870–1920.* New York: Oxford University Press, 1986.

———. *The Virtues of Liberalism.* New York: Oxford University Press, 1998.

Koven, Seth. "The Ambivalence of Agency: Women, Families, and Social Policy in France, Britain, and the United States." *Journal of Women's History* 9, no. 1 (1997): 164–73.

Koven, Seth, and Sonya Michel. "Conference Report: Gender and the Origins of the Welfare State." *Radical History Review* 43 (January 1989): 112–19.

———. *Mothers of a New World: Maternalist Politics and the Origins of Welfare States.* London: Routledge, 1993.

———. "Womanly Duties: Maternalist Politics and the Origins of Welfare States in France, Germany, Great Britain, and the United States, 1880–1920." *American Historical Review* 95, no.4 (1990): 1076–108.

Kuklick, Bruce. *The Rise of American Philosophy: Cambridge, Massachusetts, 1860–1930.* New Haven: Yale University Press, 1977.

Ladd-Taylor, Molly. *Mother-work: Women, Child Welfare, and the State, 1890–1930.* Urbana: University of Illinois Press, 1994.

Ladd-Taylor, Molly, ed. *Raising a Baby the Government Way: Mothers' Letters to the Children's Bureau, 1915–1932.* New Brunswick: Rutgers University Press, 1986.

LaFeber, Walter. *The American Search for Opportunity, 1865–1913.* Vol. 2 of the Cambridge History of American Foreign Relations, ed. Warren I. Cohen. Cambridge: Cambridge University Press, 1993.

———. *The Clash: U.S.-Japanese Relations throughout History.* New York: Norton, 1997.

Lakoff, George. *Moral Politics: What Conservatives Know that Liberals Don't.* Chicago: University of Chicago Press, 1996.

Lane, Ann J., ed. *Mary Ritter Beard: A Sourcebook.* New York: Schocken, 1977.

Lasch, Christopher. *Haven in a Heartless World: The Family Besieged.* New York: Basic, 1977.

——. *The New Radicalism in America, 1889–1963: The Intellectual as a Social Type.* New York: Knopf, 1965.

——. *Women and the Common Life: Love, Marriage, and Feminism.* Ed. Elisabeth Lasch-Quinn. New York: Norton, 1997.

Lasch, Christopher, ed. *The Social Thought of Jane Addams.* Indianapolis: Bobbs-Merrill, 1965.

Lash, Joseph P. *Eleanor and Franklin.* New York: Norton, 1971.

Leich, Jean Ferriss. *Architectural Visions: The Drawings of Hugh Ferriss.* New York: Whitney Library of Design, 1980.

Levy, David W. *Herbert Croly of* The New Republic: *The Life and Thought of an American Progressive.* Princeton: Princeton University Press, 1985.

Lind, Michael. *The Next American Nation: The New Nationalism and the Fourth American Revolution.* New York: Free Press, 1995.

Marsh, Margaret. "Suburban Men and Masculine Domesticity, 1870–1915." *American Quarterly* 40, no. 2 (1988): 165–86.

May, Elaine Tyler. *Great Expectations: Marriage and Divorce in Post-Victorian America.* Chicago: University of Chicago Press, 1980.

McBriar, A. M. *An Edwardian Mixed Doubles: The Bosanquets versus the Webbs: A Study in British Social Policy, 1890–1929.* Oxford: Clarendon Press, 1987.

McCarthy, Kathleen D., ed. *Lady Bountiful Revisited: Women, Philanthropy, and Power.* New Brunswick: Rutgers University Press, 1990.

McCarthy, Michael P. "Urban Optimism and Reform Thought in the Progressive Era." *Historian* 51, no. 2 (1989): 239–62.

McGerr, Michael E. *The Decline of Popular Politics: The American North, 1865–1928.* New York: Oxford University Press, 1986.

——. "Political Style and Women's Power, 1830–1930." *Journal of American History* 77, no. 3 (1990): 864–85.

Milne, Christopher. *The Enchanted Places.* London: Eyre Methuen, 1974.

Mintz, Steven, and Susan Kellogg. *Domestic Revolutions: A Social History of Family Life.* New York: Free Press, 1988.

Muncy, Robyn. *Creating a Female Dominion in American Reform, 1890–1935.* New York: Oxford University Press, 1991.

Nevins, Allan. *Grover Cleveland: A Study in Courage.* New York: Dodd, Mead, 1933.

Nicholson, Linda J. *Gender and History: The Limits of Social Theory in the Age of the Family.* New York: Columbia University Press, 1986.

Ninkovich, Frank. "Theodore Roosevelt: Civilization as Ideology." *Diplomatic History* 10, no. 3 (1986): 221–45.

Nore, Ellen. *Charles A. Beard: An Intellectual Biography.* Carbondale: Southern Illinois University Press, 1983.

O'Neill, William. *Divorce in the Progressive Era.* New Haven: Yale University Press, 1967.

Paulson, Ross E. *Radicalism and Reform: The Vrooman Family and American Social Thought, 1837–1937.* Lexington: University of Kentucky Press, 1968.

Payne, Elizabeth Ann. *Reform, Labor, and Feminism: Margaret Dreier Robins and the Women's Trade Union League.* Urbana: University of Illinois Press, 1988.

Ratcliffe, Richard. *Along the Banks of Brook Bezor: A History of the Spiceland Community.* N.p., 1963.

Rauchway, Eric. "Willard Straight and the Paradox of Liberal Imperialism." *Pacific Historical Review* 66, no. 3 (1997): 363–97.

Robinson, Jesse S. *The Amalgamated Association of Iron, Steel, and Tin Workers.* Johns Hopkins University Studies in Historical and Political Science 38, no. 2. Baltimore: Johns Hopkins University Press, 1920.

Rodgers, Daniel T. *Atlantic Crossings: Social Politics in a Progressive Age.* Cambridge: Harvard University Press, 1998.

——. "In Search of Progressivism." *Reviews in American History* 10, no. 4 (1982): 113–32.

Roosevelt, Theodore. *The Works of Theodore Roosevelt.* Ed. Hermann Hagedorn. National ed., New York: Scribner's, 1926.

Rosenberg, Emily S. "Revisiting Dollar Diplomacy: Narratives of Money and Manliness." *Diplomatic History* 22, no. 2 (1998): 155–76.

Rosenberg, Rosalind. *Beyond Separate Spheres: The Intellectual Roots of Modern Feminism.* New Haven: Yale University Press, 1982.

——. "In Search of Woman's Nature, 1850–1920." *Feminist Studies* 3, nos. 1–2 (1975): 141–54.

Rutkoff, Peter M., and William B. Scott. *New School: A History of the New School for Social Research.* New York: Free Press, 1986.

Ryan, Mary P. *Cradle of the Middle Class: The Family in Oneida County, New York, 1760–1865.* New York: Cambridge University Press, 1981.

Scott, Pamela, and Antoinette J. Lee. *Buildings of the District of Columbia.* New York: Oxford University Press, 1993.

Sklar, Kathryn Kish. *Florence Kelley and the Nation's Work: Women's Political Culture 1830–1900.* New Haven: Yale University Press, 1995.

——. "Hull House in the 1890s: A Community of Women Reformers." *Signs* 10, no. 4 (1985): 658–77.

Skocpol, Theda. *Protecting Soldiers and Mothers: The Political Origins of Social Policy in the United States.* Cambridge: Harvard University Press, 1992.

Smith, Mark C. *Social Science in the Crucible: The American Debate over Objectivity and Purpose, 1918–1941.* Durham: Duke University Press, 1994.

Stansell, Christine. *City of Women: Sex and Class in New York City, 1789–1860.* New York: Knopf, 1986.

Steel, Ronald. *Walter Lippmann and the American Century.* London: Bodley Head, 1980.

Steinfels, Peter. *The Neo-conservatives: The Men Who are Changing America's Politics.* New York: Simon & Schuster, 1979.

Swanberg, W. A. *Whitney Father, Whitney Heiress.* New York: Scribner's, 1980.

Swanson, Marvin C., ed. *Charles A. Beard: An Observance of the Centennial of His Birth.* Greencastle, Ind.: DePauw University Press, 1974.

Sweet, William Warren. *Indiana Asbury–DePauw University, 1837–1937.* New York: Abingdon, 1937.

Testi, Arnaldo, "The Gender of Reform Politics: Theodore Roosevelt and the Culture of Masculinity." *Journal of American History* 81, no. 4 (1995): 1509–33.

Thomas, Robert E. "A Reappraisal of Charles A. Beard's *An Economic Interpretation of the Constitution of the United States.*" *American Historical Review* 57, no. 2 (1952): 370–75.

Thompson, E. P. *The Making of the English Working Class.* New York: Random House, 1964.

Tomasky, Michael. *Left for Dead: The Life, Death, and Possible Resurrection of Progressive Politics in America.* New York: Free Press, 1996.

Turoff, Barbara K. *Mary Ritter Beard as Force in History.* Monograph Series, no. 3. Dayton: Wright State University Press, 1979.

Vidal, Gore. "Love on the Hudson." Review of *Closest Companion,* by Geoffrey Ward. *New York Review of Books* 42, no. 8 (1995): 4–6.

Wattenberg, Ben J. *Values Matter Most: How Republicans or Democrats or a Third Party Can Win and Renew the American Way of Life.* New York: Free Press, 1995.

Webb, Beatrice. *Our Partnership.* London: Longmans, Green, 1948.

Weisberg, Jacob. *In Defense of Government: The Fall and Rise of Public Trust.* New York: Scribner's, 1996.

Weisberger, Bernard A. *The La Follettes of Wisconsin: Love and Politics in Progressive America.* Madison: University of Wisconsin Press, 1994.

Westbrook, Robert. *John Dewey and American Democracy.* Ithaca: Cornell University Press, 1991.

White, Morton. *Social Thought in America: The Revolt against Formalism.* New York: Viking, 1952.

Wiebe, Robert H. *The Search for Order, 1877–1920.* New York: Hill & Wang, 1967.

Wilkins, Burleigh Taylor. "Frederick York Powell and Charles A. Beard: A Study in Anglo-American Historiography and Thought." *American Quarterly* 11 (spring 1959): 21–39.

Wynn, Neil A. *From Progressivism to Prosperity: World War I and American Society.* New York: Holmes & Meier, 1986.

Young, Michael. *The Elmhirsts of Dartington: The Creation of an Utopian Community.* London: Routledge, 1982.